POST TALIBAN AFGHANISTAN

A FRESH START

Col. S.P.Bahera (Retd.)

NEHA PUBLISHERS & DISTRIBUTORS
DELHI

Publisher
NEHA PUBLISHERS & DISTRIBUTORS
4832/24,Prahlad Lane,S-207 Ansari
Road, Daryaganj, Delhi-110002
Ph.: 43570976, 23278261
Email: nehapubdistributors@gmail.com

Edition: 2015

ISBN: 978-93-80318-58-5

Laser Typesetting
JEE-VEE Graphics, Delhi

Price: 1195/-

Printed
Vikas Computers, Delhi

Post Taliban Afghanistan: A Fresh Start

Contents

Preface

The Taliban is a predominantly Pashtun, Islamic fundamentalist group that ruled Afghanistan from 1996 until 2001, when a U.S.-led invasion toppled the regime for providing refuge to al-Qaeda and Osama bin Laden.

In 1997, Trillium Asset Management was alarmed to learn that Unocal Corporation, an international energy company, was actively exploring the construction of oil and gas pipelines through Afghanistan that might have resulted in as much as $100 million in yearly revenues for the Taliban regime. Clearly Afghanistan, devastated by years of civil war exacerbated by foreign interference, desperately needed the cash income. But the prospect of abetting the oppressive and brutal Taliban with a commercial project of that magnitude was outrageous, and we joined a growing international movement opposing the deal. Feminist opposition to the pipeline deal is widely credited with bringing about its collapse.

September 11 reopened the question of Afghanistan's future. An ironic result of the terrorist attacks is the international community's interest in reconstructing a country that had seemed doomed to subsist forever on international handouts.

The Taliban's post-2001 resurgence has partially been financed by narcotics production and trafficking, though Mullah Omar issued injunctions against opium production, and the Taliban eradicated much of the poppy crop during its rule. Insurgents and other strongmen extort *ushr*, an agricultural tithe, from farmers and levies at roadside checkpoints. Revenues from illicit mining also contribute to Taliban coffers, whichnet some $400 million a year, the UN estimated in 2012.

The book therefore, merits attention of experts on Asia, diplomats and policymakers of the developed countries.

—Editor

1

Introduction

In 1997, Trillium Asset Management was alarmed to learn that Unocal Corporation, an international energy company, was actively exploring the construction of oil and gas pipelines through Afghanistan that might have resulted in as much as $100 million in yearly revenues for the Taliban regime. Clearly Afghanistan, devastated by years of civil war exacerbated by foreign interference, desperately needed the cash income. But the prospect of abetting the oppressive and brutal Taliban with a commercial project of that magnitude was outrageous, and we joined a growing international movement opposing the deal. Feminist opposition to the pipeline deal is widely credited with bringing about its collapse.

September 11 reopened the question of Afghanistan's future. An ironic result of the terrorist attacks is the international community's interest in reconstructing a country that had seemed doomed to subsist forever on international handouts. With the Taliban now out of the way, will the pipeline deals be revived? Should socially concerned investors welcome and encourage pipeline deals and other direct foreign investments with a reconstructed Afghanistan? Can Afghanistan have an economic future without pipeline revenue?

Oil and Its DiscontentsIt is fashionable in many circles to assert that the U.S. military campaign against the Taliban is driven by the Bush Administration's alliance with Big Oil. The Caspian Sea region is home to 18-34 billion barrels in proven oil reserves, and as much as 235 billion more; possible gas reserves could go as high as 328 billion cubic feet if proven. The challenge is to export these vast reserves to foreign markets, especially to growing markets in Asia and the Pacific. Historically, the region's fuel export routes have been controlled by the Soviet Union, but since its breakup, international oil companies have been champing for a piece of the business. The geopolitics of putting together deals in this region are so complex that only one of seven new pipelines proposed since 1996 has been built. For a period in the mid- to late- 902 s, a trans-Afghan route was favored by the U.S. government and pursued by Unocal Corporation, which sought to build a nearly 900-mile gas pipeline from Turkmenistan to Pakistan through Afghanistan, to be followed in subsequent years by an oil pipeline.

While the current political climate in the U.S. has inhibited debate, the conviction that U.S. objectives have been driven by dependence on foreign oil is not limited to the far left. Even some energy executives have expressed privately their belief that the U.S. military campaign, while necessarily addressing terrorism, could be traced to Western petroleum addiction and the need to protect important fuel sources.

U.S. policy toward Afghanistan in the last decade certainly has provided rich fodder for this speculation. Following the withdrawal of the Soviet Union in 1992, the U.S. stopped funding the anti-Soviet mujahideen forces from whom today's Northern Alliance and some Taliban forces soon emerged. The Taliban movement, which took root in Afghan refugee encampments in Pakistan, gained popular support by promising to end the anarchy, plunder and widespread rape propagated by mujahideen forces.

No hard evidence has emerged that the U.S. directly supported the Taliban's ascendance. But during the critical period throughout 1996 in which the group secured its final hold on Afghanistan, the State Department openly supported the pipeline project and sent signals indicating that the Taliban offered the best prospects for its fruition. On trips throughout the region that spring, U.S. Assistant Secretary of State for South Asia Robin Raphel spoke on behalf of the pipeline. In April, Raphel stated, "This pipeline will be very good for Turkmenistan, for Pakistan and for Afghanistan." A month earlier, U.S. Ambassador to Pakistan Tom Simmons deeply offended Pakistani Prime Minister Benazir Bhutto by demanding her support for Unocal's proposal over one from its rival, the Argentinean firm Bridas. (Bhutto demanded, and received, a written apology.) Within hours of the Taliban capture of Kabul in September 1996, Washington announced that it would establish diplomatic relations, a statement that was quickly retracted.

The company's hiring of prominent ex-statesmen such as former secretary of state Henry Kissinger, and former ambassador to Pakistan Robert Oakley enhanced perceptions of coziness between Unocal and the U.S. government as lobbyists for the deal. As noted in the current bestseller Taliban: Militant Islam, Oil and Fundamentalism in Central Asia by journalist Ahmed Rashid, while such consultancies are not unusual in the U.S. context, overseas the relationships suggested that the U.S. government and Unocal's interests were wholly aligned.

Rashid separates U.S. policy toward the Taliban into several phases. Between 1994 and 1996, the U.S. supported the Taliban, viewing them as anti-Iranian, anti-Shia and pro-Western. From 1995 through most of 1997, this support intensified due to Washington's support for the Unocal project. In 1997, based on growing skepticism that the Taliban and its state sponsor Pakistan could deliver a unified Afghanistan, the US reversed its policy against accepting an alternative pipeline route that would flow through Iran. At the same time, mounting feminist opposition to the regime and new Secretary of State Madeleine Albright's condemnation of its treatment of women made diplomatic recognition of the Taliban a domestic political impossibility. These developments were major blows to the Unocal project. In the next two years, the unfavorable environment for the proposal was solidified by the Taliban's support for Osama bin Laden, and its intransigence to foreign pressure on the questions of power sharing, women's and minority rights, and the drug trade.

Unocal's withdrawal from the pipeline consortium was complete by December 1998. But new research indicates that the Bush Administration came to office with an interest in reviving it. According to an Inter Press Service wire report, a new French book, Bin Laden: The Forbidden Truth, by Jean-Charles Brisard and Guillaume Dasquie, alleges that FBI deputy director John O'Neill resigned last July to protest the hold that U.S. oil companies and Saudi Arabia had over US policy towards the Taliban. The authors say that the Bush administration secretly negotiated with the Taliban in Washington from February through August 2001. In addition the authors say that former Pakistani Minister for Foreign Affairs Naif Naik told the Taliban in July that if they accepted a "coalition government of national unity," they would be rewarded with economic aid and energy pipelines originating from Kazakhstan and Uzbekistan. Naik says Tom Simmons openly threatened the Taliban and Pakistan at these meetings with a military operation if they did not comply.

In the wake of September 11, the regional oil geopolitics have shifted yet again. Russian President Vladimir Putin's previously unimaginable decision to allow U.S. forces to operate from the Central Asian Republics reveals how deeply Moscow shares Washington's urgency to replace the Taliban. Yet, writes Ahmed Rashid, Russia is still so nervous about the U.S.'s designs on the region that National Security Advisor Condoleezza Rice felt impelled to write in a recent article, "I want to stress this: our policy is not aimed against the interests of Russia. We do not harbour any plans aimed at squeezing Russia out of there." Rashid speculates that when a stable government is established in Afghanistan, the U.S. will reconsider a trans-Afghan pipeline project, on account of the $30 billion already invested by U.S. oil companies to develop oil and gas fields in Kazakhstan, Turkmenistan, Uzbekistan, and Azerbaijan. The Afghan route would cost one-half the amount of the other alternative proposed by Washington, which would run through Georgia to Turkey's Mediterranean coast.

While there has been other such speculation in the media concerning a possible revival of interest in the pipeline after the Taliban have been removed from power, industry analysts are skeptical. According toCambridge Energy Research Associates (CERA), a consulting firm that advised Unocal when it was considering the Afghan pipeline route: Changes in the Caspian pipeline picture in the past five years have rendered this concept unrealistic for the foreseeable future...[because] there is no longer a shortage of oil export capacity in Kazakhstan; the need for a major new oil pipeline via Afghanistan or any other route will not reemerge until around 2010. Renewed opportunities for Central Asian gas to the north – to and through Russia – have removed the pressure that could have pushed gas from Turkmenistan to South Asian markets via Afghanistan.

Yet given the long lead-time required for pipeline construction, CERA's conclusion is puzzling. If market forces would support a pipeline in 2010, the time to begin construction would be now. Another skeptic is Stephen O'Sullivan, head of research for United Financial Group, who told the Moscow Times in November, "I'd be surprised if after 20 years of war the U.S. would want to build a pipeline in Afghanistan," adding that Washington is unlikely to want to disrupt its increasingly close relationship with Moscow.

One thing is certain, regardless of the timeline: as long as security remains an issue, there will be no prospect of financing pipelines through Afghanistan. Will Unocal be back? "Not us," a company spokesman emphatically told Reuters in November. Since September 11, the company's web site has posted an announcement denying any involvement in Afghanistan. Unocal contributed $100,000 to the World Trade Center relief fund.

Starting From ScratchDuring the last week of November, a conference in Islamabad co-sponsored by the United Nations Development Program, the World Bank, and the Asian Development Bank examined Afghanistan's prospects. Just prior to the gathering the World Bank released its "Afghanistan Approach" paper, which states in its introduction, "Merely restoring the pre-1978 economic situation would still leave the country one of the poorest in the world in terms of both incomes and social indicators.... [R]econstruction will need to be combined with a massive development effort...."

By every measurable social indicator, Afghanistan leads the world in suffering and deprivation. Seventy percent of the population is malnourished (including one half of all children), and most of the urban population is dependent upon foreign food assistance. Access to potable water is rare. Nearly half of all men are illiterate, as are 80% of women. In 1999 only one-third of all children were enrolled in school – and only 3% of all girls. Average life expectancy is 40 years, and over 25% of all children do not live to the age of five. An estimated six million refugees have fled the country since the Soviet invasion in 1979, including most of the professional class.

On September 27, UN Secretary General Kofi Annan appealed to donor countries for $584 million in aid to Afghanistan (to which the U.S. has pledged $320 million). But rebuilding will require much more than humanitarian aid. "Relief and recovery must go hand in hand," warms David Lockwood, UNDP deputy Regional Director for Asia and Pacific. "We have to avoid getting trapped into a relief operation only."

Afghan's physical infrastructure has been equally battered by decades of war and underinvestment. Basics such as schools, roads and rail transport, mail delivery and power generation and distribution barely exist. Consider for example, that there are currently only 9,000 telephone service subscribers of a total population of 26 million. The drug trade and landmine situation provide unique challenges.

Clearing the 10 million buried landmines that kill and maim thousands each year and inhibit agricultural development could cost $500 million over the next decade. The wildly profitable opium trade was the economy's leading agricultural commodity under the Taliban, who benefited from a 20% excise tax on the crop. Yet it will have to be wiped out, which will impoverish its cultivators.

All told, World Bank President James D. Wolfensohn has estimated that Afghanistan's reconstruction will require at least $1-2 billion of aid per year for the next decade. To put that price tag into perspective, consider the recent disclosure that the U.K. intends to propose a new $50 billion international fund as a sort of "Marshall Plan" for the entire Third World.

To prosper, Afghanistan will need to open up its economy to foreign investors. The new Afghan government will need to chart a careful course between immediate and full adoption of a Western-style economic system, which would give foreign investors a totally free reign, and total isolationism, barring all foreign investment. Sadly, after years of war, little appears to remain of the Afghani economy that could serve as the basis for economic reconstruction. Significant challenges include high rates of illiteracy, the dependency of two-thirds of the population on the agricultural sector for employment and a reliance on commodity exports, which are more vulnerable to price fluctuations and import tariff restrictions. At the same time, reducing reliance upon commodity-oriented exports will require a more educated labor force.

Afghanistan has unexploited mineral resources (including copper, iron, emeralds, zinc,and silver). It also has modest underdeveloped oil reserves (est. 95 million barrels), natural gas (est. 5 trillion cubic feet), coal (est. 400 million tons) and hydroelectric capacity. But development of these resources will be slow until the basic infrastructure needed to bring goods to market, (such as roads, worker training, power generation and security) can be put in place. Needless to say, tourism has been stagnant in recent years and will only reemerge from a lasting peace.

Afghanistan's best hope is to focus reconstruction spending on reviving its human capital – establishing schools, literacy programs, and health care, while working to repair basic infrastructure necessary to commerce, such as roads, sewers, and communications. Additionally, the new government will need to quickly establish clear and uniformly applied commercial and legal codes establishing both basic human rights and the framework under which local (and foreign) enterprises will operate. The Chinese and Taiwanese examples indicate how quickly commerce and individual skills of entrepreneurship can develop once the framework is clear and non-confiscatory.

In our view, if a government that is multiethnic and inclusive of women can be established and demonstrate staying power, social investors should encourage any emerging interest in Afghanistan by socially responsible corporations. Social investors can play a key role in monitoring corporate activities in Afghanistan to encourage appropriate community involvement and respect for human rights and the environment. We would encourage corporations to abide by the "Declaration of the Essential Rights of Afghan Women," drafted and adopted by Afghan women in Dushanbe, Tajikistan, in June 2000, among other codes of conduct developed for corporations doing business in developing nations. Our community must also be alert for opportunities to fund microenterprise and small business development opportunities.

Oxfam has called for international lenders to cancel the $48 million Afghanistan owes to the World Bank, the Asian Development Bank, and the International Monetary Fund. "Wiping out Afghanistan's debt would be a fraction of what the war has cost us so far. And it would be a welcome gesture of commitment to the development of Afghanistan," said Oxfam spokesperson David Earnshaw."

To talk about how to best help Afghanistan economically but not act to write-off its debt would be, at best, a wasted opportunity, and at worst, hypocritical," he said. The debt write-off should be linked, Oxfam says, to Afghanistan's commitment to a poverty-reduction strategy run by a broad-based interim government.

The world has learned its lesson that an Afghanistan divided is a threat to all. Surely the costs of rebuilding Afghanistan are small in comparison to the costs of continued social and military instability in a country devastated in the crossfire of global cold war interests. If only the lesson would be applied to every impoverished nation.

POST-TALIBAN AFGHANISTAN, 12 YEARS ON

Exactly 12 years ago, on November 13, 2001 — just two months after the assassination of Ahmad Shah Massoud and the al Qaeda strikes in New York and Washington D.C. — Massoud's forces entered Kabul after Taliban fighters fled the city the previous night. This came on the heels of desperate diplomatic efforts to prevent the Northern Alliance from occupying Kabul and taking over the reins of government.

Why did the United States and its allies go to Afghanistan? U.S. troops went there to get rid of the al Qaeda leadership, and combat terrorists with a global reach. Operation Enduring Freedom was launched against terrorist entities and the states that harboured them. That was the reason for targeting the Taliban regime.

INTENSE OPERATIONS

The United Nations Security Council mandated an International Security Assistance Force for the security of Kabul and its environs on December 20, 2001. ISAF has since been supported by 49 U.S. allies and partners. At its high point in 2011, there were 1,40,000 ISAF troops in Afghanistan, including 1,01,000 Americans, not counting contracted private security personnel.

After such impressive marshalling of forces and intensified military operations, Afghanistan continues to remain among the greatest security challenges of our times.

What happened? A 2009 Senate Foreign Relations Committee report blamed the 2001 Pentagon leadership for the "lost opportunity" of preventing Osama bin Laden's flight from Tora Bora to Pakistan.

Centcom Commander General Tommy Franks turned down a CIA request for a battalion of Army Rangers to assist a rag-tag force tracking bin Laden. Concurrently, in late November 2001, Pakistani planes were allowed to airlift from Kunduz hundreds of Islamabad's advisers and troops, presumably along with some of the Taliban's and al Qaeda's leading cadres. A year or so later, the U.S. shifted its attention to Iraq, leaving the Afghan and Pakistan tasks unfinished.

The U.S. and NATO initially believed that a strong Afghan Army was not required, since the Taliban and al Qaeda fighters had dispersed without a fight — as for those who fled, Pakistan would take care of them. Afghans are still reaping the consequences of this initial neglect. The blunder of sub-contracting to Pakistan the management of the Taliban resulted in the outfit's fighters being nursed, nurtured and re-infiltrated into Afghanistan from 2005.

Since then, Afghanistan has become an arena for experimentation in social and political engineering. The military campaign was first cast as a war against terror, then as a counter-insurgency operation. The advantages gained by the surging American troops and more muscular military action were defeated by the announcement of the exit strategy.

Opportunity Lost

As for building Afghan capacity, little was done for several years. U.N. representatives on the ground advocated a 'light' international footprint. Rich countries were initially parsimonious in their commitments. In early 2002, Afghanistan was a relatively clean slate on which anything could be written, so long as the country's well-wishers took account of its regional strategic space. But that was not to be.

Paradoxically, after the Taliban recovered, regrouped and re-equipped itself in its safe havens and brought violence back to Afghanistan, a stepped-up civilian effort followed. The Afghanistan Compact, put together in London in January 2006, made nation-building the main focus of the future international effort. Its conceptual flaw was the vision to transform Afghanistan into the image of its benefactors.

The instruments used to achieve this, such as the Provincial Reconstruction Teams, bypassed Afghan institutions and indigenous impulses. Afghan political leaders complained that the parallel structures created by the PRTs undermined their government. Between 2001 and 2009, the Afghan government incurred an expenditure of $5.7 billion through its own budget and institutions, compared to $41 billion committed for assistance to Afghanistan during the same period.

EXTENT OF FRAUD

Audits point to the fact that contractor profits and consultant fees absorbed a substantial part of the international assistance. The 2008 U.S. Commission on Wartime Contracting reported that fraud alone could account for as much as $12 billion spent in Afghanistan and Iraq. Some of this actually funded terrorism and insurgency in Afghanistan. "Every year, nearly $500 million flow into the Taliban kitty from western sources," the former ISI Chief, Asad Durrani wrote recently. This was mainly by way of protection money.

Moreover, all three pillars of Afghanistan's transformation — security, governance and development — were undermined by the growing security deficit. Increasing Taliban attacks immobilised the fledgling state structures at all levels and undermined Afghan growth and development. As Asadullah Khaled, former Kandahar Governor and former head of the National Directorate of Security, told me on my first visit to Kandahar in February 2008: "It is not that the Taliban is strong; it is that we are very weak."

The picture in Afghanistan today is bleak: worsening security, ubiquitous Taliban presence, poor coordination between donors and the government, a slowing economy, and increasing insecurity. A complete exit of ISAF would be a catastrophe for the country, the region and the world. Such an exit would dampen the ongoing development effort, undermine the impressive social and economic gains achieved with so much effort and sacrifice, embolden the enemies of progressive change in Afghanistan, and possibly even lead to a reversal to the *ancien regime* of 2001, with serious security implications worldwide.

So, where do we, the world community, go from here on Afghanistan?

The international community should not abandon Afghanistan. It should not encourage the country's partition or leave it to the mercy of those who are not accountable to the Afghan people. It should avoid acquiescing on exclusive rights over Afghanistan of any single power, or group of outside powers. The global community should abjure extra-territorial demands, defined in terms of a veto over decisions that Afghans themselves must make. Afghanistan's neighbours should guarantee its independence and sovereignty rather than engage in acts that subvert them.

A return to *status quo ante* should be avoided. Terrorist networks in the region, with their cult of suicide bombings, are ever more closely tied to al Qaeda and its associates. Their membership is more dispersed, diverse, and numerous than it was in 2001. Their restitution in Afghanistan might well lead to the unravelling of the state system in Pakistan, creating for India and the world an even bigger security challenge than the one we face today. We must strive to make Afghan security sustainable by supporting its security apparatus and dismantling the infrastructure of terrorism, both within the country and its border regions. Terrorism and insurgency have never ceased anywhere in the world where support, sustenance, and safe havens for terrorists and insurgents have been available in the contiguity.

On development, the world should abandon the idea that it can come from outside. An environment should be created in which Afghanistan can develop itself. Afghan voices should be heard and space allowed for national leadership. We must work towards desirable outcomes, without tangling in processes internal to Afghanistan.

Afghanistan will be economically sustainable when it becomes a trade, transportation, energy, and minerals hub in the region. The Afghan leadership had hoped to join SAARC six years ago, and that Afghanistan would soon become a land bridge linking Iran and Central Asia to China and the Indian subcontinent. The templates and action agendas for dismantling trade and transit barriers, and encouraging freer movement of goods, services, investments, peoples, and ideas, are already in place. It is the inability to operationalise them that prevents Afghanistan's sustained stabilisation.

Hard Task

In spite of multiple international back channels and the efforts of the Afghan High Peace Council, talks with the Taliban have not made much headway. Key players within the Taliban and Pakistan's state structures are yet to be convinced that they should abandon their campaign to seize power by violence. It is a hard act to fight and talk simultaneously. While a lasting and permanent solution with them on board will be difficult, without them it will be impossible. Efforts for peace, re-integration, and reconciliation with the reconcilable must, therefore, continue.

Afghanistan's fragmented polity needs to look at reconciliation — between and among ethnicities, between Afghanistan and its neighbours, and between the government and those elements of the armed opposition ready to embrace democracy and the Afghan Constitution, respect human rights, and end ideological and organisational links with al Qaeda and its associates. As Rumi, the great Afghan Sufi sage said in his *Masnawi* 800 years ago: "Believe in God, yet tie the camel's leg."

THE TALIBAN IN AFGHANISTAN

The Taliban is a predominantly Pashtun, Islamic fundamentalist group that ruled Afghanistan from 1996 until 2001, when a U.S.-led invasion toppled the regime for providing refuge to al-Qaeda and Osama bin Laden. The Taliban regrouped across the border in Pakistan, where its central leadership, headed by Mullah Mohammed Omar, leads an insurgency against the Western-backed government in Kabul. Both the United States and Afghanistan have pursued a negotiated settlement with the Taliban, but talks have little momentum as international forces prepare to conclude combat operations in December 2014 and withdraw by the end of 2016.

Rise of the Taliban

The Taliban was formed in the early 1990s by an Afghan faction of mujahideen, Islamic fighters who had resisted the Soviet occupation of Afghanistan (1979–89) with the covert backing of the U.S. Central Intelligence Agency and its Pakistani counterpart, the Inter-Services Intelligence directorate (ISI). They were joined by younger Pashtun tribesmen who studied in Pakistani madrassas, or seminaries; *taliban* is Pashto for "students." Pashtuns comprise a plurality in Afghanistan and are the predominant ethnic group in much of the country's south and east.

The movement attracted popular support in the initial post-Soviet era by promising to impose stability and rule of law after four years of conflict (1992–1996) among rival mujahideen groups. Talibs entered Kandahar in November 1994 to pacify the crime-ridden southern city, and by September 1996 seized the capital, Kabul, from President Burhanuddin Rabbani, an ethnic Tajik whom they viewed as anti-Pashtun and corrupt. The Taliban regime controlled some 90 percent of the country before its 2001 overthrow, analysts say.

The Taliban imposed its brand of justice as it consolidated territorial control. Taliban jurisprudence was drawn from the Pashtuns' pre-Islamic tribal code and interpretations of sharia colored by the austere Wahhabi doctrines of the madrassas' Saudi benefactors. The regime neglected social services and other basic state functions even as its Ministry for the Promotion of Virtue and Prevention of Vice enforced prohibitions on behavior the Taliban deemed un-Islamic, requiring women to wear the head-to-toe *burqa*, or *chadri*; banning music and television; and jailing men whose beards it deemed too short.

The regime was internationally isolated from its inception. Two UN Security Council resolutions passed in 1998 urged the Taliban to end its abusive treatment of women. The following year the council imposed sanctions on the regime for harboring al-Qaeda. Only Saudi Arabia, the United Arab Emirates, and Pakistan recognized the government. Many analysts say Islamabad supported the Taliban as a force that could unify and stabilize Afghanistan while staving off Indian, Iranian, and Russian influence.

LEADERSHIP AND SUPPORT

Mullah Omar, a cleric and veteran of the anti-Soviet resistance, led Taliban-ruled Afghanistan from 1996 to 2001 as *amir al-mu'minin*, or "commander of the faithful." He granted al-Qaeda sanctuary on the condition that it not antagonize the United States, but bin Laden reneged on their agreement in 1998 when he orchestrated bombings of U.S. embassies in East Africa. The episode was indicative of tensions that emerged between the two groups, analysts say. The Taliban was fundamentally parochial while al-Qaeda had its sights set on global jihad—yet after 9/11, Omar rejected U.S. demands that he give up bin Laden.

Ethnic minority Tajiks, Uzbeks, and Hazaras in northern Afghanistan opposed to Taliban rule formed the Northern Alliance, which assisted U.S.-led forces in routing the Taliban after 9/11. Though the regime was dismantled during the occupation, Mullah Omar and many of his top aides escaped to the frontier territories of Pakistan, where they reconstituted the Taliban's central leadership. Dubbed the "Quetta Shura" for the capital of Balochistan province, where they are believed to have taken refuge, they maintain a degree of operational authority over Afghan Taliban fighters, but appear "unwilling or unable to monopolize anti-state violence," a UN Security Council monitoring team foundin September 2013.

Many experts suspect the Pakistani security establishment continues to provide Taliban militants sanctuary in the country's western tribal areas in an effort to counter India's influence in Afghanistan. Islamabad dismisses these charges. (Tehrik-i-Taliban Pakistan, commonly known as the Pakistani Taliban, is an insurgent group distinct from its Afghan namesake; it coalesced in response to the Pakistani military's incursions into that country's tribal areas. The Afghan Taliban, by contrast, views Pakistan as a benefactor.)

The Taliban's post-2001 resurgence has partially been financed by narcotics production and trafficking, though Mullah Omar issued injunctions against opium production, and the Taliban eradicated much of the poppy crop during its rule. Insurgents and other strongmen extort *ushr*, an agricultural tithe, from farmers and levies at roadside checkpoints. Revenues from illicit mining also contribute to Taliban coffers, whichnet some $400 million a year, the UN estimated in 2012.

Public Opinion of the Taliban

More than a decade since its fall from power, the Taliban enjoys continued, if declining, support. The Asia Foundation found that in 2013, a third of Afghans—mostly Pashtuns and rural Afghans—had sympathy for armed opposition groups (AOGs), primarily the Taliban. Nearly two-thirds of Afghans, the survey found, believed that reconciliation between the government and AOGs would stabilize the country.

Afghan support for the Taliban and allied groups stems in part from grievances directed at public institutions. While the Asia Foundation survey found the Afghan National Army and Afghan National Police garner high public confidence, many civilians see government institutions such as the militia-like Afghan Local Police as predatory. Likewise, international forces' support for warlords and strongmen, an expedient in securing territory, likely also alienated many rural Afghans from Kabul, analysts say.

Many rural Afghans have come to trust the Taliban's extensive judicial network over government courts to "solve disputes in a fair war, without tribal or ethnic bias, or more commonly, without having to pay bribes," says Graeme Smith, a Kabul-based senior analyst at the International Crisis Group.

A Resilient Insurgency

As the Obama administration wound down the war in Iraq, it recommitted the United States to counterinsurgency operations against the Taliban and allied groups in Afghanistan, authorizing a surge that brought peak troop levels to about one hundred thousand in June 2011 and redoubled civilian efforts. Pakistani safe havens stymied U.S. counterinsurgency efforts, though the CIA's targeted-killing program there has sought, in part, to fulfill a "force protection" mission where the U.S. military cannot operate.

But as the Pentagon withdrew the surge troops in 2012, further drew down its military footprint in 2013, and handed lead security authority over to Afghan forces in June of that year, the Taliban-led insurgency escalated.

The United Nations Assistance Mission in Afghanistan (UNAMA) documented 8,615 civilian deaths and injuries in 2013, a 14 percent increase over the previous year and the highest toll since it began keeping these records in 2009. UNAMA attributed the vast majority of these casualties to insurgents who deliberately targeted civilians or used such indiscriminate tactics as improvised explosive devices; other civilians were caught in the crossfire between insurgents and government forces.

In some outlying districts, Afghan forces and local insurgents have reached informal ceasefires that effectively cede a degree of authority to the Taliban. The UN reported in 2014 that the Taliban maintained outright control of four districts, out of 373 nationwide, but the insurgency's reach extends much further: Afghan security forces judged in late 2013 that some 40 percent of districts had a "raised" or "high" threat level.

AN ELUSIVE ENDGAME IN AFGHANISTAN

Afghan forces have taken over nearly all combat operations, but some military analysts question whether they can keep the insurgency at bay as coalition forces draw down. Though NATO's combat mission expires at the end of 2014, a consultative *loya jirga,* a traditional grand assembly of tribal elders and community leaders, overwhelmingly endorsed a longer-term role for the U.S. military and its partners in helping secure the country.

That role is likely to be narrowly circumscribed, however. The United States has articulated a post-2014 mission focused exclusively on training Afghan forces and conducting counterterrorism operations against "the remnants of al-Qaeda." In May 2014, President Barack Obama announced a timetable calling for a complete U.S. withdrawal by the end of 2016. (This residual force is contingent on the Afghan government concluding agreements with the U.S. government and NATO; both candidates vying for the presidency have promised they would sign them.)

Some Afghans and U.S. military analysts see the U.S. withdrawal from Iraq in late 2011, which followed Washington and Baghdad's failure to agree on a renewed status-of-forces agreement, as a cautionary tale. After the last U.S. troops departed Iraq, Sunni insurgents unleashed levels of violence not seen since the height of the civil war several years prior, and made territorial gains across large swathes of the country.

Meanwhile, as an outright battlefield victory appeared unattainable, the United States came to believe by 2010 that political reconciliation "is the solution to ending the war". But talks between the Taliban and the central government have suffered repeated setbacks. Most notably, in September 2011, Kabul's chief negotiator, former president Rabbani, was assassinated. The Taliban has so far shown little interest in accepting the constitution and laying down its arms, while some civil society groups also oppose a negotiated settlement, fearing a backslide on women's rightsand other gains made in the past decade.

U.S.-Taliban talks have not fared better than those carried out by Kabul. Prospective negotiations mediated by Qatar in July 2013 were quickly scuttled after Afghan president Hamid Karzai objected to the manner in which the Taliban opened its office in Doha. The Obama administration had originally explored the prisoner swap of U.S. Army Sgt. Bowe Bergdahl for five Taliban officials as a potential confidence-building measure tethered to broader peace talks, but no such deal was in the works by the time the exchange went through in June 2014; it appears to have taken place as a one-off event.

Some of the White House's detractors contend that the surge's rigid timetable undermined U.S. leverage at a moment when maximum military pressure was brought to bear on the insurgency, and that the anticipated withdrawal has likewise diminished the Taliban's incentives to negotiate.

As coalition forces draw down, the Taliban has recast its mission from one resisting foreign occupation to one that is confronting a government it considers a Western pawn. Meanwhile, its battlefield position and financial interests further reduce its incentives to negotiate, analysts say. The UN says the Taliban and Afghan forces are at a "military stalemate." Other analyses are less optimistic about the central government's ability to hold its ground. The International Crisis Group reports that insurgents are increasingly confident as "ongoing withdrawals of international soldiers have generally coincided with a deterioration of Kabul's reach in outlying districts." An independent assessment of Afghan security forces commissioned by the Pentagon predicts that the Taliban will pick up the tempo of its operations and expand areas under its control between 2015 and 2018.

Meanwhile, strong revenues from a bumper poppy harvest in 2013 and other illicit trade have further reduced the Taliban's incentives to reach a negotiated settlement. Some Taliban factions have become less an ideology-driven armed opposition group than a profit-driven mafia, according to the UN.

But while the insurgency remained formidable, the Taliban failed at one of its chief strategic objectives of 2014: mass disruption of Afghanistan's provincial and presidential elections.

ECONOMIC, SOCIAL, POLITICAL AND SECURITY CONTEXT

10. To understand DFID's work in Afghanistan and its future strategy it is necessary to understand the economic, social, political and security context in which it currently works within country and what could potentially happen in the future.

Economic Context

Afghanistan is one of the poorest countries in the world. A third of the population lives on less than 60p per day. Aid has supported much of its economic progress since 2001 and the Afghan Government remains heavily aid dependent. While the withdrawal of international combat forces will have its own economic impact, the World Bank also projects "an expected decline in civilian aid as international attention shifts elsewhere." The average growth rate has been 9% over the past nine years but it is expected to decrease to 5-6% from 2011 to 2018. Given that 70% of the population is under 25 years old and population growth is expected to continue at 2.8% annually, this is likely to mean continued high unemployment among the youth and little progress in reducing poverty.

The Afghan economy is largely dependent on agriculture and rural trade; around 85 % of the population is entirely reliant on income from agriculture and livestock. This is despite the fact that only 12 % of the country's land is arable and only half of that is currently under cultivation. Agricultural growth over the past decade has been volatile, in part due to Afghanistan's vulnerability to disasters, and improvements remain limited. Agriculture and livestock based livelihoods remain largely dependent upon the success of rain-fed crops and pasture. Afghanistan experienced its eighth drought in eleven years in 2011, devastating rural families and threatening any potential progress in alleviating rural poverty.

Afghanistan's agricultural economy is under developed. The British and Irish Agencies Afghanistan Group (BAAG) highlighted the lack of market knowledge and modern agricultural and business skills in Afghanistan. We heard while we were in Afghanistan that many agricultural products were sent to Pakistan to be processed or stored and then sold back to Afghanistan at much higher prices.

The illicit economy, particularly around opium, remains significant. The income from opium production in 2011 was estimated to be roughly equivalent to 9% of the GDP. Afghanistan is believed to supply roughly 93% of the opium on the world market and 90% of the heroin trafficked into the UK originated in Afghanistan. While poppy eradication and alternative livelihood programmes have had mixed results, a UN Office on Drugs and Crime report finds a "strong association" between insecurity, lack of agricultural assistance and poppy cultivation.

The big hope for the future Afghan economy is its potential mineral wealth. Initial estimates from the US Geological Survey have suggested a possible $3 trillion in mineral assets, based on a partial survey of the country. However, mining profits are not likely to come online for another decade and it is an industry that generally does not result in widespread national employment. It also requires a skilled and mobile workforce and infrastructure to exploit resources that are largely located in remote or mountainous areas of the country—none of which are currently evident in Afghanistan.

GENDER AND WOMEN'S PARTICIPATION IN SOCIETY

Women in Afghanistan have made gains since the Taliban-led Government was ousted in 2001. The Constitution grants equal rights to men and women and Afghanistan is a signatory to the Convention on the Elimination of all Forms of Discrimination Against Women (CEDAW). More girls are in school now than ever before in the country's history and more than a quarter of Afghanistan's parliamentarians are female. The legal and policy frameworks protecting and empowering women have been expanded in recent years including the establishment of a National Action Plan for the Women of Afghanistan (NAPWA) in 2007 and the Elimination of Violence Against Women (EVAW) law, which criminalised rape, in 2009.

However, such gains are limited, and women and girls in Afghanistan continue to face enormous disadvantages. Afghan women's status remains amongst the worst in the world according to the UN's 2011 Gender Inequality Index. NAPWA has not been implemented and the EVAW law remains largely unenforced; 87% of women report experiencing at least one form of domestic abuse which Human Rights Watch has specified as: physical, sexual, or psychological domestic violence or forced marriage and women who participate in public life do so at significant risk to their safety.

There are worrying signs that the advancements for women and girls made in the early years after the fall of the Taliban are receding. Human Rights Watch has repeatedly expressed concerns over the Afghan Government's increasingly conservative stance on the role of women, including President Karzai's recent public statement in support of the Ulema Council that instructed women not to travel unchaperoned or mix with men in education or work. There has been a sharp rise in violent attacks on women in Afghanistan over the past year with 17 cases of "honour killings" recorded across the country in March and April compared to 20 cases recorded for all of last year.

Political Context

Afghanistan has been plagued by war and instability for more than three decades. For the past ten years, international forces and the Afghan Government have been at war with the Taliban. There has been little progress in negotiating a political settlement to the conflict. The role of the US, and Afghanistan's neighbouring countries, in establishing political talks and a realistic and successful process of security transition will be critical in averting regional interference and continued or new internal conflict.

Despite significant international support and the presence of ISAF, the control of the government is tenuous. Historically, Afghan Government has been highly centralised with significant regional devolution of power in practice. Informal power networks, such as ethnic or tribal structures and former mujahedeen commanders, are as significant, if not more so, in shaping Afghan political, social and economic dynamics. As Mervyn Lee of Mercy Corps told us "Afghanistan as a country has never really respected Kabul. The rest of Afghanistan looks a bit askance at Kabul." Government institutions at the sub-national level remain, weak and disconnected from the central Government.

Afghanistan is comprised of numerous ethnic groups, including Pashtuns, Tajiks, Hazaras and Uzbeks. Post-Taliban political affiliation has broadly followed along ethnic, tribal and regional lines as demonstrated by the composition of voting blocks in recent elections. The development of political parties has been slow, with few that can be considered pan-ethnic. There have been very few incidents of ethnic-based violence since the fall of the Taliban, but lack of rule of law (particularly in rural areas) has led to local clashes over land or economic resources between various groups that have contributed to insecurity and provided openings for the insurgency.

Afghanistan has historically lacked democratically elected institutions. The Parliament, introduced after the fall of the Taliban, is a bi-cameral structure comprised of the *Meshrano Jirga* (the Upper House) and *Wolesi Jirga* (the Lower House). It has at times taken a hard stand against President Karzai (for example, blocking the confirmation of several of President Karzai's post-2009 election ministers) and pressed for more accountable governance but has often been slow to pass legislation and enact key reforms..

Civil society has been traditionally weak, but has experienced enormous growth since the fall of the Taliban. Many civil society groups are concerned about the ways in which insecurity, transition and other factors will impact upon them.

The Afghanistan Independent Human Rights Commission (to which the UK provides funding) appears to be under increasing political pressure, with the recent dismissal of three of its Commissioners by President Karzai. There have been allegations that they were removed due to a still-unreleased report on war crimes that implicated members of the Government, including First Vice President Fahim and Second Vice President Khalili; the Afghan Government denies this.

Their positions remain vacant with the Commission severely impaired and now functioning with only five of its nine Commissioners (a fourth was killed in 2011 and not replaced). The Commission plays a vital role in monitoring rights abuses and has in the past been a vocal and effective advocate for those whose rights have been violated. The media is also under increasing pressure. Following several high profile imprisonments of journalists and Government investigations of independent media outlets, a draft media law was recently introduced that would significantly expand Government control of media and curtail press freedom.

President Karzai, elected in 2004 and re-elected in 2009, is not eligible for re-election in 2014 due to constitutional term limits. There is currently no clear successor. Some analysts believe that President Karzai will ultimately select a candidate to endorse and attempt to continue to exert his influence through this individual. Others believe that he may attempt to stay on, for example by convening a *loya jirga* to alter the constitution. President Karzai has denied such speculation and issued a public statement confirming that he would leave office once his term expired.

The prospect of security transition has exacerbated Afghanistan's already volatile political landscape. Key individuals within the Government are already positioning themselves for the withdrawal of international forces, fuelling uncertainty and unpredictability across Afghanistan's political landscape. On 4 August 2012, the Parliament voted to dismiss both the Minister of Defence, Abdul Rahim Wardak, and the Minister of the Interior, Bismullah Khan Mohameddi. President Karzai has recently identified replacements and has also replaced the head of the National Directorate for Security. While not yet confirmed, these appointments have raised some concerns from human rights activists. There is also uncertainty about the Minister of Finance, Omar Zakhilwal, who is currently under investigation for corruption. Analysts have interpreted these developments, particularly with regard to the Ministries of Defence and Interior, as political manoeuvres orchestrated by President Karzai to strengthen his position among southern Pashtuns.

CORRUPTION

Fraud and widespread corruption have undermined international confidence in the Afghan Government. The previous Secretary of State, Rt Hon Andrew Mitchell, described corruption as "endemic in Afghanistan." There are indications that the problem is getting worse: Afghanistan ranks 180 out of 183 on Transparency International 2011 Corruption Perception Index, compared to 117 out of the 158 countries ranked in 2005. We heard evidence that corruption is a growing threat not only to the effectiveness of international assistance but also the legitimacy of the state in the eyes of the Afghan people and ultimately the long term viability of the Government. David Loyn, a BBC correspondent, told us: At the moment, it is effectively a rentier state. There is quite a lot of academic work now about rentier states. They do not succeed; they are mostly in Africa; and they tend to create elites who are funded by corrupt patronage, use patronage and fund corrupt practices. That is exactly what has been happening in Afghanistan.

Since our predecessor Committee's report, several Government bodies have been created and initiatives have been launched to fight corruption. These include the High Office of Oversight and Anti-Corruption and the Major Crimes Task Force within the Attorney General's Office. Most recently, on 21 June 2012, President Karzai launched an anti-corruption push in the Afghan Parliament by appealing to donors not to give construction and businesses contracts to Afghan Government officials or their relatives. Unfortunately, the effectiveness of these initiatives has been extremely limited, and often obstructed by interference from senior officials. An Asia Foundation study commented that:

Efforts at curbing corruption to date appear too modest, often ill-suited, badly-informed, and narrow-minded. As a result, if there are some anti-corruption successes, they look like islands of integrity.

Similarly, the recent Independent Commission on Aid Impact (ICAI)'s audit of DFID's programme in Afghanistan warned:

Anti-corruption measures in Afghanistan are ineffective. There are multiple agencies with ill-defined roles and limited independence. Afghan agencies such as the Ministry of Justice and the police force have a history of reported corruption.

David Loyn argued that the massive influx of international aid in recent years had exacerbated corruption. The Asia Foundation study commented that:

Oversight mechanisms have been overwhelmed, while insecurity makes it impossible for many donors to go visit the projects that they fund. Some have even institutionalized the absence of oversight. Massive inflows of aid also mean pressure to spend quickly, which has often led to parallel systems lacking in accountability, and non-participatory or discretionary decision-making.

While David Loyn thought there would be a significant reduction in corruption when aid decreased, other witnesses felt that the deeply entrenched patronage networks that drive corruption were unlikely to simply go away. These networks may continue to play a significant political and economic role, and the ways in which they might adapt to the withdrawal of troops and a likely decrease in aid was of concern. Dr Gordon of the LSE commented: I think the real concern in terms of many of the institutions is the way in which they adapt to the tap being turned off and the way in which they reconnect, or connect more firmly, to the narcotics industry.

Kabul Bank Scandal

The Kabul Bank scandal has perhaps been the most visible and damaging case of corruption to date in Afghanistan. Prior to the scandal, Kabul Bank held accounts for several key ministries and paid the salaries for civil servants, teachers, police and other Government employees. It is reported that the bank's management had ties to key powerholders including Vice President Marshall Fahim and the brother of the President, Mahmoud Karzai, who allegedly received a significant loan from the Kabul Bank to buy his share in the bank. In September 2010, when hundreds of millions of dollars in losses were reported, primarily from shareholder investments in Dubai, there was effectively a run on the bank. Public confidence in the banking system was severely eroded. The International Monetary Fund (IMF) suspended its credit programme to the Afghan Government, requesting an audit of Afghan banks, and several donors (including the UK) suspended, but have since resumed, funding to the Afghanistan Reconstruction Trust Fund.

DFID has been working with the Afghan Ministry of Finance to help recover some of the assets. The Minister of Finance, Omar Zakhilwal, assured us when we met him in Kabul that he was taking action not only to recover assets but to bring the perpetrators to justice. While some of the funds have been traced, there has been little concrete action to date to bring those believed to be responsible to justice. David Loyn told us: $120 million of the Kabul Bank money that was stolen has been traced. There is more widespread acceptance that they will not get a huge amount more of it back. There has been a property market collapse in Dubai. No one knows quite how much money there really is. If it had been invested, it would now be $900million, but the belief is that it is probably around $500million that they would be looking for. Since our visit it has been reported that the Finance Minister himself has also come under investigation for separate allegations of corruption.

The Kabul Bank crisis is but one of many examples that illustrate just how significantly corruption threatens to undermine the state. High profile scandals continue to emerge. In June 2012, the EU suspended funding to the Law and Order Trust Fund, which supplies funds for 120,000 Afghan police salaries, due to allegations of corruption. The fund has received $2.9billion in aid from multiple nations, including the UK, since 2002. With less aid money flowing into Afghanistan, donors may gain greater leverage to hold the Afghan Government to account on these issues and impose stronger conditions on funding to the Government. Doing so requires strong coordination, vigilant monitoring and sustained political will within the international community to tackle the problem.

ELECTIONS

Presidential elections were last held in 2009 and Parliamentary elections in 2010. Both elections were marred by widespread violence and fraud. The next round of Presidential elections will be held in 2014, prior to the end of security transition, and Parliamentary elections are due to be held in 2015, following the end of the formal security transition process. 2014 will be the first post-Taliban Presidential election in which President Karzai will not stand.

It has been reported that urgently needed reforms to the electoral law and structure of the Independent Electoral Commission have been slow moving. There is also significant concern that it is already too late to correct voter lists in time for the Presidential election, given the challenges of widespread illiteracy, a high proportion of the population without formal identity documents and worsening security problems. Witnesses questioned the Afghan Government's capacity—and indeed willingness—to support transparent, inclusive, fair and credible electoral process. David Loyn commented that "There will be, over the next two years—we have already seen it—significant pressure from President Karzai to keep the international community out."

Security

The Committee received a positive briefing from British and ISAF military commanders while in Afghanistan which indicated that they believed security had improved during the past year.

Their position was that it was now much safer for Afghans to travel around and there was much more freedom of movement. In addition Dr Gordon of the London School of Economics told us of a recent trip to Helmand: I went on a patrol with the American military in Sangin, and unlike on earlier trips there was no shooting and no IEDs. We managed to walk through the bazaar for the best part of two hours. You could never have done that 18 months or so before that. There has been a change.

The United Nations Assistance Mission in Afghanistan (UNAMA) Human Rights Unit also found that violence had dropped slightly in the first six months of 2012. In all, 1,145 civilians were killed and 1,954 wounded in the first half of 2012, down 15% on the same six-month period in 2011.

However, UN officials called the reduction a "hollow trend" and warned that civilians were still being killed at "alarmingly high levels", with four-fifths of deaths attributed to attacks by the Taliban-led insurgency. Nicholas Haysom, the UN's Deputy Special Representative to Afghanistan, said: The reduction in civilian casualties is welcomed, but these gains are fragile. They do not reflect a move towards a peaceful society. This report does not suggest that Afghans are necessarily safer or better protected in their communities. Nor does is suggest any real or concerted attempt by anti-government elements to minimise civilian casualties.

While the proportion killed by Afghan Government or ISAF forces has dropped to around 10%, a significant reduction from previous years, targeted killings by insurgents of civilians, such as Government employees, tribal elders and contractors, working with the Government or ISAF forces rose by 53%. Moreover, the UN indicated that violence had increased in July 2012.

Regardless of the reduction of violence in the first half of 2012 other organisations argued that the security situation had significantly deteriorated overall since 2006. The International Committee of the Red Cross (ICRC) described the current situation: Widespread conflict continues to devastate the live of Afghans in many districts and villages. The threat of civilian casualties, internal displacement, and insufficient access to medical care, are only some of the challenges. All of them occur against a backdrop of a splintering of armed groups, night raids, air strikes, suicide bombing, and the laying of improvised explosive devices. The expansion of the conflict to previously quiet areas has increased people's difficulties and left whole communities trapped between warring parties. The south, east, north, north-west and central regions are the worst affected.

Despite the surge in international troops since 2010 and increased civilian and military aid, 2011 was the most violent year since 2001. The Afghan NGO Safety Office (ANSO) reported that opposition attacks increased to 40 a day in the first six months of the year, up 119% since 2009 and 42 % since 2010. Insurgent attacks reached previously secure areas including Parwan and Bamiyan as the war spread to many new parts of the country. In addition, 2011 saw the highest number of civilian casualties since 2001. UNAMA recorded 3,021 conflict-related civilian deaths in 2001, an 8% increase since 2010. Some 80% were attributed to anti-government forces, most commonly caused by IEDs.

The International Rescue Committee noted that this deterioration was true both for "classic" security related to conflict and violence, but also for personal security. As evidence, they pointed to record low returns of Afghan refugees from other countries, record high numbers of Afghan asylum seekers in other countries, record high internal displacement and increasing migration from rural to urban areas in search of economic opportunities.

BAAG reported that the deteriorating security situation was threatening the ability of NGOs to operate in many areas of the country, including major cities. ANSO also reported a 73% increase since 2010 in attacks against aid workers. David Page of Afghanaid said: We are already experiencing a deterioration of the security conditions in the provinces where we work. One hears that in Helmand things are a great deal better, but in Ghor to the north of Helmand, or even in Badakhshan in the north-east, you have got a great deal more instability as people position themselves for this 2014 deadline.

The Afghan diaspora in the UK told as that they increasingly feared kidnappings when returning to visit family in Afghanistan and therefore kept a very low profile. This was echoed by the businessmen we met at the Afghan Chambers of Commerce who spoke of their fear of kidnapping and of violence against themselves and their families.

ANTI-GOVERNMENT GROUPS

The Afghan Taliban consists of a complex network of several linked groups. After the Taliban collapsed in 2001, many of its leaders fled to Pakistan and have reorganised under the leadership of the Quetta shura. In addition, the Haqqani network, Hezb-i-Islami Gulbuddin and several other insurgent groups function throughout the country with different levels of integration, coordination and cooperation with one another. The reliability of estimates of the size of the Taliban's fighting force are questionable, but publicly reported ISAF estimates have remained consistent in recent years at approximately 25,000-35,000 fighters. The leadership of many of these groups, including the Islamic Emirate and Haqqani, are believed to reside in Pakistan and there are strong allegations that they receive support from individuals, including Pakistani intelligence officials, with links to the Pakistan Government. There is mounting evidence that Pakistan's support may extend further. A leaked 2012 ISAF report asserted that "the Government of Pakistan remains intimately involved with the

Taliban" and that "Pakistan remains fundamentally opposed to GIRoA [Government of the Islamic Republic of Afghanistan]."

Other criminals and warlords not allied with the Taliban continue to threaten security. Motivations are not ideological but primarily economic, and often linked to the resurgent poppy economy. The UN Office on Drugs and Crime estimates that the Taliban and criminal groups derive $150million a year from the narcotics trade.

AFGHAN NATIONAL SECURITY FORCES

At the London Conference in 2010 the troop-contributing countries agreed, together with the Afghan Government, that the international forces would gradually transfer responsibility for security across Afghanistan to the Afghan National Security Forces (ANSF). The NATO mission aimed to train a 157,000 strong police force and 195,000 soldiers by the end of 2012 to take over from international forces and this is believed to be on track, with 149,600 police and 194,500 army as of mid-May 2012.

Transition began in July 2011 and is happening in phases with tranches of districts and provinces being handed over to the Afghan forces. Three tranches have already begun the handover process, with two remaining. All tranches will have completed transition by the end of 2014.

Afghan National Army

There was a notable difference in the use of language we heard from the British military on our visit to Afghanistan compared to that of 2007—there was no longer talk of beating the insurgents and winning hearts and minds but instead creating a situation where the Afghan Government and the Afghan National Army (ANA) could control the situation.

Brigadier Skeates, deputy commander of Regional Command (Southwest), told us that no one would win militarily and that peace had to come through a political settlement. We were told by Task Force Helmand that there would always be insurgents with over 25,000 over the border in Pakistan—their aim was therefore not to beat them but to tip the balance towards the

Afghan Government and ANA so they would be in a better position to maintain security.

ISAF is backing away from direct counter insurgency work and instead is training and advising the ANA as well as providing capabilities such as medical support and helicopters. We also heard many references to the work of DFID from the military and its importance in changing livelihoods to provide incentives to discourage people from growing poppies or joining the Taliban. There were also discussions about the slow pace of progress and being realistic about what 'success' looked like as opposed to discussions of fast gains.

David Loyn believed there had been improvements with the Afghan Army: They are better than they were. The trainers I talked to say that they are better than they thought they were going to be by now. The mid ranking ANA officers whom I have spoken to are in a completely different league to where they were only four or five years ago. They seem to be an impressive and cohesive national force.

Whether they will be able to guarantee security particularly in the absence of a political settlement to end the conflict remains unclear. David Loyn conceded "They are not anything like as good as the forces that the Russians had put together by the same period; they are nothing like as ruthless. We are leaving Afghanistan in a much less secure state than it was left in 1989."

Afghan National Police

With regard to the Afghan police, our predecessor Committee concluded that "corruption and bribery are rife and this is hampering acceptance of the police as a force for good." While we recognise that there have been some improvements in training and recruitment, we share the same concerns as our predecessor Committee with regard to the capacity and accountability of the Afghan police. On our visit to Afghanistan, we heard strong fears from Afghans about corruption and the ineffectiveness of the police force. A survey released by the UN earlier in 2012 found that more than half of Afghans see the police as corrupt. While the survey notes that public opinion has slightly improved in recent years, only 20% believe that the police will be able to keep order once international forces leave.

There were also concerns that the Afghan police continue to play a paramilitary role rather than one focused on civilian policing and tackling criminality. Civil society groups believed that the police—particularly those outside of Kabul—were trained on counter insurgency rather than on civilian policing models, focused on protecting civilians and upholding the law.

They also suggested that many police were loyal to their local commander rather than to the Government. These local commanders did not have a sense of responsibility to the community but saw their position as the reward of a larger patronage system. They were therefore reluctant to report crimes, as they did not want their area to be seen as dangerous and therefore that they were failing in their role.

The Afghan female civil society activists we met in Kabul were very critical of the police attitude towards women. That told us that women did not trust the police as they often shouted insults and were viewed as unaccountable for their actions. This echoes results from a 2011 survey of the views of women in Kabul on the Afghan police, which found that women rarely felt that they could turn to police for help. This survey also found that there was significant resistance to gender or human rights-focused training or policies within the Ministry of Interior and that much of the albeit modest progress in recruiting women police and gender-sensitising policing was a result of consistent international pressure.

Oxfam recommended reforms such as better training and awareness regarding human rights and women's rights, accelerated recruitment of female security personnel, and much greater attention to women's needs such as increased awareness and enforcement of laws addressing violence against women. Our predecessor Committee also recommended that "the recruitment, training and retention of female police officers" should be "given appropriate priority". In addition Oxfam would like to see established a well-publicised, transparent and independent complaints review mechanisms for the ANP, accessible to both men and women.

Afghan Local Police

Human Rights Watch were concerned by the Afghan Government efforts to combat insurgency by arming and providing money, with little oversight, to militias that have been implicated in killings, rape, and forcible collection of illegal taxes. The Afghan Local Police (ALP), village-based defence forces trained and mentored primarily by US Special Forces but which report to the Ministry of Interior, have been created in parts of the country with limited police and military presence. There are believed to be approximately 13,000 ALP, with 30,000 planned to be recruited and trained by the end of 2014. In its first year ALP units were implicated—with few consequences for perpetrators—in killings, abductions illegal raids, and beatings, raising serious questions about Government and international efforts to vet and train these forces There is little to no oversight and accountability and the ANSF in general lacks sufficient, accessible complaints mechanisms. Our predecessor Committee raised concerns about such militias, stating: We have reservations about the suggestion of arming local communities to defend themselves. While we accept that there are many people who already have weapons, we believe that it is important that donors do not encourage or exacerbate factionalism and tribalism.

Afghan National Security Forces

While there has been significant progress with the ANSF, the effort faces serious challenges, including attrition, insurgent infiltration, illiteracy and substance abuse among recruits. Incidents in which ANSF have attacked and killed their international mentors known as 'green on blue' attacks are of growing concern. There have been 34 such attacks so far this year resulting in the deaths of 45 international troops and accounting for a quarter of UK military deaths to date in 2012.

What is increasingly clear is that the current target for the ANSF will be financially unsustainable. As Robert Fox told the Defence Committee recently "nobody believes for a minute that that number could be sustained on the funding that is likely to be available after 2014." Prior to the NATO summit in Chicago, a conceptual model for the Afghan security forces after 2014 was endorsed that foresaw a target of 228,500 police and army personnel by the end of 2017—a reduction of 123,500—with an annual estimated budget of $4.1billion. This figure is equivalent to a quarter of Afghanistan's gross domestic product and is two and half times total annual Government revenue. It is currently unclear how much money goes to the ANSF due to lack of donor coordination and transparency, but retaining the current force size is estimated to cost $5billion annually. Even if this reduction is gradual, it presents a number of challenges in terms of disarmament, creating viable alternative employment for those dismissed and sustaining international financial support for the annual budget requirements to support the ANSF. As Gerard Russell, an analyst on Afghanistan, highlighted: Afghan forces will rise to a peak of 350,000 people, but will that be sustainable? [...] Or is this going to end up being a system by which many people are recruited—perhaps hastily recruited—and trained in how to use a weapon and then made unemployed?

There are also concerns about whether troops will remain loyal to the central Government after 2014, particularly if funding for security forces is reduced. Dr Gordon of the LSE said: If you remove the funding, what you have got is a well trained militia. There are already signs, in parts of Helmand and elsewhere, in particular, of some of those security forces, particularly the ANA and some of the militia, realigning with some of the local power brokers; the old strongmen. I think it is that fragmentation along tribal and patronage network lines that is the real concern.

The ANSF is mostly a defence matter and a subject that the House of Commons Defence Committee is currently inquiring into. However, its success is important to the delivery of development in Afghanistan. In addition, DFID has a role to play in this. DFID funds £7,230,000 on 'Strategic Support' advice to the Ministry of Interior, 2010-14, which aims to support the capability and accountability of the ministry. The Ministry of the Interior is responsible for both the Afghan National Police and the Afghan Local Police. The then Secretary of State also informed us that DFID provides funding to the Afghanistan Independent Human

Rights Commission which investigates human rights abuses. In its oversight advice role to the Ministry of Interior on accountability, we recommend that DFID insist on the creation of an external oversight body to provide a way to investigate and follow up allegations of violations by not only Afghan Local Police but the whole of the Afghan National Security Force. This body could potentially be managed by the Afghan Independent Human Rights Commission which is also supported by the UK Government. Such a body should be empowered to receive and investigate complaints, make public their findings and make recommendations about how to redress individual complaints.

PEACE AND RECONCILIATION

Little progress has been made on working towards a political settlement that would end the conflict between the Afghan Government, international forces and the various factions of the insurgency. A High Peace Council was appointed by President Karzai in September 2010 to facilitate peace talks and to lead reconciliation. The Council was initially chaired by former President of Afghanistan, Burhanuddin Rabbani and membership included some former members of the Taliban, former mujahedeen leaders and nine women. Outreach efforts by the High Peace Council have been undermined by ongoing violence in many parts of the country. This culminated in the September 2011 assassination of Rabbani and the subsequent assassination in May 2012 of High Peace Council member Arsala Rahmani effectively halting its work.

In January 2012 the Taliban announced it would open an office in Doha, Qatar, which led commentators to believe they were ready to negotiate. But by March 2012 the Taliban said it was suspending negotiations with the USA. It is thought that this was because the Taliban did not accept the presence of the Karzai Government at the talks which it sees as illegitimate, or due to the US failure to agree to a proposed prisoner swap.

Another challenge has been the role of regional powers, particularly Pakistan but also Iran and India. The Afghan Government has accused the Pakistan Government of obstructing the peace process in the past and Pakistan continues to deny the existence of high level insurgent leaders in its territory. However, there have been recent signs of progress. In July 2012, the Afghan Government and Pakistan Government agreed to regular meetings for a bi-lateral Peace Commission. Pakistan has also agreed to help facilitate talks with Taliban leaders and Afghan Government officials recently confirmed a meeting with a member of the Taliban leadership in Pakistan.

The Afghan Peace and Reintegration Programme (APRP) was created following the Kabul conference in June 2010 to try to reintegrate mid and low level fighters through financial incentives and training. APRP is supported directly through a trust fund administered by the United Nations Development Programme, which has received donations from 12 nations including the UK. The success of APRP has been limited. We were told by Brigadier Skeates in Helmand that only 62 out of a potential 5,000 insurgents in Helmand had joined the programme. The UN reported that as of May 2012, just 4,641 former insurgents had reintegrated through APRP nationally. BAAG and Christian Aid expressed concerns about APRP. They cited limited gains in recruiting genuine reintegrees, human rights concerns, failure to provide insurgents with jobs and assistance, little credibility among the Afghan people and documented cases of individuals then returning to the insurgency.

POST 2014 SCENARIO

The impact of the withdrawal of international troops remains to be seen and the opinions of analysts and other experts vary. Dr Gordon told us the most likely scenario was "somewhere towards status quo and partial meltdown in some areas, but with a central degree of authority and stability". The UN has forecasted "a continued escalation of violent conflict fuelled by the departure of foreign security forces in country and subsequent increased humanitarian need, coupled with nominal humanitarian access or assistance." Mercy Corps, an NGO working across Afghanistan and funded by DFID for its work in Helmand, was concerned by the potential spread of insecurity as tranches were handed over to ANSF, and the ISAF presence reduced. It told us that without a relatively secure environment, it was unlikely that economic and development progress would be achieved or maintained and that if fighting and conflict spread at the local level, the economy would almost certainly suffer.

Security during and after transition depends on a number of variables, including the capacity of the ANSF in 2014, the support and the role of the ISAF contributing countries and the military advisers that remain on after 2014. Naysan Adlparvar, a researcher on Afghanistan, said peace hinged on: the amount, continuity and modalities of aid committed to Afghanistan; sources of growth; the emerging investment climate; the outcome and acceptability of the pending presidential elections; the role played by regional powers including Pakistan; and whether a political settlement with the Taliban, and other armed groups, is achieved and accepted by the Afghan people.

While much of Afghanistan's future economic stability depends on an improvement, or at minimum a halt, to the continued deterioration, of security, it also depends on continued financial support from the international community. The World Bank expects economic growth to slow up to 2025, and said that "sudden sharp drops in aid can be particularly destabilising by changing perceptions of the Government's strength and encouraging political actors and armed groups to challenge the state's authority." Afghanistan has one of the highest aid dependencies in the world with 71% of its GDP funded by external assistance. Key donors have made significant, if reduced, pledges to support both the security forces as well as development and humanitarian assistance. As part of the $4.1billion pledged annually for security forces at the NATO Summit held in Chicago in May 2012, the British Government has pledged to provide £70million (approximately $110million) annually. The Afghan Government aims to assume responsibility for these costs by 2024. The Tokyo Conference resulted in donors pledging $16billion in civilian aid to Afghanistan up to 2015—a 35% decrease from current funding levels.

There is also a concern that as a result of the withdrawal of international combat forces there will be a reduction in spending by the military which currently bolsters the Afghan economy. There will no longer be the high level of demand for food and provisions from local Afghan businesses which supply the foreign military forces and there will also be the loss of wages for civilian staff, security guards and interpreters who work for ISAF. A dramatic fall in GDP at the point of transition would undermine security, fuel perceptions of the international community turning its back on the country and ultimately threaten stability. ISAF troop-contributing countries (including the UK) should therefore quantify the likely economic impact of military withdrawal and commit to spend part of the peace dividend they gain when they bring troops home on ODA to Afghanistan, particularly in the years immediately following withdrawal.

It is currently unclear where any reduction in aid after 2014 will be focused or how quickly aid will decline. There is a risk of both security and development being underfunded, with a resultant deterioration in public services. Global Witness projected that "a reduction in foreign development assistance will correlate directly to a reduction in the Government's ability to provide services, infrastructure projects, Government salaries, and security [...] There is a significant risk to development gains made in the past ten years if the transition is not carefully planned, and alternative and sustainable sources of funding are not secured." Dr Gordon said that one of his main concerns was if the amount of international oversight of Kabul's expenditure was reduced there would be a further reduction of money flowing from Kabul down to the district level. He predicted that if that occurred it would have a dramatic impact on governance arrangements and make it more likely that other patronage systems would become more dominant and the informal sector of governance would end up dominating the formal. It is not just a potential decrease in aid money and the drawdown of troops that is likely to affect the economy. The World Bank noted: Recent performance has been on a downward trend [...] transition presents serious threats to growth and economic stability, but these do not directly stem from declining aid itself. Key economic vulnerabilities are risks of drought (which would adversely affect volatile agricultural production) and of falling business confidence as a result of worsening insecurity, corruption, governance and uncertainty over Afghanistan's political future.

Impact at the local level is likely to vary, with provinces heavily dependent on aid tied to security objectives and on funding from the PRTs likely to be most severely affected. Mercy Corps highlighted that a large percentage of construction and related industries in Helmand were significantly bolstered by contracts awarded by the PRT. These range from the building of police checkpoints, road repair and school construction to repairs and maintenance of generators and electrical apparatus. It believed that without an international presence providing funding and overseeing these contracts the number and value would sharply decrease. Those which remained were likely to be awarded to a small number of companies, often based outside of Helmand and even Afghanistan, that have political support or links to Government officials. This meant that the construction boom that Helmand had experienced was likely to stall and previously working men of fighting age would be faced with fresh economic challenges.

A concern we heard whilst in Afghanistan was that the young and educated Afghans were already preparing to leave due to fear of what was going to happen post 2014. Ahmed Rashid believed that the exodus had already started and that this would have a detrimental effect on the civil service in which they were often working as well as the economy as it was losing its skilled labour.

As this chapter demonstrates, the situation in Afghanistan is very complex. There are great uncertainties about the political, security and economic future of Afghanistan, notably: the outcome of the 2014 elections; whether there will be a political settlement; economic growth; and the role of Afghanistan's neighbouring countries. In the light of these uncertainties DFID will need to be able to adapt. DFID will also need to continue to lead donors in pledging and disbursing aid so that there will not be any sudden drops in funding which could exacerbate an extremely fragile situation. Based on the assessment of the likely economic impact of military withdrawal, the UK Government should be prepared to do whatever it can to address this potential shortfall in spending including urging other governments to increase their aid commitments to Afghanistan to fill the economic gap.

THE REALITY OF LIFE IN AFGHANISTAN SINCE THE FALL OF THE TALIBAN

Afghanistan under American Invasion

The United Nations organisations (UNDP, UNICEF, UNHCR, and ILO) and international NGOs (amongst others, Human Rights Watch, the Aga Khan Foundation and the Afghan Research and Evaluation Unit) provide reliable reports and statistics. However, their experiences are limited to their own specific projects. Also their environment is sterile, as they have to protect themselves against possible hostilities from the remnants of the Taliban and al-Qaeda. They are not allowed to mix with ordinary Afghans, although some of them are brave enough to do so as they find it frustrating not being able to be reflective and learn the truth about the reality in Afghanistan. I am grateful to these organisations for helping me. As a researcher and writer, I studied the information provided by them, but I learned a great deal more about the experiences of women and men by staying and travelling with Afghan friends in Kabul, Jalalabad and Mazar-e Sharif, here I share with you my experience and findings.

Years of wars and violent conflicts left Afghanistan with massive loss of life, displacement and physical and environmental destruction. With the fall of the Taliban in 2001, many Afghans expected to attain peace and development. However, after four years of American led invasion, in the words of the United Nations Development Programme, reconstruction and development is urgently needed otherwise this fragile nation could easily slip back into chaos and abject poverty. Very little has been invested in reconstruction. Out of 21,000 kilometres of roads, only 2,793 kilometres are paved. There are 47 airports, but only 10 have paved runways, and only 3 of them are over 3,047 meters.

No investment has been made to make the Ariana Airline (the Afghan national airline) a viable airline to travel with. The workers of the UN and international NGOs are not allowed to travel on the Ariana Airline, because it is not safe. Instead a number of western private airline companies provide services for foreign workers under the name: 'provision of services for humanitarian, relief and development projects and organisations'. They charge between US$60-1600 per journey depending on the distance and the security of the area. In the eyes of many Afghans the invasion forces are not reconstructing, they are making a huge amount of profit out of Afghanistan's destruction.

In Kabul and a few other urban centres, big houses and businesses are being built. Many believe that these lands and properties belong to those Afghans who escaped their country during the years of war and violent conflicts and have not returned yet. According to the Afghans I interviewed, the warlords who killed raped and terrorised the population for years, are now working with some foreign contractors, confiscating these properties and building big houses and businesses for themselves.

Damaged buildings are not demolished and rebuilt. In some cases 2 or 3 floors are built on top of damaged foundations. As a result a number of schools and hospitals have collapsed, killing children, teachers, sick people and workers.

The government has given the private sector responsibility for the reconstruction. This means that in the absence of Afghan entrepreneurs, the limited reconstruction which takes place involves foreign companies and warlords. Many Afghans are concerned about the future of their economy based on a combination of foreign and warlord's capital. The international NGOs are responsible for provision of services. But like everywhere else in the world, they are only able to provide a degree of health, education and other services at local levels. According to the UNDP Report, 39% of the population in urban areas and 69% in rural areas do not have access to clean water. One in eight children dies because of contaminated water.

People living in Kabul and other urban areas have electricity only a few hours per day, mainly in the evenings. Around 40 international organisations, including the World Bank, the IMF, the WTO, the UN and various international NGOs, are operating in Afghanistan. There are also foreign embassies and the ISAF (International Security Assistance Force). They are all under heavily armed protection and are situated in central Kabul and a few other cities. They have their own supply of electricity, water and gas.

Afghan people are resentful of the fact that after four years they do not have access to electricity, gas and clean water, while foreigners enjoy these facilities.

The Human Development Index also presents a gloomy picture: life expectancy is 44 years; 53% of the total population lives below the poverty line; the adult literacy rate is 29%; only 3% of women are literate and in some areas less than 1% of the population is literate; one woman dies from pregnancy-related causes every 30 minutes; one out of five children dies before the age of five.

Three million school children (grades 1-12) and four million high school students have enrolled and 70,000 teachers have returned to work. However, the majority of schools which were damaged in the war years have not been rebuilt and are not safe. There are shortages of teachers, books, tables, chairs, paper and pencils, let alone other equipment. Many children go to school at 8.00am and return home by 10.00am. University courses are closing down because of lack of teachers and equipment.

Without literacy, education and skills, many have difficulty obtaining work. In Kabul and a few other urban areas, a small minority of people with limited skills and education work for international NGOs, UN organisations, foreign embassies and the ISAF. These organisations pay a higher wage than Afghanistan's state and private institutions.

The average monthly wage is US$40.00. The average monthly rent is US$200 and the average monthly food/expenses cost is US$200. Poverty has led to massive corruption. Nothing can be done without paying the 'middle man'. Being a 'middle man' is a job and a way to survive.

Poverty and years of war, violent conflicts and displacement mean that 3 generations live under the same roof. Many feel a great need to support each other and to be with each other after so many years of separation and displacement. However, overcrowded houses and apartments mean that young people in particular suffer from lack of space and privacy. No-one dares to be out in the streets after sunset. Drugs, violence and the kidnapping of children and young women are widespread. Moreover, there is a danger of being shot by security forces or run over by their fast cars patrolling the streets.

3 million refugees have returned from Iran and Pakistan. They live in tents in Kabul and other urban areas. They face unemployment and a lack of education and healthcare facilities. I came across a young man who was begging in the streets. He recognised my Afghan friends who run an NGO in Peshawar. When he was in Peshawar he went to the school provided by this Afghan NGO. Back in Kabul he is a beggar. He felt that he was better off in Peshawar as a refugee.

Around 1.5 million people come to Kabul from other parts of Afghanistan every year looking for work. Kabul's population was 500,000 just after the fall of the Taliban, today it is 5 million. The majority of these people are landless and homeless. Those who can afford it, mainly men, emigrate to Iran and Pakistan to work and earn money for their families. Many families move from cold areas to warm areas, as they do not have any way of keeping themselves protected from the cold weather in winter. The extreme poor cannot emigrate and live in absolute poverty.

THE POPPY ECONOMY

For the majority of people the only available option to consistently secure food is to become involved in the poppy economy. Many are locked into debt. They sell or mortgage their land; they sell their household belongings; even their daughters and their sons in order to cultivate opium to pay for their debt plus interest. In other cases, families send their young boys to work in the fields of traders in the form of bonded labour. Many young girls are married off to richer, older men in return for money which can be used to repay debts. Despite unprecedented high prices for opium, they only ever succeed in partially paying off their debt and systematically fail to regain their land. So they sell their belongings again to pay off the rest of their debt. They are highly dependent on the opium poppy as a means of survival.

According to the Aga Khan Development Network research on opium production in Badakhshan, some areas are consumption areas and some areas are production areas. In the consumption areas a large number of the population are addicted. The consumption is high, ranging from 18 grams per 15 days to 18 grams every day. People use opium to fight the unbearable amount of sickness and pain, caused by years of poor nutrition, sleeping in cold conditions and, for women, constant cycles of pregnancy. Pregnant addicts give birth to either still born babies or babies which themselves become addicted when they breast feed. Opium consumption is relatively low among families with higher standards of living and is higher among the poorer households. They give opium to their children to curb their hunger, to keep them quiet and calm, and in times of sickness. Older children cannot go to school without a dose of opium. Accidental death from overdose is common among children. Also, opium addiction is often the source of husband-wife conflicts. When men are addicted they cannot provide adequately for their families, and when women are addicted they face disapproval from their husbands. Both cases lead to violence against the women. In many cases male opium addicts who become impotent force their wives to become addicts, with the aim of reducing the chances of infidelity. According to my interviewees, these experiences are not specific to Badakhshan. For the majority of the population the opium economy is the only available option for survival. Poverty and the absence of healthcare have led to widespread opium addiction.

The Position of Women

A major justification for the war was that it would improve the position of women. Four years after the US led invasion of Afghanistan, there is very little evidence to demonstrate improvements for women and girls. As was mentioned above, girls can go to school, but school buildings are unsafe and there are severe shortages of teachers, facilities and equipment. The new constitution guarantees women equal rights. However, continuing religious and cultural conservatism and a dangerous security environment are real obstacles to women's participation in the economy, politics and society.

The regional and local warlords, who were the key allies of America against the Taliban and al-Qaeda, are not women's rights advocates and the invasion forces are not interested in the warlords' treatment of women. In most of Afghanistan, the rule of the warlords' guns is more of a reality than the rule of law. Women suffer under conditions of violence, fear and intimidation, and they remain at risk from sexual violence. With the exception of Kabul city centre women do not go out of the house or travel without Borqa and without being accompanied by a male member of their family. According to Human Rights Watch reports, in many parts of the country parents do not send their daughters to school because it is not safe enough for them to walk to school. The practice of exchanging girls and young women to settle feuds or to repay debts continues, as do high rates of early and forced marriage.

The western media have reported the Afghan people's access to satellite TV, Bollywood films, mobile phones and the internet as a positive development. Taking into consideration the level of poverty and lack of electricity, very few Afghans have access to the television stations across the country. For those who can afford this luxury the choice is to watch American style cop violence movies or Bollywood movies which advocate the subjugation of women to men and their families. Many Afghan women's rights activists are worried about the messages of Bollywood romance films, which are all about the woman's submission to the husband and his family's tradition. Love affairs between a rich man and a poor girl will start with romance, music and dance and end up in traditional marriage, the wife obeying the husband and his family or else facing domestic violence.

The relative availability of cheap mobile phones for a minority of young men and women in Kabul and a few other urban centres may mean that boys and girls can text each other and meet each other in internet cafes. However, many religious, conservative families do not consider internet cafes an appropriate place for their daughters, as pornography is freely available online. There are many young girls in jail who have been put there by their male relatives. Feze, one of my interviewees explained: "I was put in jail by my father, uncles and cousins for being a 'bad girl'". Although she passed the virginity test which is done in jail to all 'bad girls', she was kept there for months. In jail, she was approached by the jail keeper. When she was finally released, she was approached by the local policeman. "When a young woman is accused of being a bad girl by her own father, the word goes around town that she is available to men." Out of jail she is under constant threat of being murdered by her family as the issue of a woman's honour is linked to the family's honour and can frequently escalate to killings and violence.

THE PRESENCE OF FOREIGN TROOPS

People resent the presence of foreign troops. The 'war against terrorism' costs the US more than US$1 billion each month. George Bush and Tony Blair created the phenomenon of 'humanitarian aid' as part of the War on Terror. Provisional Reconstruction Teams (PRTs) are a mixture of soldiers and civilian aid workers. This means that soldiers shoot and kill people in the morning and the aid workers distribute aid in the evening.

The majority of people are hostile to the presence of foreigners. A woman, whose blind husband was dragged from their home as an al-Qaeda suspect, was cursing the Americans as 'Kafar' (the infidels) who raided her home, disrespected her religion and culture and created misery and fear for her and the neighbourhood.

Many believe that the Americans are building military installations and camps and/or stealing Afghanistan's resources all over the country. Najia explained: "They are building massive walls around large areas where Afghans are not allowed to enter. My husband works for them.

He and his friends fill the lorry with sand and earth and drive the lorry to the area near the walls and empty them all day long. They pay in dollars, so even those people who hate them work for them, as they have to feed their families".

American soldiers kick, swear and beat people up in the streets and terrorise them when traffic jams are created. In fact the traffic jams are created by the large vehicles of the UN, NGOs, and the ISAF which are filling Kabul city centre and other city streets all day long. The word 'motherfr' is used so often that many Afghan men use it for the foreigners. They don't even know the meaning of the word, but they know it is a derogatory term.

The Warlords

There has recently been an increase in open fighting between the foreign troops and the insurgents. The US has concentrated on maintaining Karzai in control of Kabul. The warlords have grips on large chunks of the country and on the population. Some of the old warlords are now registered and paid as part of the security contingent. Of course, this may be considered as a good move because these groups may have changed their positions and reformed.

However, many Afghans that I interviewed do not believe this, as these groups, on the one hand, are working with the government and on the other hand working with anti-government groups in other parts of Afghanistan. They are all armed with their own privatised security forces and resist state authority. The process of their disarmament has not been successful.

They are also connected with the opium economy and impose forced labour on communities, making the people work on their land.

They control large areas which are outside the law of the state and are used for drug trafficking. They are engaged in corruption, confiscating lands and properties belonging to those who left the country during the war years and have not yet returned.

There are over 60 registered political parties approved by the Ministry of Justice. Most of them remain allied to the warlords and their military factions and are in conflict with local government officials.

The UN, the NGOs and Human Rights Watch, while working on gender issues have reported that they have faced hostility and their work has been undermined by the conflict between local government institutions and political parties.

Afghanistan has massive natural resources (natural gas, petroleum, coal, copper, chromite, talc, barites, sulphur, lead, zinc, iron ore, salt, precious and semiprecious stones).

Afghanistan also has skilled labour, ranging from professionals to those with industrial and agricultural skills. These qualified people have lived in diasporic communities over the last 25 years, the majority in Iran and Pakistan and a minority in the West and Australia. But 4 years after the fall of the Taliban, the Afghan economy is still not functioning and is unable or unwilling to absorb this skilled labour.

Davoud, an American educated engineer explained: "I have offered my services; the American client state administration does not want us to participate in the reconstruction. The Americans co-operated with the warlords to defeat the Taliban and still they are co-operating with them, they have mutual interests in sharing the country's resources". And Shahla, an educated businesswoman from Britain, said: "I have come to help with the reconstruction of my country. But there is no place for me here. There is no reconstruction; there is just a terrible rush to make quick money. I don't know how long I will be able to remain here".

Hundreds of thousands of refugees who lived in Pakistan and Iran have returned. They are skilled workers but have not been absorbed into the Afghan economy. Therefore, they have no choice other than to go back to Iran and Pakistan and work illegally, because they are no longer categorised as refugees. According to research by the Afghanistan Research and Evaluation Unit, in only one area of the border with Pakistan (Torkham), 160,000 people per day go from Pakistan to Afghanistan and 190,000 people per day go from Afghanistan to Pakistan. They bring hundreds of thousands of US dollars per month to Afghanistan and for them this is just survival.

The warlords are engaged in the opium economy and the majority of the population is engaged in survival activities. International organisations and western governments keep changing their position between a military anti-drugs campaign and a long-term approach combining law enforcement issues with alternative economic opportunities. Either way, no real attempt has been made to develop Afghanistan's economy.

THE INTERNATIONAL COMMUNITY

It has been argued that the presence of international security forces is positive. This is because international organisations and

NGOs feel safe working to create jobs and security for the population, especially for women and girls.

In the eyes of many Afghan women's rights activists that I interviewed, the lack of any meaningful reconstruction and the presence of military invaders have created resentment and hostility.

The UN organisations and NGOs have no power or resources for development. They are not in Afghanistan just out of good will. In order to attract more funds and continue their businesses they have to exaggerate the degree of success of their programmes.

Najia explained: "Women's rights, human rights and democracy issues are cosmetically imposed from above. There are so many international organisations, some are trying their best, but they are miles away from understanding our cultural issues. Also when people are hungry and sick these issues are meaningless for them".

Some felt that even their language and culture was under threat.

Considering the level of illiteracy, they found the spread of English language terminology by NGOs, UN organisations, television programmes and the internet oppressive. Terms such as gender, development, participatory rural appraisal, democracy, planning etc are rapidly used by illiterate or partially educated men and women who are involved in UN and NGO projects.

Many do not understand the real meaning of these terms and do not have any chance to learn the Dari or Pashto equivalents. Many are questioning whether these organisations, with all their good intentions, are contributing to the improvement of people's lives in Afghanistan or unwittingly cooperating in neo-colonial reconstruction.

They also feel that their culture is under threat as many projects on gender, human rights and democracy are based on individuality and fail their cultural needs.

Fatima believed that, "Women's rights and human rights issues have become tools and slogans for those in power to use for their own agenda. I work with ordinary women and men and try to explain to them that Islam has given rights to women. This is the only way to fight for women's rights in Afghanistan, to show to women and men the positive side of Islam and Islamic culture, not from outside and not by insulting people's culture and religion".

The Western invasion of Afghanistan was and still is about strengthening US political and economic hegemony and control of the energy resources of the region.

Afghan women and men do not have the power to combat them on their own. But they have the power to think and to implement what is best for them and how to construct and develop their country. They need the people around the world to stop the neo-conservatives' imperial programmes which continue a vicious circle of war and terrorism.

2

Taliban: Network and Ideology

The exact location of the supreme leadership of the Taliban movement, however, cannot be established with any self-evident clarity. Irrespective of where the rahbari shura (leadership council) centered on Mullah Omar and his closest associates found shelter in the immediate aftermath of their defeat, Afghan military and civilian intelligence officials as well as NATO commanders today believe that this coterie eventually found refuge in Quetta, the largest city and capital of Pakistan's Baluchistan Province, from where they continue to operate to this day. As Col. Chris Vernon, NATO's chief of staff for southern Afghanistan, declared forthrightly, "The thinking piece of the Taliban [operates] out of Quetta in Pakistan. It's the major headquarters— they use it to run a series of networks in Afghanistan." These networks, in turn, are judged to be directed by four subsidiary shuras based in Quetta, Miran Shah, Peshawar, and Karachi: the first three actually control or coordinate most of the ongoing terrorist operations occurring, respectively, along the southern, central, and northern "fronts" in Afghanistan, whereas the fourth is believed to connect the Taliban with the logistics, financial, and technical assistance conduits emanating from the wider Islamic world. The pattern of terrorist attacks occurring in Afghanistan from 2002 to 2007, again corroborates this judgment.

Because the Pakistani state was most intimately involved in the creation of the Taliban before their fall, Musharraf's antiterrorism campaign after September 11, 2001, deliberately avoided any concerted targeting of this group and, in particular, its senior leadership. No other explanation is consistent with the fact that, although Pakistani military, intelligence, and paramilitary forces apprehended scores of al-Qaeda operatives, including numerous key individuals in the al-Qaeda hierarchy, the senior Taliban leaders killed or captured in southern Afghanistan or in the FATA have numbered literally a handful in comparison.

This asymmetry in seizures is all the more odd because, prior to Operation Enduring Freedom, Pakistani military and ISID liaison elements were deeply intertwined with all levels of the Taliban mand structure and its war fighters in the field. In contrast, the Pakistani intelligence relationship with al-Qaeda in Afghanistan was more tenuous, yet Pakistan's military forces were able to apprehend far more al-Qaeda cadres than Taliban operatives.

These successes in regard to al-Qaeda have invariably been attributed by Pakistanis, including General Musharraf, to the fact that it was always easier to identify the ethnically alien al-Qaeda elements along the frontier in comparison with the Taliban who, being ethnically Pashtun, were able to disguise their identities by assimilating into the larger tribal population.

While this explanation is only partly true— non-native fighters have lived in and become amalgamated into the social structures of the Afghan-Pakistani frontier since at least the anti-Soviet jihad of the 1980s— it is also disingenuous because the Pakistani ISID was not only deeply involved in the recruitment, training, arming, and operations of Taliban fighters at multiple bureaucratic levels, but it also maintained an intense liaison relationship with the Ghilzai tribes whose population has been disproportionately represented in the Taliban.

Since protecting these relationships was deemed to be especially critical for Pakistan's national security interests in the aftermath of the Northern Alliance victory in Kabul, the large number of Taliban foot soldiers who made their way into the FATA were largely ignored by Pakistani counterterrorism operations so long as they did not engage in any untoward activities that either called attention to their presence or magnified the troubles confronting the Pakistani state. All told, then, the Taliban network, just like the Pakistani-aided terrorist groups operating in Kashmir and elsewhere in India, was deliberately permitted to escape the wrath of General Musharraf's counterterrorism operations in the initial phase of the war on terror.

Such an approach, however, could not be extended to the fourth group, al-Qaeda, which had also taken up sanctuary in the FATA, particularly in South Waziristan initially. Although al-Qaeda continued to have sympathizers within the extreme fringes of Pakistani society even after the terrible events of September 11 were conclusively attributed to its operations, the Pakistani military establishment did not enjoy the luxury of slackening its campaign against this target because of the consequences for U.S.-Pakistani relations at a time when bilateral ties were just recovering after a decade of U.S. disfavor and when Washington had just embarked on a ferocious campaign against al-Qaeda worldwide. Most senior Pakistani military officers at the corps command level were also genuinely horrified by the destruction that al-Qaeda wreaked in New York and Washington and, fearing for their country's own future in the face of the monster now present in their midst, supported Musharraf's decision to engage and destroy this terrorist organization of global reach.

Pakistan's military, accordingly, began to prosecute the war against al-Qaeda with great vigor, if not always with finesse, through multiple instruments. These included providing the United States and its military with facilities and access for the prosecution of Operation Enduring Freedom in Afghanistan, and conducting various law enforcement and internal security operations (sometimes in cooperation with their U.S. counterparts) aimed at interdicting terrorist financing and apprehending and rendering terrorist targets for prosecution abroad. Most important, however, the Pakistani military initiated Operation Al Mizan, a large-scale effort that involved moving major military formations from the Army's XI Corps and elite Special Services Group (SSG) battalions into the FATA, an area where regular army units had not ordinarily been deployed for decades. These infantry forces joined the Frontier Corps regiments— the paramilitary formations usually located in the region— as a show of force in order to both reassert the strong state presence that historically was lacking and apprehend the al-Qaeda elements that had taken shelter within the area.

This military campaign, which took the form of a gigantic cordon-and-search operation, had several consequences. First, it resulted in the capture of numerous al-Qaeda and other extremist operatives— some 700 at last count— who have since been turned over to the United States. Because these individuals are mostly foreigners— non–South Asian arrivals living in what are essentially Pashtun lands— detecting their presence, while not easy because of the local support they receive from the natives for ideological reasons and sometimes simply out of greed or fear, was certainly easier.

Second, it forced some though by no means all senior al-Qaeda operatives— for example, Khalid Sheikh Muhammad and Ramzi Binalshibh— to leave the relatively secure FATA sanctuary and disperse further inward into Pakistan, where their insertion into less ideologically congenial surroundings and their need to rely on more complex means of communication increased their susceptibility to detection and arrest.

Third, the dramatic irruption of the Pakistani state into the FATA, through a significant military presence of the kind not seen in more than a century, resulted in making conditions sufficiently inhospitable for al-Qaeda such that its senior leadership and cadres were compelled to relocate under fire from South to North Waziristan and beyond, where they operate to this day. This forced displacement, which unfortunately remains at continuous risk of reversal, nonetheless had the beneficial effect of disrupting many planned terrorist operations, but the dispersal of the organization's leadership in the northern FATA, especially in the Bajaur Agency where the terrain is inhospitable, the population is violently pro-Taliban, and the presence of the Pakistan Army is thin, has inadvertently made the task of destroying the al-Qaeda core all the more difficult.

In any event, these outcomes suggest that although Pakistan began as a reluctant entrant into the global war on terrorism, it has since become an active participant in the struggle. More than 85,000 Pakistani troops remain garrisoned along the Afghanistan-Pakistan border— a deployment that predates the initiation of the global war on terror. A significant fraction of these forces, however, is engaged today in counterterrorism operations in the border areas, and more than 600 soldiers have already sacrificed their lives in this effort. Further, Islamabad itself has now become a victim of terrorism as a variety of groups, ranging from those previously nurtured and now discarded by the Pakistani state, such as the al-Alami faction of the Harkat-ul-Mujahideen, to more distant beneficiaries of past Pakistani policies, such as al-Qaeda, seek to wreak an orgy of revenge against institutions and individuals whom they had previously counted among their sponsors and friends.

That Pakistan has made significant contributions to defeating various terrorist groups is therefore undeniable, yet its larger campaign against terrorism has also been conspicuously selective and perhaps self-serving. While it has secured major gains in eradicating some domestic anti-national sectarian terrorist groups and has contributed disproportionately to the ongoing campaign against al-Qaeda, it has been much more reluctant to conclusively eliminate those terrorist entities operating against India in Kashmir and elsewhere and against Afghanistan both in the FATA and in transit back and forth to the southern and eastern Afghan provinces. Further, the protection of the terrorist infrastructure that supports these groups has produced undesirable blowback because the actors traditionally involved in perpetrating terrorism in Kashmir increasingly either coordinate with or directly assist the Taliban and al-Qaeda in operations against not only Afghanistan but also the United States and even Pakistan itself.

Clearly, strategic and geopolitical calculations play an important part in accounting for this segmented Pakistani response. Islamabad, for example, has long viewed the terrorist groups operating in Kashmir and now in other Indian states as useful instruments for executing its policy of "strategic diversion" against New Delhi. For this reason, Pakistan has been reluctant to target and eliminate these groups conclusively, preferring instead to alternately tighten and loosen control over their operations depending on how much satisfaction it receives from India at any given moment. The decision to avoid targeting the Taliban was born of similar calculations. Initially, it was owed simply to the inclinations of senior Pakistani military commanders who were just not prepared to add insult to injury by physically eliminating the very forces they had long invested in, especially because they had now suffered the ignominy of having to consent to their client's defeat.

Over time, however, the reasons for protecting the Taliban only grew stronger: India's growing prominence in Afghan reconstruction, its increased influence and presence in Afghanistan more generally, the weakening of the Hamid Karzai government in Kabul, the progressive souring of Pakistani-Afghan relations (including those between Karzai and Musharraf personally), and the disquiet about a possible U.S. exit from Afghanistan (a prospect inferred from the mid-2005 announcement that the United States would divest full command of Afghan combat operations to NATO) once again increased Pakistan's paranoia about the prospect of a hostile western frontier. It was exactly the desire to avert this outcome that led to the initial Pakistani decision to invest in sustaining the Taliban. And with fear of the wheel turning full circle gaining strength in Islamabad since at least 2005, the temptation to hedge against potentially unfavorable outcomes in Kabul— by protecting the Taliban as some sort of a "force-in-being"—only appeared more and more attractive and reasonable to Pakistan.

THE TALIBAN'S CREATION DURING PREMIERSHIP OF BHUTTO

Pakistan figures prominently in any discussions related to the Taliban in terms of creating this medieval monster in Afghanistan and the subsequent inhuman repression that the Taliban has imposed on the Afghans themselves. ISI also figures prominently in relation to provision of Pak Army cadres, military advisers and military hardware. However what does not figure is Benazir Bhutto's role in its creation. The Taliban emerged forcefully on the Afghan scene in the period 1993-94 and captured the whole of Afghanistan, less the Northern Provinces by September 1996. It requires to be noted that all these developments took place during Benazir Bhutto's second tenure as Prime Minister, i.e., 1993-1996. As one author puts it: "Furthermore, there was considerable evidence to suggest that the Taliban were being strongly supported by the Pakistani government led by Benazir Bhutto, ironically a woman educated at Oxford and Harvard."

Initially, more than the ISI, it was the Bhutto party machine both at Islamabad and in the provincial capitals at Peshawar (NWFP) and Quetta (Baluchistan) which were active in the reinforcement and furtherance of Taliban operations. It is indicated that: "When the Taliban captured Kandahar, the ISI was initially more sceptical than the Government about the chances of further success. While General Babar(Bhutto's Interior Minister) and the Jamiat-e Ulema-i Islam pushed for support to the Taliban, the ISI took a back seat. Thus Babar had a free hand in "civilianising" the initial support to the Taliban."

Benazir's newly created Taliban ensured that they had the right connections in Pakistan to enable continued support as this would suggest: "And the Taliban soon developed close relations with several businessmen close to Asaf Ali Zardari-the husband of Benazir Bhutto, who in turn were given the highly lucrative permits to export fuel to Afghanistan. As the Taliban's war machine expanded, permits for fuel supplies from Pakistan became a major money earner for Pakistani politicians"... The linkages and implications are self evident.

Benazir's pretentious pronouncements are avidly lapped up in Washington and New Delhi as emanating from a committed democrat, a Pakistani politician of moderate hues and above all a Muslim with western educated secular values, in short someone New Delhi could trust in political dealings. The above record of Benazir Bhutto however does not match up with what she would like us to believe about her.

Bodansky states that: " Pakistan's ascent in the Islamist terrorist system is particularly important in a strategic context. Pakistan's growing involvement resulted in both escalation of the war by proxy in Kashmir and the rise of Taliban in Afghanistan, two movements that still provide shelter and closely cooperate with Osama bin Laden." What Bodansky has not added to complete this summation is that in terms of contextual time-spans both these developments emerged during the two tenures of Benazir

Bhutto as Prime Minister of Pakistan. Benazir's duplicity against the United States of America of forming a Trans-Asian anti-US alliance while mouthing platitudes on democracy during Washington visits indicates a fatal flaw in her political credibility. Comparatively speaking, former PM Nawaz Sharif appears far superior to Benazir's Bhutto. He had at least the courage to fight an election in Pakistan on the agenda of improvement of Indo-Pak relations and won on this issue with an overwhelming majority.

Regrettably, Benazir Bhutto's record on Islamic fundamentalism of Pakistan, escalation of the proxy war in Kashmir and the creation of the Taliban leads one to the conclusion that Washington's assessments of Pakistani politicians and Pakistan's political scene tend to be faulty and unreliable as inputs for any Track II diplomacy. Both these conclusions are pertinent presently for those advising and espousing the continuation of India's cease fire in Kashmir.

TALIBAN EMIRATE AND THE UNITED FRONT

The Taliban started shelling Kabul in early 1995 but were defeated by forces of the Islamic State government under Ahmad Shah Massoud. Amnesty International, referring to the Taliban offensive, wrote in a 1995 report: "This is the first time in several months that Kabul civilians have become the targets of rocket attacks and shelling aimed at residential areas in the city."

The Taliban's early victories in 1994 were followed by a series of defeats that resulted in heavy losses which led analysts to believe the Taliban movement had run its course. But Pakistan provided increased support to the Taliban. Many analysts like Amin Saikal describe the Taliban as developing into a proxy force for Pakistan's regional interests. On 26 September 1996, as the Taliban with military support by Pakistan and financial support by Saudi Arabia prepared for another major offensive, Massoud ordered a full retreat from Kabul. The Taliban seized Kabul on 27 September 1996, and established the Islamic Emirate of Afghanistan. They imposed on the parts of Afghanistan under their control their political and judicial interpretation of Islam issuing edicts especially targeting women. The Physicians for Human Rights (PHR) analyse:

"To PHR's knowledge, no other regime in the world has methodically and violently forced half of its population into virtual house arrest, prohibiting them on pain of physical punishment."

After the fall of Kabul to the Taliban on 27 September 1996, Ahmad Shah Massoud and Abdul Rashid Dostum, two former enemies, created the United Front (Northern Alliance) against the Taliban that were preparing offensives against the remaining areas under the control of Massoud and those under the control of Dostum. The United Front included beside the dominantly Tajik forces of Massoud and the Uzbek forces of Dostum, Hazara factions under the command of leaders such as Haji Mohammad Mohaqiq andPashtun forces under the leadership of commanders such as Abdul Haq or Haji Abdul Qadir. The Taliban defeated Dostum's Junbish forces militarily by seizing Mazar-i-Sharif in 1998. Dostum subsequently went into exile.

According to a 55-page report by the United Nations, the Taliban, while trying to consolidate control over northern and western Afghanistan, committed systematic massacres against civilians. UN officials stated that there had been "15 massacres" between 1996 and 2001 and that "hese have been highly systematic and they all lead back to the [Taliban] Ministry of Defense or to Mullah Omar himself." The Taliban especially targeted people of Shia religious or Hazara ethnic background. Upon taking Mazar-i-Sharif in 1998, 4,000-6,000 civilians were killed by the Taliban and many more reportedtortured. The documents also reveal the role of Arab and Pakistani support troops in these killings. Bin Laden's so-called 055 Brigade was responsible for mass-killings of Afghan civilians. The report by the UN quotes "eyewitnesses in many villages describing Arab fighters carrying long knives used for slitting throats and skinning people".

Pakistani President Pervez Musharraf – then as Chief of Army Staff – was responsible for sending thousands of Pakistanis to fight alongside the Taliban and bin Laden against the forces of Massoud. According to Pakistani Afghanistan expert Ahmed Rashid, "between 1994 and 1999, an estimated 80,000 to 100,000 Pakistanis trained and fought in Afghanistan" on the side of the Taliban. In 2001 alone, there were believed to be 28,000 Pakistani nationals, many either from theFrontier Corps or army, fighting inside Afghanistan. An estimated 8,000 Pakistani militants were recruited in madrassas filling the ranks of the estimated 25,000 regular Taliban force. A 1998 document by the U.S. State Department confirms that "20–40 % of [regular] Taliban soldiers are Pakistani." The document further stated that the parents of those Pakistani nationals "know nothing regarding their child's military involvement with the Taliban until their bodies are brought back to Pakistan."

From 1996 to 2001 the al-Qaeda terrorist network of Osama bin Laden and Ayman al-Zawahiri became a state within Afghanistan.Bin Laden sent Arab recruits to join the fight against the United Front. 3,000 fighters of the regular Taliban army were Arab and Central Asian militants. In total, of roughly 45,000 Pakistani, Taliban and al-Qaeda soldiers fighting against the forces of Massoud in mid-2001, only 14,000 were Afghans.

Ahmad Shah Massoud remained the only leader of the United Front in Afghanistan. In the areas under his control Massoud set up democratic institutions and signed the Women's Rights Declaration. Human Rights Watch cites no human rights crimes for the forces under direct control of Massoud for the period from October 1996 until the assassination of Massoud in September 2001. As a consequence many civilians fled to the area of Ahmad Shah Massoud. In total, estimates range up to one million people fleeing the Taliban. National Geographic concluded in its documentary *"Inside the Taliban"*:

"The only thing standing in the way of future Taliban massacres is Ahmad Shah Massoud." In early 2001 Massoud addressed the European Parliament in Brussels asking the international community to provide humanitarian help to the people of Afghanistan.

He stated that the Taliban and al-Qaeda had introduced "a very wrong perception of Islam" and that without the support of Pakistan and bin Laden the Taliban would not be able to sustain their military campaign for up to a year. On this visit to Europe he also warned that his intelligence had gathered information about a large-scale attack on U.S. soil being imminent.

RECENT HISTORY (2001–PRESENT)

On 9 September 2001, Ahmad Shah Massoud was assassinated by two Arab suicide attackers inside Afghanistan and two days later about 3,000 people were killed in the September 11 attacks in the United States. The US government identified Osama bin Laden, Khalid Sheikh Mohammed and the Al-Qaeda organization based in and allied to the Taliban's Islamic Emirate of Afghanistan as the perpetrators of the attacks. From 1990 until this date over 400,000 Afghan civilians had already died in the wars in Afghanistan. The Taliban refused to hand over bin Laden to US authorities and to disband al-Qaeda bases in Afghanistan. In October 2001, Operation Enduring Freedom was launched as new phase of the War in Afghanistan (1978-present) in which teams of American and British special forces worked with ground forces of the United Front (Northern Alliance) to remove the Taliban from power and dispel Al-Qaeda. At the same time the US-led forces were bombing Taliban and al-Qaida targets everywhere inside Afghanistan with cruise missiles. These actions led to the fall of Mazar-i-Sharif in the north followed by all the other cities, as the Taliban and al-Qaeda fled over the porous Durand Line border into Pakistan. In December 2001, after the Taliban government was toppled and the new Afghan government under Hamid Karzai was formed, the International Security Assistance Force (ISAF) was established by the UN Security Council to help assist the Karzai administration and provide basic security to the Afghan people.

While the Taliban began regrouping inside Pakistan, more coalition troops entered the escalating US-led war. Meanwhile, the rebuilding of war-torn Afghanistan kicked off in 2002. The Afghan nation was able to build democratic structures over the years, and some progress was made in key areas such as governance, economy, health, education, transport, and agriculture. NATO is training the Afghan armed forces as well its national police. ISAF and Afghan troops led many offensives against the Taliban but failed to fully defeat them. By 2009, a Taliban-led shadow government began to form in many parts of the country complete with their own version of mediation court. After U.S. President Barack Obama announced the deployment of another 30,000 soldiers in 2010 for a period of two years, Der Spiegel published images of the US soldiers who killed unarmed Afghan civilians.

At the 2010 International Conference on Afghanistan in London, Afghan President Hamid Karzai said he intends to reach out to the Taliban leadership (including Mullah Omar,Sirajuddin Haqqani and Gulbuddin Hekmatyar). Supported by NATO, Karzai called on the group's leadership to take part in a loya jirga meeting to initiate peace talks. These steps have resulted in an intensification of bombings, assassinations and ambushes. Some Afghan groups (including the former intelligence chief Amrullah Saleh and opposition leader Dr. Abdullah Abdullah) believe that Karzai plans to appease the insurgents' senior leadership at the cost of the democratic constitution, the democratic process and progess in the field of human rights especially women's rights. Dr. Abdullah stated:

"I should say that Taliban are not fighting to be accommodated. They are fighting to bring the state down. So it's a futile exercise, and it's just misleading.... There are groups that will fight to the death. Whether we like to talk to them or we don't like to talk to them, they will continue to fight. So, for them, I don't think that we have a way forward with talks or negotiations or contacts or anything as such. Then we have to be prepared to tackle and deal with them militarily. In terms of the Taliban on the ground, there are lots of possibilities and opportunities that with the help of the people in different parts of the country, we can attract them to the peace process; provided, we create a favorable environment on this side of the line. At the moment, the people are leaving support for the government because of corruption. So that expectation is also not realistic at this stage."

Over five million Afghan refugees were repatriated in the last decade, including many who were forcefully deported from NATOcountries. This large return of Afghans may have helped the nation's economy but the country still remains one of the poorest in the world due to the decades of war, lack of foreign investment, ongoing government corruption and the Pakistani-backed Taliban insurgency. According to a report by the United

Nations, the Taliban and other militants were responsible for 76% of civilian casualties in 2009, 75% in 2010 and 80% in 2011. In 2011 a record 3,021 civilians were killed in the ongoing insurgency, the fifth successive annual rise.

After the May 2011 death of Osama bin Laden in Pakistan, many prominent Afghan figures began being assassinated, including Mohammed Daud Daud,Ahmed Wali Karzai, Jan Mohammad Khan, Ghulam Haider Hamidi, Burhanuddin Rabbani and others. Also in the same year, the Pak-Afghan border skirmishes intensified and many large scale attacks by the Pakistani-based Haqqani Network took place across Afghanistan. This led to the United States warning Pakistan of a possible military action against the Haqqanis in the Federally Administered Tribal Areas. The U.S. blamed Pakistan's government, mainly Pakistan Army and its ISI spy network as the masterminds behind all of this.

"In choosing to use violent extremism as an instrument of policy, the government of Pakistan, and most especially the Pakistani army and ISI, jeopardizes not only the prospect of our strategic partnership but Pakistan's opportunity to be a respected nation with legitimate regional influence. They may believe that by using these proxies, they are hedging their bets or redressing what they feel is an imbalance in regional power. But in reality, they have already lost that bet." —Admiral Mike Mullen, *Chairman of the Joint Chiefs of Staff*

U.S. Ambassador to Pakistan, Cameron Munter, told Radio Pakistan that "The attack that took place in Kabul a few days ago, that was the work of the Haqqani Network. There is evidence linking the Haqqani Network to the Pakistan government. This is something that must stop." Other top U.S. officials such as Hillary Clinton and Leon Panetta made similar statements. On 16 October 2011, "Operation Knife Edge" was launched by NATO and Afghan forces against the Haqqani Network in south-eastern Afghanistan. Afghan Defense Minister, Abdul Rahim Wardak, explained that the operation will "help eliminate the insurgents before they struck in areas along the troubled frontier".

In anticipation of the 2014 NATO withdrawal and a subsequent expected push to regain power by the Taliban, the anti-Taliban

United Front (Northern Alliance) groups have started to regroup under the umbrella of the National Coalition of Afghanistan (political arm) and the National Front of Afghanistan (military arm).

Governance

The government of Afghanistan is an Islamic republic consisting of three branches, executive, legislative and judicial. The nation is currently led by the Karzai administration with Hamid Karzai as the President and leader since late 2001. The National Assembly is the legislature, a bicameral body having two chambers, the House of the People and the House of Elders.

The Supreme Court is led by Chief Justice Abdul Salam Azimi, a former university professor who had been a legal advisor to the president. The current court is seen as more moderate and led by more technocrats than the previous one, which was dominated by fundamentalist religious figures such as Chief Justice Faisal Ahmad Shinwari who issued several controversial rulings, including seeking to place a limit on the rights of women.

According to Transparency International's corruption perceptions index 2010 results, Afghanistan was ranked as the third most-corrupt country in the world. A January 2010 report published by the United Nations Office on Drugs and Crime revealed that bribery consumes an amount equal to 23 % of the GDP of the nation. A number of government ministries are believed to be rife with corruption, and while President Karzai vowed to tackle the problem in late 2009 by stating that "individuals who are involved in corruption will have no place in the government", top government officials were busy stealing and misusing hundreds of millions of dollars through the Kabul Bank. Although the nation's institutions are newly formed and steps have been taken to arrest some, the United States warned that aid to Afghanistan would be reduced to very little if the corruption is not stopped.

Elections and Parties

The 2004 Afghan presidential election was relatively peaceful, in which Hamid Karzai won in the first round with 55.4% of the votes. However, the 2009 presidential election was characterized by lack of security, low voter turnout and widespread electoral fraud. The vote, along with elections for 420 provincial council seats, took place in August 2009, but remained unresolved during a lengthy period of vote counting and fraud investigation.

Two months later, under international pressure, a second round run-off vote between Karzai and remaining challenger Abdullah was announced, but a few days later Abdullah announced that he is not participating in the 7 November run-off because his demands for changes in the electoral commission had not been met. The next day, officials of the election commission cancelled the run-off and declared Hamid Karzai as President for another 5-year term. In the 2005 parliamentary election, among the elected officials were former mujahideen, Islamic fundamentalists, warlords, communists,reformists, and several Taliban associates. In the same period, Afghanistan reached to the 30th nation in terms of female representation in parliament. The last parliamentary election was held in September 2010, but due to disputes and investigation of fraud, the sworn in ceremony took place in late January 2011. After the issuance of computerized ID cards for the first time, which is a $101 million project that the Afghan government plans to start in 2012, it is expected to help prevent major fraud in future elections and improve the security situation.

Administrative Divisions

Afghanistan is administratively divided into 34 provinces (*wilayats*), with each province having its own capital and a provincial administration. The provinces are further divided into about 398 smaller provincial districts, each of which normally covers a city or a number of villages. Each district is represented by a district governor.

The provincial governors are appointed by the President of Afghanistan and the district governors are selected by the provincial governors. The provincial governors are representatives of the central government in Kabul and are responsible for all administrative and formal issues within their provinces. There are also provincial councils which are elected through direct and general elections for a period of four years. The functions of provincial councils are to take part in provincial development planning and to participate in monitoring and appraisal of other provincial governance institutions.

According to article 140 of the constitution and the presidential decree on electoral law, mayors of cities should be elected through free and direct elections for a four-year term. However, due to huge election costs, mayoral and municipal elections have never been held. Instead, mayors have been appointed by the government. As for the capital city of Kabul, the mayor is appointed by the President of Afghanistan.

The following is a list of all the 34 provinces of Afghanistan in alphabetical order and on the right is a map showing where each province is located:

Foreign Relations and Military

The Afghan Ministry of Foreign Affairs is responsible for managing the foreign relations of Afghanistan. The nation has been a member of the UN since 1946, and has maintained goodrelations with the United States and other NATO member states since the signing of the Treaty of Rawalpindi in 1919.

The United Nations Assistance Mission in Afghanistan (UNAMA) was established in 2002 under United Nations Security Council Resolution 1401 to help the nation recover from decades of war and establish a normal functioning government. Today, more than 22 NATO nations deploy about 140,000 troops in Afghanistan as part of the International Security Assistance Force (ISAF). Apart from close military links, Afghanistan also enjoys strong economic relations with NATO members and their allies.

Afghanistan also has diplomatic relations with neighbouring Pakistan, Iran, Turkmenistan, Uzbekistan, Tajikistan, the People's Republic of China, including regional states such as India, Turkey, Kazakhstan, Russia, United Arab Emirate, Saudi Arabia, Iraq, Egypt, Japan, South Korea, and others. Afghanistan's relationship with Pakistan has often fluctuated since 1947. They have cultural, security and economic links with each other but disputes between the two states remain. Afghanistan continues to reject the porous and poorly marked Durrand Line as its international border with Pakistan, and has repeatedly accused Pakistan of supporting the Taliban insurgents, Haqqani Network, and other anti-Afghanistan terrorist groups. Economically, Afghanistan is highly dependent on Pakistan in terms of imports, supplies and trade routes. Conversely, Pakistan considers Afghanistan as an important trade route for access to Central Asian resources.

Pakistan harbours concerns over the growing influence of its rival India in Afghanistan. Relations between the two states were strained further after recent border skirmishes. Afghan officials allege that Pakistani intelligence agencies are involved in terrorist attacks inside Afghanistan. Pakistan has denied supporting the Taliban and claimed that a stable Afghanistan is in its interest. India and Iran have actively participated in reconstruction efforts in Afghanistan, with India being the largest regional donor to the country. Since 2002, India has pledged up to $2 billion in economic assistance to Afghanistan and has participated in multiple socio-economic reconstruction efforts, including power, roads, agricultural and educational projects. There are also military ties between Afghanistan and India, which is expected to increase after the October 2011 strategic pact that was signed by President Karzai and Prime Minister Manmohan Singh.

The military of Afghanistan is under the Ministry of Defense, which includes the Afghan National Army and the Afghan Air Force. It currently has about 180,000 active soldiers and is expected to reach 260,000 in the coming years. They are trained and equipped by NATO countries, mainly by the United States Department of Defence. The ANA is divided into 7 major Corps, with the 201st Selab ("Flood") in Kabul being the main one. The ANA also has a commando brigade which was established in 2007. The National Military Academy of Afghanistan serves as the main educational institute for the militarymen of the country. A new $200 million Afghan Defence University (ADU) is under construction near the capital.

Crime and Law Enforcement

The National Directorate of Security (NDS) is the nation's domestic intelligence agency, which operates similar to that of the

United States Department of Homeland Security (DHS) and has between 15,000 to 30,000 employees. The nation also has about 126,000 national police officers, with plans to recruit more so that the total number can reach 160,000.The Afghan National Police (ANP) is under the Ministry of the Interior, which is based in Kabul and headed by Bismillah Khan Mohammadi. The Afghan National Civil Order Police is the main branch of the Afghan National Police, which is divided into five Brigades and each one commanded by a Brigadier General. These brigades are stationed in Kabul, Gardez, Kandahar, Herat, and Mazar-i-Sharif. Every province of the country has a provincial Chief of Police who is appointed by the Ministry of the Interior and is responsible for law enforcement in all the districts within the province.

The police are being trained by NATO countries through the Afghanistan Police Program. According to a 2009 news report, a large proportion of police officers are illiterate and are accused of demanding bribes. Jack Kem, deputy to the commander of NATO Training Mission Afghanistan and Combined Security Transition Command Afghanistan, stated that the literacy rate in the ANP will rise to over 50% by January 2012. What began as a voluntary literacy program became mandatory for basic police training in early 2011. Approximately 17 % of them test positive for illegal drug use. In 2009, President Karzai created two anti-corruption units within the Interior Ministry. Former Interior Minister Hanif Atmar said that security officials from the U.S. (FBI), Britain (Scotland Yard) and the European Union will train prosecutors in the unit.

The south and eastern parts of Afghanistan are the most dangerous due to the flourishing drug trade and militancy. These areas in particular are often patrolled by Taliban insurgents, and in many cases they plan attacks by using suicide bombers and planting improvised explosive devices (IEDs) on roads. Kidnapping and robberies are also often reported. Every year many Afghan police officers are killed in the line of duty in these areas. The Afghan Border Police are responsible for protecting the nation's airports and borders, especially the disputed Durand Line border which is often used by members of criminal organizations and terrorists for their illegal activities. Reports in 2011 suggested that up to 3 million people are involved in the illegal drug business in Afghanistan, many of the attacks on government employees and institutions are carried out not only by the Taliban militants but also by powerful criminal gangs. Drugs from Afghanistan are exported to Iran, Pakistan, Russia, India, the United Arab Emirate, and the European Union. The Afghan Ministry of Counter Narcotics is dealing with this problem.

HOW PROGRESSIVES GOT AFGHANISTAN WRONG

Against the sunny predictions of the cruise missile left, Afghanistan is in ruins. Western bombings in Herat, Farah, and Kunduz have led to mass civilian death, while nighttime house raids murder more intimately in Ghazi Khan and Khatabeh.

The casualty figures should shame the war's supporters. Bob Dreyfuss and Nick Turse of the *Nation* calculate that even by conservative counts, the deaths of 6,481 civilians were directly attributable to ISAF and the Afghan government with which it is allied. Thousands more have been killed by insurgents, fighting a war of the West's making.

Nor has this blood soaked path led to a promising post-Taliban future. Afghanistan has the worst rate of infant mortality in the world. Half of Afghan children suffer irreversible harm from malnutrition. The UN's 2013 Human Development Index ranks Afghanistan 175 out of 186 countries. Thomas Ruttig of Afghanistan Analysis Network writes that "economic activity in general [is] falling," unemployment and crime are rising, and that 60 percent of children are malnourished. Just 27 percent of the population has access to safe drinking water.

The record of Hamid Karzai's government is blighted by torture, corruption,warlords, and a fraudulent 2009 election. Nor has freedom and safety for Afghanistan's ever-instrumentalized women come about.

In March of 2013, the ISAF-backed Karzai endorsed a statement that refers to women as "secondary," bars violence against women only for "un-Islamic" reasons, and advocates gender segregation in schools, workplaces, and public spaces. In 2012 the burn unit of an Afghan hospital admitted a record number of women who tried to set themselves on fire. And Suraya Pakzad, who runs women's shelters in the country, has described cases of women being publicly stoned while ISAF-trained Afghan troops looked on.

Moreover, the war's hideous violence has benefited the ultra-misogynistic Taliban. A November 2013 study conducted by a team of scholars from Yale and Princeton finds that among Afghans "Harm inflicted by the International Security Assistance Force (ISAF) is met with reduced support for ISAF and increased support for the Taliban, but Taliban-inflicted harm does not translate into greater ISAF support."

All of these outcomes are perfectly predictable and were in fact anticipated by many. As the United States prepares to withdraw most of its forces from Afghanistan, it is worth looking back at the debates many had during the lead-up to and early phases of that war.

While it is easy to say in hindsight that such writers as Tariq Ali and Marjorie Cohn were correct to oppose the intervention and that others like Michael Bérubé, Michael Kazin, Todd Gitlin and Michael Walzer were wrong to endorse it, an examination of how the latter group got it wrong is necessary. Clarifying the analytic errors made by the imperialist "left" at the time are important because some have since taken similar approaches to Iraq and more recently to Libya and Syria.

"Progressive" boosterism for the Afghan war had several calling cards. Chief among them was how authors touted their credentials in opposing past cases of US aggression, in some cases professed concern for the Palestinians, and bragged of a left-of-center track record on social and economic issues.

However, the left-imperialists believed that differences in the tactics and ideological orientation of the US' enemies in Afghanistan were major reasons that the Afghan war was legitimate whereas the ventures in Vietnam and Nicaragua were not. Cruise missile leftists ignored that while the context of US military action had changed, no moment of rupture had taken place within the American state that directs that military.

By contrast, leftists who opposed the war in Afghanistan did so because they understood that the character of US power and its allied states is such that wars against the smaller and poorer nations are exercises in accumulation and imperialism by their very nature.

The cruise-missile leftists also made sure to attack those who were not so eager to drop cluster bombs on Afghan villagers. For example, Chomsky accurately pointed to a September 16, 2001 report that the US government "demanded" that Pakistan end "truck convoys that provide much of the food and other supplies to Afghanistan's civilian population." Chomsky used Burns' report to decisively show that the US was taking actions that it knew would harm Afghan civilians, and that it was therefore unreasonable to believe the war was going to liberate Afghans or even attempt to do so.

In response to this, Bérubé raged that Chomsky was exhibiting "a repellent mix of hysteria and hauteur," without even attempting to refute the argument.

Progressive warmongers frequently accused anti-imperialists of claiming in a simplistic way that the US is incapable of helping the world's oppressed. Yet in the same breath such cruise missile leftists would demand simplistic, unequivocal declarations of the US' moral superiority.

Gitlin wrote that the anti-imperialists were "Like jingoists who consider any effort to understand terrorists immoral, on the grounds that to understand is to endorse, [because these leftist] hard-liners disdain complexity." For Gitlin, the problem is that anti-imperialism is a "cartoon view of the world [where] there is nothing worse than American power — not the woman-enslaving Taliban, not an unrepentant Al Qaeda committed to killing civilians as they please."

According to Gitlin's one-dimensional view, there was no room for considerations such as the degree to which bombing and occupying Afghanistan and propping up a warlord regime with its own rather patriarchal tendencies might have adverse effects on the people of that country, particularly Afghan women. To Gitlin, it was necessary to overlook complications such as the fact that ISAF's (ultimately failed) "rescue" of Afghan women would inevitably mean killing, detaining or horribly wounding thousands of their fathers, grandfathers, brothers, community members, and friends—and quite a few Afghan women themselves.

Anti-imperialist arguments against war in Afghanistan can be roughly divided into three categories. The first category of anti-war argument was to point out, asChomsky and Cohn did, that the invasion of Afghanistan violated international law and was also fundamentally unjust.

The second involved identifying the US state as imperialist, and thus pre-occupied with the standard concerns of imperialism: militarized accumulationand geostrategic advantage — goals which tend to harm the peoples of the South.

Arguments of this variety were supported by the third approach, which showed that Western policy in Afghanistan belied the idea that ISAF's actions would better the lives of Afghans. For example, Chomsky pointed to the UN's Food and Agriculture Organization, who advised that the bombing of Afghanistan "had disrupted planting that provides 80 percent of the country's grain supplies." And Arundhati Roy took the same approach when she noted, just before the war began, that "the UN estimates that there are eight million Afghan citizens who need emergency aid. As supplies run out – food and aid agencies have been asked to leave – the BBC reports that one of the worst humanitarian disasters of recent times has begun to unfold."

By contrast, much of the "progressive" defense of the war in Afghanistan, and the War on Terror more generally, was based on vacuous excoriations of the Left for its failure to "live up to its core values."

Similarly, then-*Dissent* editor Michael Walzer explained that he had "a modest agenda: put decency first." Bérubé dismissed "morally odious" the idea that "the bombing of Afghanistan was the moral equivalent of the 9/11 attacks." Gitlin described Roy as "in the grip of a prejudice invulnerable to moral distinctions" because she compared the corruption and brutality of Bush to that of bin Laden. In place of engagement with details and complexities, what the progressive imperialists offered were arbitrary, content-free, ill-defined concepts being put forth by tut-tutting, finger-wagging white guys with tenure.

Little has changed. The pro-war progressives have made the same points amid the 2011 NATO bombing of Libya and leading up to the military campaign that the US nearly undertook in Syria in 2013 and may attempt again in the future.

For example, in the spring of 2012 Bérubé was denouncing anti-imperialists who opposed NATO's war in Libya. He boasts that the intervention prevented a massacre — even though NATO and the forces whose victory they enabled actually carried out multiple massacres. In so doing, Bérubé resurrects Walzer's question of whether a "decent left" was possible, though Bérubé thinks the phrasing could be tweaked:

> The question, rather, should have been whether there can be a rigorously internationalist left in the U.S., a left that will promote and support the freedom of speech, the freedom to worship, the freedom from want, and the freedom from fear—even on those rare and valuable occasions when doing so puts one in the position of supporting U.S. policies.

Set aside that in Libya NATO did no such thing. Bérubé blithely assumes, as pro-war progressives had in Afghanistan, that NATO states act in pursuit of the freedom of oppressed peoples. It is holding idealist beliefs such as these despite all evidence to the contrary that causes Bérubé to celebrate in Libya, as he had in Afghanistan, an empire shedding of the blood of dark-skinned people.

On Syria, *Dissent* editor Michael Kazin was upset by the tenor of Dreyfuss's opposition to Western intervention. Though Kazin is equivocal about the merits of bombing Syria, he thinks it reasonable "to want to punish the Syrian government for violating a ban on [sarin gas] the first weapon which nearly every nation agreed, back in the 1920s, never to use again."

As with Bérubé's misdiagnosis of the Libyan war, there's no need to dwell on Kazin's easy acceptance of the claim that it was Bashar al-Assad's government who used sarin gas in August 2013 despite significant evidence to the contrary.

Kazin's basic error is to principally focus on the nature of Assad's regime while ignoring the character of the institutions that determine policy within Western states and overlooking how that could undermine the chances that their bombing of Syria will create a just peace in that country.

Furthermore, Kazin took exception to leftists who he felt opposed bombing Syria in overly strident terms, on the grounds that this allegedly "dishonors the vision of a left which, at its best, has always adhered, in essence, to the motto of the late, great New York City daily PM: 'We are against people who push other people around, just for the fun of pushing, whether they flourish in this country or abroad.'"

Presumably the civilians who would die in a US-led bombing campaign, and in the likely escalation of the Syrian war, might feel "push[ed] around" by the cruise missiles falling on them but Kazin could not see that.

An opposition to those who "push other people around" is the vaguest of vague abstractions, belied most of all by its inattention to the biggest bully on the block: the American ruling class. Indeed, while it may be a fine principle on which to supervise recess, it completely overlooks the myriad complexities and contingencies that characterize any war and most certainly the one in Syria.

In the debates over the West's imperialist aggression against Afghanistan, the assessments made by the radical Left proved correct primarily because they derived from observable phenomena.

And among the most significant lessons to draw from progressive support for the war in Afghanistan is one that progressives had to no excuse not to know by 2001: while there is often a shortage of immediate results-yielding ways to support people in the Global South dealing with problems of inequality and human rights, one surefire way to not be of use is to rally support for imperial armies to invade, bomb, militarily occupy, jail en masse, torture, and kill the people in question.

3

Civil-Military Cooperation in Post Taliban Afghanistan

INTRODUCTION

The debate on Civil-Military Cooperation in Post-Taliban Afghanistan dates from the introduction of Provincial Reconstruction Teams (PRTs) model in 2003, with the primary goal to assist the central government in providing security at the sub-national level, facilitating civil-military cooperation and implementing small scale reconstruction projects (Hugh, 2004). In practice, the simultaneous involvement of international civilian actors and military institutions along with increased integration of relief operations into political and military strategies have seriously elevated a series of problematic issues concerning the present Civil-Military Cooperation trend in Post-Taliban Afghanistan (Jenny, 2007).

The armed humanitarian division of international military have continued operating in unsecure Afghan local communities claiming to assist NGHAs mission by providing humanitarian and development assistances. However, NGHAs have consistently expressed their concerns by pointing out a number of negative implications, as a result of military involvement in relief operations (Sedra, 2005). The repeatedly expressed concerns by NGHAs are: undermining of humanitarian principles, overlapping and unsustainability of projects, increasing figures of targeted NGHAs by insurgents and ultimately, limiting the space for humanitarian actors in the local communities (Dziedzic & Seidl, 2003). This paper focuses on the present approaches of Civil-Military Cooperation in Afghanistan and attempts to answer the following questions:

"How has the present Civil-Military Cooperation approach in Post-Taliban Afghanistan affected the Non-governmental humanitarian agencies in providing humanitarian relief? How can this trend be improved?"

This essay begins by evaluating the role of the military, represented by the PRTs, in delivering humanitarian and development aid in Post-Taliban Afghanistan and highlights a variety of destructive consequences for NGHAs, caused by military involvement in relief operations. In addition, the essay takes a step forward and employs Theory of Shared Responsibility (Blend,1999) and Theory of Regime (Krasner, 1983) to sketch out the possible courses of action for improving Civil-Military Cooperation in post-Taliban Afghanistan in future humanitarian and development joint-efforts.

DEFINING TERMINOLOGIES AND INTRODUCING ACTORS

For reasons of conciseness of this article and particularity of the context of Post-Taliban Afghanistan, the paper intentionally divides the engaged actors in civil-military cooperation in two general groups: 1, Provincial Reconstruction Teams (PRTs) and 2, Non-governmental Humanitarian Agencies (NGHAs). Each of the groups –in some cases indirectly – encompasses all the international military and non-military actors who are operating in Afghanistan. The term, Non-governmental Humanitarian Agencies (NGHA), which is deliberately used in this paper, encompasses national and international non-governmental organizations (NGOs), International Committee of the Red Cross (ICRC) and humanitarian agencies within the UN system (Sedra, 2005). Likewise, Provincial Reconstruction Teams (PRTs) includes the all the international military forces including NATO, ISAF and coalition Special Forces. Similarly, it includes all other armed institutions operating under structures of PRTs in Afghanistan.

Since the nature of PRTs and NGHAs are remarkably different with each other in terms of organisational structure, operational culture, and their goals and approaches in addressing reconstruction and development in Post-Taliban Afghanistan (Brzoska, 2008), it is essential to separately have a deeper look at both of the actors.

Provincial Reconstruction Teams (PRTs)

Shortly after the fall of the Taliban regime in late 2001, the coalition forces created a Joint Civil-Military Operations Task Force (CJCMOF) to manage and coordinate the civil-military interactions in Afghanistan (Sedra, 2005). The second step was establishment of Coalition Humanitarian Cells (CHLCS) under the auspices of CJCMOF in several key provinces. The main objective of the CHLCs was to conduct 'winning hearts and minds' operations by implementing humanitarian and development programs in Afghanistan. In addition, the political agenda of these cells were obtaining positive publicity for the war efforts in the United States, on the one hand, and securing the support of local Afghan populations, on the other.

Finally, in mid 2002 the need to accelerate the reconstruction and development efforts in Post-Taliban Afghanistan has led the U.S Led Coalition Forces to seek ways of decentralising ISAF at the provincial level.

As a result, the United States Agency for International Development (USAID) developed the concept of civil-military field units throughout Afghanistan. The concept was supposed to be implemented under the name of Joint Regional Teams (JRTs); however, due to the suggestion of the Afghan President, Hamid Karzai, the teams started operating under the name of Provincial Reconstruction Team (PRT) in Gardiz province for the first time in 2003 (Dziedzic & Seidl, 2003).

At the time of writing this paper, there are 26 PRTs operating across the country. Structurally, PRTs are composed of various military and civilian bodies including diplomats, specialists in economic development and governance and a few representatives of the Afghan government.

Non Government Humanitarian Agencies (NGHAs)

The involvement of NGHAs in Afghanistan in delivering humanitarian assistance goes far beyond the collapse of the Taliban regime. The first officially registered non-governmental humanitarian agency in Afghanistan was International Committee of Red Cross (ICRC), which started operating in 1979. According to the figures given by the United States International Grantmaking (USIG), a total number of 4,280 NGHAs are currently operating in Afghanistan. (USIG, 2012)

In general, any national or international non-governmental humanitarian organization operating in armed conflicts or post-conflict contexts are committed to comply with the core humanitarian principles namely: a, Principle of Humanity, meaning that all victims should be treated and respected equally at any circumstances by saving lives and alleviating suffering. b, Principle of Impartiality, meaning that humanitarian assistance should be based on need, and must not be based on race, religion, nationality or political view. c, Principle of Neutrality, meaning that no sides should be taken with any warring parties during or after the armed conflict (Anderson, 1999).

However, it is an internationally accepted principle that NGHAs neither follow any political agendas nor is it supposed to be utilized as a political instrument by any government for any purpose; some argue that that since the end of the cold war, humanitarian aid has increasingly been politicised. A counterargument is always opposed to this by claiming emerge of "new humanitarianism" which aims to assist peace building trends in fragile states by addressing poverty (Brzoska, 2008).

CIVIL MILITARY COOPERATION IN POST-TALIBAN AFGHANISTAN

After the fall of Taliban regime, development and humanitarian assistances have been recognized as one of the essential commitments of the international community towards reconstruction and development of Afghanistan. Another aspect of this strategic commitment was launching counterinsurgency and peacekeeping operations to ensure security (Runge, 2009).

Therefore, one of the initiatives of the international coalition was introducing the PRT model with the objective of providing security and facilitating humanitarian and development interventions at the provincial level. After this model was successfully implemented in Garzdiz Province in 2003, the PRTs soon expanded and started operating in 26 provinces under the command of North Atlantic Treaty Organization (NATO).

Establishment of PRTs in Afghanistan rapidly led to the massive involvement of military, through the PRTs, in delivering humanitarian and development assistances. This humanitarian nature of PRTs raised intense debates concerning Civil-Military Cooperation trend among the humanitarian actors, especially due to the fact that the military humanitarian activities has blurred the line between humanitarian and military actors in the ground and seriously affected the neutral and impartial image of NGHAs among the local Afghan communities. It is worth to mention here that in recent years several civil-military cooperation guidelines have been developed by the UN agencies and other NGHAs to improve the trend but none of these guidelines proved to be effective in improving Civil-Military Cooperation in Post-Taliban Afghanistan. In contrast to what Thomas G. Weis, the author of *Military-Civilian Interactions* (1999) argues that the main role of military in the humanitarian space is to provide security and logistics. In Afghanistan, the PRTs have conversely accelerated their "winning hearts and minds" operations by launching a huge number of quick-impact programmes, aiming to gain community support. These operations, however, did not adhere to the humanitarian organizations standards, as constantly claimed by NGHAs ((Hugh, 2004).

Surprisingly, it is not only the NGHAs who criticise the PRTs involvement in development and humanitarian affairs, very precise criticisms were made by the Afghan president, Hamid Karzai who mentioned that:

"Afghanistan clearly explained its viewpoint on Provincial Reconstruction Teams and structures parallel to the Afghan government ... bodies which are hindering the Afghan government's development and hindering the governance of Afghanistan" (BBC, 2011).

However, NGHAs are concerned and the Afghan Government is frustrated concerning the deficient civil-military cooperation in Post-Taliban Afghanistan, the United States has officially endorsed – in addition to PRT's three main areas of responsibilities: security, reconstruction and support to the central government – the principle of military engagement in humanitarian operations in certain circumstances (Runge, 2009). The issue was further publicised last year by International Security Assistance Forces (ISAF) press release emphasising that:

"ISAF is also directly involved in facilitating the development and reconstruction of Afghanistan through Provincial Reconstruction Teams throughout the country" (NATO Annual Report, 2011).

THE NGHAS PERSPECTIVE ON PRTS

In order to assess the present civil-military cooperation trend in Post-Taliban Afghanistan, it is very essential to examine the perception of NGHAs on the involvement of PRTs in delivering aid. The establishment of PRTs in Afghanistan has seriously increased the discontent of the NGHAs operating in Afghanistan under the international humanitarian principles. One of the commentaries made by NGHAs and further supported by ICRC is the issue of blurring line between the responsibilities of military and NGHAs in most of the local Afghan communities. The ICRC, while criticising this trend, described the "blurring line" phenomenon as follows:

"The distinction between humanitarian, political and military action becomes blurred when armed forces are perceived as being humanitarian actors, when civilians are embedded into military structures, and when the impression is created that humanitarian organizations and their personnel are merely tools within integrated approaches to conflict management" (Rana, 2004, p. 586).

In another scenario, the simultaneous dropping of bombs and aid packages by the US military in 2001, which were later justified as military relief operations, is another instance showing how has the line between responsibility and identity of military and civilian humanitarian actors been blurred. This situation manifests that the civil-military cooperation has been affected and weakened from the very beginning, after the international community and coalition forces intervened in Afghanistan.

Furthermore, the uncoordinated humanitarian interventions, launched and implemented by PRTs, have contributed in endangering the lives of NGHAs aid workers in many ways. The civilian divisions of military teams, for instance, have made it difficult to physically distinguish the military personal from the aid workers. This ambiguity has led the insurgents to target NGHAs staff, quite frequently assuming them as military. Similarly, when the UN Under-Secretary General for Humanitarian Affairs and Emergency Relief Coordinator, John Holmes, visited Afghanistan in June 2008, he expressed:

"I agree that there has been and there is to some extent a blurring of lines between military operations and, for example, humanitarian assistance by the PRTs. I think it is very important that PRTs do not involve themselves in humanitarian assistance unless there is absolutely no other alternative for security reasons" (Runge, 2009).

However, such emphasis never proved effective for convincing PRTs to terminate their relief operations. At this point, the essay outlines four specific areas where NGHAs have increasingly suffered from the instrumentalisation of humanitarian aid by the military, on the one hand, and the blurred line of responsibilities between civilian and military actors, on the other. The current military approach towards the civil-military cooperation trend and the military involvement in development and humanitarian activities undermined the humanitarian principles, overlapped the implemented projects, fuelled the violence and finally reduced the space for humanitarian actors in most of the Afghan local communities to operate.

Undermining Humanitarian Principles

Humanitarian aid is based on the principles drawn in the humanitarian code of conduct in which all NGHAs are committed to act accordingly. The essence of these principles – Humanity, Neutrality and Impartiality – is to deliver humanitarian assistance to the vulnerable and needy population regardless of race, ethnic, nationality and political background. Since the PRTs are deployed in Afghanistan for a military and political purpose, therefore; they cannot be perceived as humanitarian actors. The humanitarian actors expressed their concerns continuously about the issue. Save the Children Fund, for instance, declared the humanitarian involvement of military as: *"inappropriate and contrary to the fundamental humanitarian principles of independence and impartiality"* (Hugh, 2004). Some may argue that the military occupying power has a mandate to ensure the safety and security of the civilian population or NGHAs in the unstable and unsecure environments based on International Humanitarian Law and the 4th Geneva Convention. This never means that the occupying military power can deliver humanitarian aid directly, nor it can legally justify involvement of military in relief operations. In contrast, the present military involvement in delivering humanitarian and development assistance is in violation of international humanitarian principles.

In another instance, a press release by NATO/ISAF on December 2007, declared that: "Humanitarian assistance operations are helping both the people of Afghanistan and coalition forces to fight the global war on terror" (ISAF, 2007). The integration of humanitarian assistances with a political agenda of war on terror has significantly undermined the principle of neutrality of NGHAs among the local Afghan population. Moreover, according to Donini (2009, p.2) ICRC is the only international organization that is able to operate neutrally, impartially and independently on both sides of the warring parties. However, thousands of NGHAs are operating in Afghanistan after the fall of Taliban.

Overlapping Interventions

In principle, the roles and responsibilities of PRTs and NGHAs are sharply different, however; in practice these responsibilities are extremely blurred. Under this circumstance, development and humanitarian actors have expressed their concerns about the overlapping of certain implemented projects in the field (Hugh, 2004).

An assessment conducted by the Asian Development Bank (ADB) on Security of ADB Projects in Afghanistan in 2007 revealed a couple of substantial PRT interventions that contradict Article

32.4 of the United Nations Guideline for Civil-Military Cooperation. Here, the paper quotes some of the ADB assessment findings:

"Some PRTs include projects linked to health care, education, water supply or waste clearance, in this, there is an overlap with NGO programmes" (Marsden & Arnold, 2007; p.30)

"There is some evidence that some PRTs have provided cash to power holders or individual villagers in an effort to win influence" (Marsden & Arnold, 2005; p.31).

"Some PRTs, including those led by Spain and Italy, use military personnel for development work" (Marsden & Arnold, 2007, p.30).

As a result of PRT's constant intrusions without respecting the enacted civil-military cooperation guidelines, the United Nations Office for the Coordination of Humanitarian Aid (UNOCHA) described the increasing influence of military in humanitarian activities as follows:

"In NATO and elsewhere there has been an evolution of the doctrine of military–civilian operations, with an increasing tendency for military forces being used to support the delivery of humanitarian aid, and sometimes even to provide this aid directly (Barry and Jefferys,2001, p. 1).

Moreover, another critique against the PRTs involvement in the development and humanitarian sphere is their unprofessionalism. The military actors are not well-trained to implement complex cross-cutting and mutually reinforcing projects at the community level. This awkwardness is bolded in the areas of rebuilding the political institutions and effectively engaging with civil society actors (Jenny, 2007).

Fuelling Violence

Increased violence against humanitarian aid workers is another consequence of the current ineffective civil-military cooperation in Post-Taliban Afghanistan. In the list of fragile countries where the level of violence against aid workers is enormously high, Afghanistan is positioned in third place. Relief operations by PRTs notably raised acts of violence against NGHAs. In 2004, for instance, five employee of Médecins Sans Frontières (MSF) were targeted and killed by insurgent. As a result, MSF evacuated its staff and stopped operating in Afghanistan. Moreover, an assessment conducted by the German Institute for International and Security Affairs, revealed that the security environment in northern provinces of Afghanistan has deteriorated and level of violence against aid workers has increased since the deployment of the German Military (Lange, 2008). It is noteworthy that the northern provinces of Afghanistan were considered highly secured regions after the fall of Taliban regime.

Appendix one is produced by Afghanistan NGO Security Organization (ANSO) which shows a 60% increase in the abduction of aid workers over the year 2009 (ANSO Annual Report, 2011). According to the Afghanistan NGO Safety Office (ANSO) the increased nature of insurgents' attacks on NGHAs, are functionally linked with a misperception that NGHAs have political and military agendas (Cornish & Glad, 2008). Such views were strongly publicised by the various international high officials like Colin Powell, the former US Secretary of States, who said: "NGOs are the force multiplier" (Runge, 2007). Ultimately, the consequences of such publications were the death of 1500 civilians who were targeted by different insurgency attacks in 2010. Furthermore, a report by UNAMA contrasts the level of violence in 2001 with the level of violence in 2007. According to the report, in 2001 only 3 suicide attacks were carried out in Afghanistan, while after five years of international military presence in Afghanistan, this figure increased 53 times. In other words, 160 suicide bombing attacks were conducted by insurgents in 2006 (UNAMA, 2007).

Reducing Humanitarian Space

The increased level of violence, is a restricting factor for the presence of NGHAs in most of the local Afghan communities. Humanitarian actors need "Humanitarian Space" (Runge, 2007) in the conflict affected areas to independently and impartially identify conflict victims to assist them. This humanitarian space is getting limited, especially when PRTs interfere in providing aid by wearing civilian uniforms and driving unmarked vehicles in the local communities. This humanitarian nature of the military posed another serious threat to the security of NGHAs since there is no distinguishing indicator left between them and the PRTs. MSF, for instance, was among those NGHAs that found itself in an eroded humanitarian space. The justification given by MSF, after evacuating its staff and stopping all its operations in Afghanistan, was increased level of violence against their employees as a consequence of military involvement in providing humanitarian aid in the ground. In another instance, a UK quartered NGO left its projects and withdrew from Kamdesh District because a US armed team visited the community without informing the local authorities in advance and prior consultation with the NGO (Afghanistan Group, 2008, p. 22).

In appendix two, the figures shown in the circles are the total number of armed NATO forces in each province. Regions that are coloured in red means a 50% of growth in Armed Opposition Groups (AOG) attacks. It is interesting to see in Herat Province, for instance, the number of NATO forces is fewer – 6,700 forces – compared to Helmand – 31,000 forces – but still the level of violence in Helmand had a 50% growth over the year 2009. This shows that the presence of military in the local Afghan communities have contributed to the growth of violence.

To condemn the erosion of humanitarian space in Afghanistan, The Agency Coordinating Body for Afghan Relief (ACBAR) released a statement in 2007, mentioning that:

"Humanitarian actors are increasingly unable to provide adequate protection and assistance to displaced people and other populations at risk in the south and east of Afghanistan due to the significant deterioration in the security situation. Humanitarian space and humanitarian access continues to be seriously limited" (ACBAR, 2007).

Moreover, existence of great insecurity against the NGHAs significantly decreased the possibilities of accessing the needy population in most of the Afghan communities. Studies carried out by UNHCR and ICRC demonstrates that large part of the country is inaccessible by NGHAs. UNHCR claimed that in 2008, they only had access to 55% of the country and ICRC declared that the humanitarian access situation was the worst in the last 27 years in Afghanistan in 2008 (Norton-Tylor, 2008).

THEORISING CIVIL-MILITARY COOPERATION IN POST-TALIBAN CONTEXT: A KEY FOR IMPROVING

The Theory of Shared Responsibility, posed by Douglas L. Bland (1999) argues that Civil-Military Cooperation can effectively be improved by sharing responsibilities between civilian and military actors. Theory of Regime, which Bland (1999) borrowed from International Relations, provides a conceptual framework and strong instrument to arrange and maintain the shared responsibilities between the civilian and military actors. Theory of regime emphasises an evolved regime of norms, principles, rule and decision making procedures in order to restrict the actors to respect the rule of the game and operate within the limits of their responsibilities. Considering the results of above analysis on the present Civil-Military Cooperation trend in Afghanistan and its harmful implications on NGHAs activities, at this point, the paper takes a step forward, and utilizes Theory of Shared Responsibility (Blend, 1999) and Theory of Regime (Krasner, 1983) to sketch out the potential courses of action for improving Civil-Military Cooperation in the future humanitarian and development joint-efforts in Post-Taliban Afghanistan.

In order to address the legitimate concerns of the NGHAs, caused by a deficient civil-military cooperation approach and a blurred line of responsibilities among the actors, the study strongly suggests a clear division of responsibilities between PRTs, represented by military, and NGHAs. To restrict the PRTs and NGHAs to operate according to their sharply distinguished roles, this paper recommends that a series of legitimate principles – accepted by both sides – should be enacted and reinforced by a third party from the top, preferably by a joint committee of humanitarian and military divisions of the United Nations (UN).

Considering the context of Post-Taliban Afghanistan, the study suggests that PRTs should restrict their role into two main areas: First, PRTs should concentrate in providing security in unsecure communities rather than delivering humanitarian or development aid in stable areas. It is frequently observed that presence of PRTs in stable communities has deteriorated the security situation rather than improving it. Secondly, PRTs engagement in humanitarianism should be transformed into a logistical backup only in humanitarian catastrophes or disasters. It is an obvious fact that in Post-Taliban Afghanistan, NGHA are in a better position to deliver humanitarian aid than the PRTs. Most importantly, PRTs should immediately terminate and handover their interventions in the areas of education, water and food aid to NGHAs (Sedra, 2005).

The Civil-Military Cooperation model, proposed above, will allow NGHAs to access the conflict victims on time and effectively deliver the assistances to the affected communities. Moreover, this approach will contribute in enhancing community participation in delivering aid and will mitigate the hostilities, mistrust and suspicion between the local Afghan communities and international society.

In order to encourage civil-military academics and practitioners in dedicating their future research to finding alternatives and effective ways for improving the civil-military cooperation trend in Post-Taliban Afghanistan, the study ends up this section by quoting a short but meaningful sentence by Mary Anderson, the author of DO NO HARM: "...the range and variety of ways should be identified, in which international assistance worsens the situation rather than relief" (Anderson, 1999).

4

Political Leadership in Post Taliban Afghanistan

THE CRITICAL FACTOR

A hasty, fluid, and poorly conceived process of creating leadership in a post-war situation mainly provides the space for rich and powerful — mostly corrupt — individuals to prevail because their roles, styles, and abilities overshadow concerns about their background, characteristics, homogeneity, and behavioral patterns. Regrettably, such is the case in post-Taliban Afghanistan.

The hasty entry of Hamid Karzai, his cabinet colleagues and regional leaders eight years ago is proving a costly deal. The resources of Afghan non-governmental organizations (NGOs) are used at will for individual benefits, because donors rarely condition their aid on an assessment of background, characteristics, and behavioral patterns of key staff of the recipient. So-called Afghan civil society is predominantly comprised of the rich and powerful whose abilities (speaking English, understanding Western culture and values) and lifestyles (luxurious homes, mobility, and access to technology) enable them to communicate better with donors and other representatives of the international community than grassroots or other sectors of society with the same field of specialization are able to.

This essay explores the subject of the post-Taliban political leadership in Afghanistan by addressing two related questions: First, why is the quality of political leadership, especially of individuals occupying high office, a critically important ingredient for a successful post-conflict transformation? And second, which features of political leadership are most conducive (and in the Afghan case have been present or missing) to furthering peace and reconstruction?

POLITICAL LEADERSHIP IN AFGHANISTAN — ESSENTIAL BUT DEFICIENT

Political leaders who occupy a high office in a legally sanctioned government have more power than political leaders who do not, simply by virtue of the legitimacy of government and the resources at their disposal. In a post-war situation and in a unique case like that of Afghanistan, political leaders are of particular importance. They may possess more power than those in an orderly institutional setting because they mainly engage on behalf of their constituents in an environment where fewer checks and balances are in place for accountability and transparency.

Institutionally, political leaders in post-war settings will eventually determine the fate of reconstruction efforts. They set the institutional rules of the game, breaking them at any point, or not agreeing upon them at all. As Ashraf, Ghani, and Clare Lockhart have written:

> [They] must demonstrate that they can forge and maintain international partnerships for generating legitimacy in the international system and opportunity in the economy, understand and navigate the opportunities and constraints of globalisation, and maintain the trust and loyalty of citizens at home by generating a belief that the state can enhance their lives and capabilities. They must be able to conceive of an architecture of change that operates across functions on global, national and local levels. They show to their citizens that they participate in the world as respected global leaders, as well as representatives of distinctive cultural identities.

Equally important is the role of political leadership in inspiring and rallying everyone, including interveners, around a vision with which both government organisations and broader society, as well, can identify. Additionally, their persistent and deep involvement in all levels of development programs and familiarity with details further encourages success.

FOUR CRUCIAL FEATURES OF EFFECTIVE POLITICAL LEADERSHIP

Purposefulness and Determination

Lack of determination and decisiveness can easily be pointed out as Hamid Karzai's main weakness. Ordinary Afghans, foreign diplomats, aid workers, political leaders and even armed opponents of the Karzai government are aware of it and have spoken about it. But how much does it matter? Take as an example the National Solidarity Programme (NSP) — arguably the only success story in post-Taliban Afghanistan. The NSP, which covered almost all of rural Afghanistan, was comprehensive: It addressed issues of governance, focused on rebuilding or building small infrastructure, and gave local communities "ownership" (block grants were transferred directly to members of the community who planned, implemented, and accounted for projects of their own design after receiving thorough training in planning, administration, accounting, and meeting management).

Aware of his precarious position in the government, the lead minister, who had been included in the cabinet merely on the back of his technical know-how, was aware of the fact he did not have sufficient popular support to sustain his position. That, along with his background as a long-time humanitarian worker, made him determined to create an exemplary ministry. This cannot be divorced from his technical skills, knowledge, and experience in the fields of humanitarian assistance and development. To achieve success, he had to bank heavily on members of the NGO community. In this effort, he appointed a former professional adversary as his Deputy Minister and a fellow member of NGO community as the Chief Coordinator. Their collaboration proved instrumental to the NSP's success.

All three are cabinet colleagues now. However, they have yet to come up with something similar to, or better than, the NSP. The reason is clear: They do not have common goals, towards which they generate determination of the same levels. In fact, they are seeking to undermine one another in order to wield or retain more power, emboldened by the ill counsel of advisors, all of whom are foreign nationals. In one case, an Australian advisor actively and blatantly tweaked the donors to divert funds from their previous ministry to the new one to great dismay of their former boss and in spite of abundance financial resources. Important for the two offshoot ministers is also to create identities of their own and banish the *protégé* tags.

Intimate Relationship with the Bureaucracy

The success of the Minister of Rural Rehabilitation and Development (MRRD) to execute the NSP successfully was also due to his intimate relationship with the bureaucracy which he nurtured during his time in MRRD. His model was initially criticized. Karzai's Chief of Staff told one of the authors in 2005 that creating a parallel structure of advisors by the Minister was costly, temporary, and counterproductive to the efforts institutionalization. However, what he had not foreseen was the plans of the Minister to embed the capable legion of advisors, on temporary consultancy contracts, into the main bureaucracy. His Deputy Minister was his senior advisor for a year until he was incorporated into the civil services structure. The trend went on, and the new elements presented a perfect example of a modern bureaucracy responsive to the demands of a post-war reconstruction phase.

In contrast, the inability of Karzai's Chief of Staff not only hampered his efforts to reform his office but even cost him his job. The argument is reinforced by the case of the newly establish Independent Directorate for Local Governance (IDLG) whose director has kept the rotten bureaucratic structure intact and installed some new inept individuals. His advisory team — the Strategic Coordination Unit, or SCU — which consists of some capable individuals, has struggled to push their agenda. The SCU consistently has been undermined by the civil servants whose authority derives from their positions of power. In late 2006, the lead Inwent consultant and the FES Resident Representative sought one of the author's advice on why their capacity-building and organizational development program for the Ministry of Foreign

Affairs was failing. We jointly concluded that the Minister's incompetence and lack of integrity and determination were the reasons.

Similarly, the current Minister of Education (MoE) has complained in closed circles about the loyalty of his top bureaucrats who were installed by his predecessor, a supposed adversary. He says, "they are my deputies during the day and his deputies at night," one of his confidants admitted to me this year. The former Minister (the same man who had successfully led MRRD) had created a synergy at MoE, replicating that success. However, the model is dependent on its agents. And the current Minister's antagonistic relationship with the former Minister shapes his suspicions of his colleagues. Mutual lack of trust has thrown the ministry in disarray and impact of change is clear in its performance. This means that the intimate relationship with the bureaucracy, a crucial denominator for success, has ceased to exist, depriving it from achieving its goals.

Despite Internal Differences, United for a Cause

Afghanistan's political leadership lacks a common vision and are only unified by one thing: political survival, as the cases of the five ministers discussed in this essay reveal. The moment they realized that the link between their personal ambitions and their counterparts' weakened, their alliances fell apart and they formed destructive alliances against each other.

Furthermore, Karzai's fragile administration has only responded in unity when threatened. They are united against insurgents because the latter threaten their very existence and hold on power. This is and has been the main reason for Karzai's tolerance of a few disloyal governors who make personal gains of their government positions but never threaten Karzai's central authority. The mere fact that every political leader in Afghanistan pins his/her survival to their favorable relationships with interveners has made the political leaders reluctant to work for what should have been a key demand of the international community — a common Afghan vision or goal. The difference between political leadership of Afghanistan and their counterparts in other developmental states seems to be their perception of tools for preserving their power. The former sees tainted alliances with drug barons and warlords and reliance on interveners as their salvation. The latter saw economic growth and social progress as their salvation because it earned them the support of their constituents.

Relative Autonomy from Special Interests

As is the case in many post-conflict countries, Afghanistan has yet to formulate its set of national interests. And as is typically the case in aid-receiving countries, the Afghan government is completely driven by the interests of aid providing countries. During my time with the five ministers, I saw them regularly bow to both internal and external special interests. One Minister had to retain an entire department for the sake of only one person who was supported by Karzai's Second Vice President. The department cost hundreds of thousands of dollars over a number of years and its head was a constant source of conflict in the ministry, slowing down or, at times, completely damaging the implementation of crucial development projects. A second Minister was so obsessed with keeping the ethnic balance that he appointed numerous incapable individuals, which not only demoralized others but also badly factionalized the Ministry, making the delivery of services almost impossible.

The Ministry of Agriculture has been one of the most incompetent government entities in a country where 70% of the population is dependent on agriculture for livelihood. Yet, its Deputy Ministers have held onto their positions due to their affiliations to two political parties accused of war crimes before and during the Afghan Civil War. One Deputy Minister famously solicits and engages in physical intimacy with his subordinates to the point of harassment. A number of his family members are employed in the Ministry in violation of standard procedures. The same is the case with the Afghan Development Association (ADA), one of the main Afghan recipients of donor funding, where 80% of staff are hired based on their membership of or goodwill towards a particular political party or their relationship with its management. Consequently, the institutions in question constantly have labored to execute their mandates or reach their potential capacity instead of just serving the interests of a few.

Conclusion

The political and civil society leadership of Afghanistan lacks the popular support required for achieving peace. It is the responsibility of the leadership to facilitate the emergence of a common purpose in a society through creating reciprocal and equitable relationships among community participants. In Afghanistan, such a situation has not yet prevailed. Moreover, it may never happen since the leadership is almost totally disconnected from the society and incapable of understanding this crucial reality and working towards it.

FAILURE OF POST-TALIBAN POLITICAL SYSTEM

Peace process begun at Bonn in November 2001 for establishment of a democratic government in Afghanistan after collapse of Taliban. Bonn agreement scheduled three steps for reestablishment of democratic government institutions. First step was an Emergency Loya Jirga charged for electing the Afghan Transitional Administration (ATA). The second step was Constitutional Loya Jirga and the third step was election. In the era of Post-Taliban period Afghanistan had two presidential and parliamentary elections. With consideration to this period established constitution and structure of Afghan government failed to bring accountability. Afghanistan constitution have opted a strong central government. According to the new constitution, "the president of the Islamic State of Afghanistan combines the powers which had been exercised by the king and by the prime minister under the constitution of 1964" (Grote) The Afghan constitution which followed the constitution of 1964 did not make a major contribution to the further development of the concept of separation powers. (Grote) vagueness in the sphere of authority and framework of institutions cut accountability in their actions. Absence of clear determination of vertical and horizontal separation of powers in constitution, limited constraining roles of legislative and judiciary, fraud elections in the absence of high-quality electoral system, led to failure of post-Taliban political system.

Horizontal separation of powers is ill defined and horizontal accountability cannot be implemented. Constitution in article 60 states "President is the head of the state of the Islamic Republic of Afghanistan and conducts his authorities in the executive, legislative and judiciary branches in accordance with the provisions of the constitution. (The Constitution of Afghanistan) While Montesquieu argued, separation of powers prevent from misuse of any branch or tyranny by having checks and balance among them. (Montesquieu) Concentration of power on the head of the state grants the president to have influence over the functions of other two branches.

Determined authorities between executive and legislative do not provide checks and balances between them. The several 30 days deadlines to confirm the entire appointees, passing budget, and approval of fundamental policies of the state. If the WJ failed to approve or reject it within 30 days the budget would be considered approved. These unrealistic timelines for approval of executive proposes enhance discard between these two branches. (Afghanistan's New Legislature: Making Democracy Work) at the same time, control of parliament over budget is bounded by initiating its proposal only to government. "The national assembly is obliged to give priority to the discussion of bills and treaties introduced by the government if the latter formally request their urgent consideration." (Aricle 97) This shows clear influence of executive over working agenda of parliament. As well, the passed law by the National Assembly should be signed by the President which is claimed to keep parliament accountable to the executive. But, it allows the president to exert influence over legislative. Also, under 2004 constitution president is manipulated to appoint 1/3 of MJ which enhances his influence over legislative. For instance, when president sent the electoral law decree to the WJ, didn't get approved by its members. But, the MJ (where president have more influence on) deputy and its pro governmental members agreed that constitution doesn't allow the lower house to amend or discuss the electoral law over last year of their term. (Afgahnistan's Election Stalement)

In other side, parliament as the highest legislative organ is responsible for making laws and oversight of government. Checks of legislature over the executive are vote of no confidence to minister, impeachment of the president, and establishing special commission to investigate the actions of government. (Article 81-89) Vote of no confidence to ministers were not that much applicable and investigative commission were not established because of lack political parties. And, impeachment of president is nearly impossible because there is need for 2/3 approval of parliament and convene of Loya Jirga. So, the designed system does not support fair checks and balances between executive and legislative.

Furthermore, executive enjoy a strong influence over judiciary too. Supreme Court should review the constitutionality of the laws, legislative decrees and international treaties. But it cannot do it on its own strategy, only upon request of government or of the lower courts. (Article 121). "President has the authority of appointing, retiring and accepting resignation and dismissal of the judges" (Article 64).

According to reports, the executive used budgetary constraints as a means of applying pressure on the Supreme Court, which controls the appointment, promotion, dismissal reward, and punishment of all judges in the country. (Lister)

Appointments of judges by president make them loyal to him then their attitude would seek what is politically feasible for the government. Dr. Spanta former foreign minister didn't get vote of confidence by parliament but the decision of WJ vetoed and he remained as foreign minister. Karzai referred the law to the Supreme Court for review, which, not unexpectedly resulted in the executive's favor. Clearly, the made legal frame work allow executive for interference in system and influence on actions of judiciary.

Moreover, there are three main institutions of rule of law in Afghanistan are the Supreme Court, the attorney general's office and the ministry of justice. In theory, each one has distinct responsibilities but in practice lack of clarity on the legal authority, overlapping mandates, and persistent political interference have led to constant turf wars. Also, relationship between three legal foundations: Islamic Sharia law, Secular Statuary law, and customary law have been problematic. (Reforming Afghaistan

Broken judiciary) These contradictions of laws not only complicate the justice on national level but also allow powerbrokers to use it for their own political interest.

One of the big obstacles for accountability of the government is lack of political parties. "The citizens of Afghanistan have the right to form political parties in accordance with the provisions of the law" (Article 35) However, "the electoral law all but remove such groups from any formal role in electoral process; this has stifled their development and process within the assembly" (Afghaistan's New Legislature: Making Democracy Work) Due to Non-Transferable Voting (SNTV) system people run as independent candidates. The concentration of power on hands of the party leaders and lack of a platform to unite the members caused some MPs leave their parties after getting into parliament. Also, it leads MPs to bargaining and promoting personal interest with government. (Wafaey) This fragmentation made the parliament a weak institution. Obviously, in such condition there is no clear stances and decision making become complicated and ineffective. For instance, this absence of discipline caused the WJ to not pass the internal rules of procedures in longer than one and half year and elected deputy speaker in one year. WJ didn't succeed to establish commission to oversight the functions of government. In one year only could select 2 out of 25 members of it. (Wafaey) Lack of political parties in parliament resulted to absence of discipline and defined stances for decision making. As a result, parliament failed to oversight actions of government and keeps it accountable.

Government administration failed to provide policies to preserve interest of community. Afghanistan National Development Strategy (ANDS) was responsible for setting objectives and benchmarks for all ministries and important governmental institutions..it was to reflect the interest of Afghans with their participation in the process but the process became dominated by the foreign technical advisors and met donor requirements. It didn't specified how the presented guides to actions should be achieved. (Sarah) Clearly, these policies won't be applicable in a situation where institutions neither have sufficient capacity nor were involved in the process. Afghanistan is not only politically but fiscally and administratively one of the most centralized countries in the world.

All budgetary and most staffing decisions are made in Kabul, and provincial departments of line ministries, as well as the governor's office, have virtually no discretionary spending power and limited input into planning. The governor, who is accountable in theory to the ministry of interior, has only a loose coordinating role and formally does not have authority over representatives of other ministers.

Administration system is fashioned based on old patronage system not merit. Because, positions are given to power holders in order to prevent from their disagreement with government. As result, PAR system which mainly threatens patronage networks failed since lacked political backing.

Overall, design of new political system in Afghanistan failed to bring accountability. Concentration of power in the center and ambiguity of authorities of branches cut the accountability in the government. The 2004 constitution articles are not well defined. Duties and responsibilities of judiciary and legislative are under influence of executive. Concentration of power in the center and poor administration system in sub national government resulted to the failure of the Post-Taliban political system.

CONSTITUTIONALISM IN POST CONFLICT AFGHAN SOCIETY

When seen from the Western lens, constitution serves as the foundational document for any legal system, it is almost incomprehensible for the modern liberal democratic state to exist without a constitution. However prior to the twentieth Century, Afghanistan had no written constitution, the governance was characterized by the Islamic *Shari'a* and the customary laws passed by the *Jirga/Shura* which composed of the local tribal leaders.

The concept of nation state with a constitution started to become the order of the day, this was and is imposed on the non-European countries through colonization and the western imperialism. Consequently there began to exist plural legal systems, in today's Afghanistan, despite having a written constitution, the hangover of the past still lingers and hence customary law, Islamic law and the statutory law coexist. This is otherwise known as legal pluralism.

Seemingly, they have inherent contradictions and thus they do not always complement each other, hence the challenge of the constitutionally validated judiciary is to reconcile the differences and yield the much needed legality in the modern nation state framework.

Hence, firstly, we look at the political, legal and constitutional history of Afghanistan, this helps in providing a theoretical framework for our understanding of the current situation in Afghanistan and the mechanisms provided for in the constitution and the evolution of Islamic jurisprudence.

POLITICAL HISTORY OF AFGHANISTAN

The monarchy of Zahir Shah which began in the 1933 ended in 1973 with Mohammed Daud declaring himself as the first president of the Republic. Mohammed Daud's reign lasted till 1978, he was overthrown by the Saur revolution led by the Communist People's Democratic Party of Afghanistan, the uncertainty in the communist rule led to soviet occupation in 1979, Soviet entered the country with the Red Army and Barbarak Kamal was installed as the ruler in the year 1980.

The communist social reforms clashed with the long established social standards of Afghanistan and hence the support for the PDPA soon crumbled. To counter the Soviet invasion, the Mujahideen i.e. The guerilla fighters from the rural areas of Afghanistan organized themselves into an army and fought back the Soviet, this tumultuous period of struggle was characterized by bloodshed leading to the killing of a million of Afghans.

The Mujahideen were organized into many political factions, it was armed and supported by Saudi Arabia, Pakistan and the US. It was during this time that Osama Bin Laden had entered the politics of Afghanistan, he was leading the Mujahideen. It needs no mention that the Mujahideen was mainly supported by the US as a strategic foreign policy to check the spread of communist regime and have a control over the region.

In 1986, Najibullah was replaced as the head of the Soviet backed regime. And in 1988, when the war was ongoing, Afghanistan, USSR, the US and Pakistan had signed peace accords; subsequently, the Soviet Union of Russia began pulling out its troops. The last troop left in 1989, however the civil war still continued as the Mujahedeen tried to topple Najibullah's government. After the overthrowing of the Najibullah's government in 1992, the factions of the Mujahideen fought amongst themselves until the Taliban seized control of Kabul and solidified its rule in 1996. The Taliban ruled the country from 1996-2001.

Theoritical connections can be made to the "state of nature" proposed by Thomas Hobbes, he was the earliest philosophers, who witnessed the terrors of the English Civil War and thereby concluded that the inherent nature of the man is "short, brutish and nasty" hence he conceptualised the notion of a "Levaithan", whose purpose is to protect the man from spilling into the state of nature, ever since the communist coup in 1978, Afghanistan has been the ground for warring factions, this has allowed for the budding of extremist muslim groups, the international community's response to the chaos and the stringent rule of Taliban has been a Hobbesian's approach, this lead to the installation of Hamid Karzaia as the Levaithan in 2001.

How and why did this happen? In 1998, the USA launched missile strikes in the militant bases of Osama Bin Laden as he was accused of bombing the US embassies in Africa. It was followed by the UN imposing an embargo and financial sanctions on the Afghanistan to handover Osama Bin Laden, this was the beginning of USA's uncomfort with the Mujahiadeen. Later, as a response to the September 112001 Pentagon attacks, US led bombing started in Afghanistan, the pseudonym of the "global war against terror" had become the policy of the United States and hence it started targeting the Taliban. The Anti-Taliban Northern Alliance which fought a war against the Taliban entered during the same time. The Taliban was over thrown in 2001. As the result of the negotiations that happened in Bonn, Germany; Afghan groups agreed for the establishment of an interim government. *Loya Jirga* elected Hamid Karzai as the interim head till 2004. In 2004 the *Loya Jirga* adopted the new constitution which provided for a strong presidency.

CONSTITUTIONAL HISTORY OF AFGHANISTAN

Having tracked the political history, it is evident that Afghanistan's fragile politic barely gave any opportunity to actually implement the constitutional principles. However it had too many constitutions. Since the first constitution in 1923, Afghanistan had eight different sets of constitution. The first two constitutions of 1923 and 1931 were established by the monarchy but they barely had any public participation and were totally elitist conferring all the power on the monarchy without leaving any room for popular vote. In 1963, after thirty years of stability under the regime of King Zahir, he called in for the formation of the constitution. This constitution was drafted democratically over a period of eighteen months, it provided for a popularly elected parliament, provincial advisory councils, elected city councils, and an independent legislature. This era marked the beginning of democracy in the region, two parliamentary elections were also held, however it was short lived. In 1973, Sardar Daoud, took power by coup, Afghanistan was declared Republic and the constitution that was drafted in 1963 was suspended. A new constitution was promulgated in 1977 without popular consultation; again, during the communist coup, the 1977 constitution was suspended. Another constitution was put in place in 1980 by Babrak Karmal, this came to an end with the Soviet invasion, the government of Najibullah introduced yet another constitution in 1987, it only lasted till the exit of the Soviet union. After the Soviet withdrawal in 1992, the new interim Mujahideen government proposed a new constitution, but it never came into fore as the fighting broke out between the internal elements, and later on the Taliban never introduced a constitution at all.

Thus in this whole period, Afghanistan had three spells of unconstitutionalism between 1973-1977, 1980-1987 and 1992-2001. Hence due to the instability in political structure and governance, people took to the local *Jirga* and *Shura* for their dispute resolution as there was no continuity in the legal system.

LEGAL PLURALISM IN AFGHANISTHAN

Jirga and *Shura* fall outside the purview of state institutions, the chthonic law that is adjudicated upon in such institutions is diverse due to different ethnicities and varies with regions, it isn't a uniform system of law, however it plays a significant role in dispute resolution.

Prolonged conflict in the society, multiple constitutions and a lack of centralized authority propelled people, particularly people living in the rural areas to take up to non-state chthonic law, rural population constitutes eighty percent of the Afghan population and hence one cannot dismiss the pervasive and binding effect of chthonic law in Afghanistan.

Even today, Hamid Karzai's government is largely composed of the old war lords of Northern alliance, and hence due to the lack of separation of powers people are still dependent on the local non state entities for the purposes of security and justice.

The reasons as to why people prefer chthonic law over the state law boils down to the following:

a) Chthonic law focuses on substantive justice instead of procedural justice;
b) It focuses on compensation and reconciliation instead of punishment;
c) The parties have a sense of faith in the institution and hence are bound by it.

Pashtuns are the dominant ethnic tribe in Afghanistan, their chthonic law is the pasthunwali, it is an amalgamation of *Shari'a* law, customs and ethical values of the tribe. The decision making process in a *jirga* is driven by consensus rather than voting; parties to the dispute and the communities meet for the resolution of a dispute. It has an appeal procedure as well, the first level of appeal is taken to another *jirga* with more elder members, the second level of appeal is taken to a tribal assembly which has representatives of pashtuns from other lineages.

In a Shura, the *Shari'a* plays a significant role when compared to a *jirga*, it is composed of imams and the "local religious figures" for the resolution of dispute, the local practices of the geography play a major role in dispute resolution. Now, with the emergence of a constitution, there surfaces a problem of deeply embedded legal pluralism, the question then remains, how do we reconcile the state and non state entities? Specifically in a culture which lacks constitutional morality. The normative laws guiding a constitutionally validated judiciary would inevitably come into conflict with the diverse normative framework of a non state entity.

United States Institute of Peace proposes the interaction of both, in cases where chthonic law isn't in congruence with the state law, the state should ensure that the chthonic law doesn't violate "the basic human rights" or "principles within the law", thus the government should act as a bridge between the both, the model posits that the government should prescribe the areas where non state institutions can be beneficial and work positively, the state shall have supremacy on important realms such as criminal law and property law, the rationale for such supremacy is the conception that the state's objective is to further justice and hence it must have finality over issues of such issues of significance, the *jirgas* have their own conceptions of justice, but however the model ascribes finality and supremacy to the state conception's of justice.

Wardak on the other hand proposes for an active human rights unit along with *jirga/shura* and the formal legal institutions. The role of the human rights unit is to interact with the educational institutions at the local level for the production of material pertaining to issues that are culturally sensitive in nature and sensitise people on human rights abuses such as domestic violence and so on, thus it works at the ground level. The formal mechanism of the state on the other hand is to deal with civil issues that are usually not dealt by the informal mechanisms and other major criminal offences. It is to aid the informal institutions and the human rights unit in their functioning.

In some way, both the models hierarchize the institutions at hand, despite giving due recognition to chthonic institutions, major powers are given to the state instilled formal legal institutions; however the ground reality remains that, even in the matters pertaining to major criminal offences, the mechanisms adopted by the informal institutions secure more authority.

Hence, the judge then, while assessing the decisions must weigh it in terms of two different normative frameworks: legal and chthonic. He must analyse the extent to which it is consistent or comes into contradiction with such frameworks. While doing so, he must also incorporate into his decisions, the universal principles of international human rights and the *shari'a* law. A standard set of priori rules will not be able to resolve the conflicts that arise due to legal pluralism; hence an assessment has to be done on a case-by-case basis depending upon the facts and circumstances of each case.

The constitution of Afghanistan also provides for fundamental rights such as the freedom of expression, presumption of innocence, right to liberty, right to form social organization, and the right to legal defence if accused of an offence under the law ; the philosophy of fundamental rights is to encapsulate human rights, the aim of the state is to protect the fundamental rights, thus the discourse of fundamental rights can also serve as a framework to evaluate the decisions of *jirga/shura*. A concern can be raised if there is a deviation of fundamental right.

The state may as well identify major avenues i.e. Issues related to women, major criminal offences etc. that could potentially give space for conflict and then oversee the rulings of*jirga/ shura* pertaining to such matters.

Judicial review needn't always be one sided, decisions can also be made from the vantage point of chthonic law. For an instance, in the south African case of Bangindawo and Other v Head of Nyanada Regional Authority & Another, the court while deciding on the role of a traditional ruler- who was a judge and the legislator, opined that such duality could hamper judicial independence, however, it was careful enough to not impose the western notion of separation of powers and held that, such duality can be allowed as the adherents of such customary law trust the impartiality of the ruler when he is a judge. Mechanisms have to be developed to provide for the working multiple legal systems, trying to annihilate entities outside the purview of state can turn counter productive.

Now, we are going to examine the legal history of Islamic law in Afghanistan and track the making of the current constitution.

LEGAL HISTORY OF AFGHANISTAN

The population of Afghanistan is 80–85% *sunnis* and 15–20% *shei'ite.* The majority of*sunnis* in Afghanistan are followers of the *hanafi* school and the *Shias* follow the *jafari*jurisprudence.

In the 1950's and 1960's the rulers started to modernize the justice system in line with the Western world, hence during this process of consolidation, *Hanafi* version of *Shari'a* law along with the customary laws provided the foundation for the legal system in Afghanistan. Islamic scholars acted as Judges in the state courts. During the process of modernization, a lot of these laws were also codified, since then, the state law rather than the Islamic law began to be the primary source of the law.

Thus, Afghanistan substantially altered its structure of governance through the 1964 constitution, the political atmosphere during the time was relatively peaceful and hence there was public participation at the time of making the constitution.

In the 1964 constitution, Article 69 explicitly stated that in the event of no codified law, the*Hanafi* jurisprudence of the *Shari'a* law will be considered as the law. Thus this justice system tried to reconcile between the Islamic *Shari'a* law and the modern state law, it regulated the interaction between the both. State law was recognized as the primary source of law and the Shari'a law to be the secondary source of law. The impact of this transition in reality is minimal; the corruption embedded in the legal system and the lack of faith in the state authority distanced people from formal legal structures.

Later, the reforms that were introduced during the communist regime were totally at odds with both Islam and Afghan traditions, hence the whole system of governance and its judicial reforms (decrees) were rejected by the people, and instead they took to the local traditional institutions for the purposes of dispute resolution.

After the collapse of the Marxist government, the Mujahideen government (1992–1996) declared*Shari'a* as the substructure of their "Islamic State of Afghanistan". They attempted to impose a totalitarian theocracy. The Taliban'stheocratic regime (1996–2001) imposed an even more regressive version of *Shari'a*

BONN AGREEMENT AND THE 2004 CONSTITUTION: AN ANALYSIS

Thus owing to the relevance of *Shari'a* in the justice system, the Bonn agreement emphasized on rebuilding the justice system in accordance with Islamic principles, the rule of law and the Afghan legal traditions. In other words, it tried to put in *Shari'a* that is compatible with the Afghan traditions and the fundamental principles of human rights that are in vogue in the contemporary international arena.

Article 3 of the Constitution makes it explicit that no statute can be contrary to the "beliefs and rulings" of the sacred religion of Islam, it is important for us to mark the phrase "beliefs and rulings" as it awards the Supreme Court with ample discretion so as to decide on what a belief is, *Shari'a* law has been given a due constitutional recognition, fears were expressed that this clause can have the potentiality to introduce Taliban like theocratic regime.

Under the new constitution, the Supreme Court, "can review compliance of laws, legislative decrees, international treaties and international conventions with the Constitution and interpret them, in accordance with the law." The constitution grants the Supreme Court in Article 121, the power of judicial review i.e. "power to reject virtually any law or treaty as un-Islamic.

On the other hand Article 7 states that "The state shall abide by the UN charter, international treaties, international conventions that Afghanistan has signed, and the Universal Declaration of Human Rights."

The constitution has been aspirational to include relevance of the Universal declaration of Human Rights and make it a mandate to abide by it. But, if a law has to pass through the filters of Article 3 it is subject to much skepticism as to whether both the Articles can be reconciled and implemented.

Thus, it is important for us to examine whether article 3 is justiciable or non justiciable. Most of the Islamic constitutions have a *Shari'a* clause of this kind in their constitution and had explicitly made it non justiciable, which means that the Supreme Court cannot enforce it, or otherwise the courts have read the clauses to be non justiciable;

When it comes to Afghanistan, it is not explicit in the constitution as to whether this clause is justiciable or non justiciable, all Afghan judges and scholars believe that the clause is justiciable, if so, then it is important to arrive at a mechanism as to how the review of laws has to be done so that they are in consonance with Islam. Due to multiple ethnicities, and different Islamic jurisprudential schools in place, there is no consensus on the interpretative mechanism in Afghanistan.

Article 130 states that the court would decide in accordance with *Hanafi* jurisprudence in the instance when there is no provision in the Constitution or other laws pertaining to the ruling on an issue. Majority of *Sunnis* follow the *Hanafi* school of jurisprudence and hence the *Hanafi* school of jurisprudence has been given a priority in the constitution.

However, the Article merely makes a reference to the instance when there is no particular ruling on an issue but doesn't prescribe for the interpretation of laws in general. Article 130 is problematic as not all *Sunni* Muslims follow the *Hanafi* school and this is not agreeable to the minority *Shias* either, moreover Article 3 doesn't make any reference to the adherence to*Hanafi fiqh, it merely states "beliefs and rulings" of the sacred religion of Islam*. It is important to give space for these concerns and hence while evaluating the "islamicness" of any legislation, it is advisable for the courts to not stick to one classical school but instead they have to take to the broader principles that reinforce the protection of human rights. Now, it is important for us to make a reference to the interpretation of Islamic law, the difference between classical view and the modern view; this would help us in understanding how Islamic principles are to be synchronized with liberal values of a democratic state. A reference is made to Egypt so as to examine how modern Islamic jurisprudence has evolved.

Shari'a is basically an Arabic word which simply means "the path to follow".

The primary sources of *Shari'a* are the Quran and the *Sunnahs*;

Quran is the Holy book and the *Sunnahs* are the Statements and Deeds of the Prophet Mohammed which are used to interpret the Quran.

The secondary sources for the Islamic law are the *Qiyas*, anological reasoning i.e. Reasoning deduced from the cases in Quran and *Ijma* is the consensus of Islamic jurists.

The science of interpreting *Shari'a* is called *'ilm usul al-fiqh*, a scholar's interpretation of it is known as *fiqh*.

Classical jurists adopted two methods to interpret *Shari'a* and develop *fiqh*.

Namely, *Ijitihad* and *taqlid*.

Ijtihad understands God's law through four sources, namely the.

The Qur'an,

The *hadith* literature: Account of events in Prophet's life.

The juristic logic *(qiyas)* and

The juristic consensus (*ijma*).

Taqlîd entails adopting the jurist's rulings despite having no evidence; it is the personal religious view of the jurist and is trusted to be correct.

Using the sources, a scholar had to look at the scripture and then evaluate the authenticity of the text and the clarity of its command. Thus only few scriptures were finalized to be certain with respect to authenticity and clarity, these came to be known as "*qat'i*", the rest are presumptive in nature, and are believed to be "*Zanni*".

Whenever there is no evidence, the classical jurists using the *Taqlid* form of interpretation believed that the principles of *Zanni* also highly reflect God's will and hence are presumptively binding, the modern jurists deviate from such a conception, they believe that the classical interpretation of Islamic law must be only relied to the extent of *"qat'i"*. This departure gives the leverage for the modern jurists to interpret Islamic law from a utilitarian perspective and also accommodate the customs of the State. The benchmark that was set to be achieved by the modern jurists are the "goals of *Shari'a*"

On this note, a reference must be made to the Egyptian constitution; Article 2 of the Egyptian constitution requires all the legislations to be consistent with the Islamic principles. The constitutional court in Egypt while resorting to modern jurisprudence required the laws to be furthering the principles of "justice" and "public utility", it advocated legal liberalism and thus protected negative liberties in the arena of human rights and economic regulation. Through this, the court expanded the scope of Islamic review and tried to harmonize the liberal values with Islamic principles.

Country's system for implementing a *Shari'a* Clause reflects the country's institutional, political and social environment. Hence when such an interpretation as like in Egypt is advocated by the Supreme Court in Afghanistan, it would build judicial power and bolster the constitutionalist culture that protects many liberal rights.

The power of judicial review in Afghanistan is subject to debate, it doesn't rest solely with the Supreme Court, the constitution through its article 157 created a constitutional commission to supervise the implementation of the constitution. However like in Egypt it doesn't have specialized constitutional benches to deal with the issues of *Shari'a*.

Now, let us look at the political structure in the country and the rationale for adopting such structure.

THE CURRENT POLITICAL STRUCTURE IN AFGHANISTAN AND ITS RATIONALE

The Separation and balance of powers in the Government

Afghanistan's political system is presidential in nature with a directly elected President, two vice presidents, a bicameral legislature, and an independent judiciary. The president can choose his cabinet but it is subject to the approval of the legislature. The legislature and the judiciary also have a significant role to play in the constitution. The lower house of the bicameral legislature requires a minimum of 68 members to be women out of the total 249 members, this is to safeguard and ensure the political participation of women and is constitutionally mandated by Article 83 of the constitution. This is definitely a progressive step towards the empowerment of the women especially after the regressive policies towards women in the Taliban regime for a period of ten years.

However in a country like Afghanistan, it is skeptical as to how much a meaningful political choice can people make as to the direct election of president as the electoral politics are still in the budding state and the means of communication to be able to approach people is still underdeveloped. The concentration of power in the hands of a single person is dangerous especially in an unstable political situation as the rewards for illegitimate capture of the presidency stands high, and thus increases the risk of it happening. The President cannot even be impeached by the legislature which can make him a strong Monarch. Moreover, in a Presidential system, the executive and the legislature usually belong to two different parties and hence the legislature's control over the budget can be a medium to brake the executive and hence lead to dead lock between the both and delay the decision making process. The president has been given wide discretionary powers to pick and choose members for the purposes of allocating ministries, the ground reality remains that the key ministries in the post Taliban government have been given to the anti taliban Northern alliance leaders who were once involved in pillaging Kabul. Nepotism, institutional abuse of power fructuate the promises of reconstruction, protection of human rights and the progress of democracy in the country.

On the other hand, given the atomic structure of the Afghanistan's society, when we think of the political structure in terms of a parliamentary system, it is highly probable that no one party would attain majority in the legislature and it would be composed of multiple political parties, the executive would be a fragile coalition leading to slow decision making process.

People of the Country wanted a system where in there would be strong prime minister and the President as the ceremonial head acting as a mediator; this is more akin to India and is a partial parliamentary system. The political considerations of USA which was a party in the constitution making cannot be denied, it has a significant role to play in determining the political structure of the country, to have a control over the region, presidential system in Afghanistan is best suited to its interests rather than a strong parliament, because presidential system entails dealing with a single person and the executive is under the control of the President.

Fear that the country would break apart lead to the creation of a centralized authority having firm control at the top. The tragedy of policy making in Afghanistan is that it has largely been Hobbesian, Jefferson's Republican vision of decentralized authority, checks and balances on power or the Gandhian vision of village level panchayat justice system didn't inform the constitution making.

Usually, the Supreme Court acts as the check to the power of the constitution through its power of the judicial review and interpretation. The Supreme Court of Afghanistan has been awarded with the same power, through the power to interpret the constitutionality of laws and treaties and may even review them; however the nascent judges interpret it according to their own religious view which can be often conservative owing to the Taliban regime in the region.

For instance, ten days after the constitution had been ratified, the Supreme Court announced that airing a female singer on Kabul TV is unislamic and hence unconstitutional, the Supreme Court had neither a case before it nor a law which could back such an order. Hence the court's decree wasn't enforced; this sort of makes the legality of the Supreme Court a little shaky.

Unitary State

The State to be a "unitary state" owing to the fragmented nature of the country in the past. Ethnic groups that were disenfranchised in the past now have autonomous military and political, structures. The party structures that came up during

Jihad times (the war with the Russian government) almost functioned as mini state governments and indulged in activities like issuing the visas, carrying foreign relations and printing currency. The interference of the foreign neighbor states that is leading to the disintegration of the country also prompted the constitution makers to call it an "independent, indivisible and a unitary state."

Owing to the historical past of authoritarianism and brutality, the local populations always resented the decisions made by the centre and thus they have developed their own independent social organization and a culture of self governance, the country even lacked the requisite infrastructure to run the government from the Centre. The war period created the Gap between the Centre and the local provinces, Among Pashtun tribe, the *jirga* or tribal assembly is consensus-building device for resolving disputes and for non pastuns councils called as (*shura*) However, without consolidation of the State, establishment of fiscal control and legitimate power structures, there is high probability of the country being torn apart and hence despite the circumstances in the past, Afghanistan aspired to be a unitary structure.

Elements of consociationalism in Afghanistan's constitution

Consociationalism gives space for the recognition, representation and political participation of all major social segments in the governance of the Country. Afghanistan is an ethnically divided society and the period during the Taliban regime witnessed the division of the society on ethnic lines and of their own political consciousness. For instance during the Taliban regime, "Jihad" was declared on the minority Shia Hazaras, they were severely persecuted, and other minorities like the Tajik, Uzbek who formed a part of Northern Alliance which aimed at overthrowing the Taliban were also badly targeted by the Taliban and severe human right violations had been perpetrated on them. Hence giving them a constitutional recognition would help in assuaging their fears of the tyranny of majoritarian democracy.

Recognizing this need, Article 4 of the Afghanistan's constitution makes it explicit that "The nation of Afghanistan is comprised of the following ethnic groups: "Pashtun, Tajik, Hazara, Uzbak, Turkman, Baluch, Pashai, Nuristani, Aymaq, Arab, Qirghiz, Qizilbash, Gujur, Brahwui and others." This is understood to be the constitutional recognition of minorities and guaranteeing them citizenship in Afghanistan.

Moreover, Article 6 of the Constitution makes it an obligation on the part of the state to ensure "equality among all ethnic groups and tribes and to provide for balanced development in all areas of the country."

Liberal consociational rules aim at broadening the spirit of inclusion and leave the decision to the electorate to decide upon the terms of such inclusion. On the other hand, corporate rules perceive individuals as group members and make explicit provisions for power sharing, like the case of Bosnia and Herzegovina. Afghanistan in such sense can be called a liberal consociation as it allows for diverse participation through its provisions but doesn't make explicit provisions for power sharing among the ethnicities.

Moreover, the 2004 Afghanistan constitution contains several components that could induce power-sharing, such as the Single Non-Transferable Vote electoral system for legislative elections and the proviso for two vice-presidents, this could be utilized to provide for ethnic diversity in the executive, however, the discretion rests with the President.

A COMPARTITIVE ANALYSIS: INDIA AND AFGHANISTAN

The historical trajectories of Afghanistan and India differ greatly, the constitution highlights the contemporary political problems in a country and it's to-do aspirations, Indian constitution had no foreign interference in its decision making process and was democratically drafted, the constitution in Afghanistan despite being drafted by the interim government, the foreign forces had a definite role to play, this can be partially deduced through its adoption of a presidential model despite people having an inclination to choose a parliamentary model. If they had adopted parliamentary system, it would have eliminated the fear of power concentration in a single person and would have better suited for the current political culture in Afghanistan, for instance, the Indian system allows for a proper check on the executive through its no-confidence motion. The epochs in which the respective constitutions were born also differ, the Afghanistan's constitution made it a mandate to enforce various UN conventions similar to the South African constitution but India has no such provision as international treaties weren't in their full sway during the 1940's.

India has diverse religious communities; communal card was played by the British in their divisive politics during the colonial period and due to the painful partition with Pakistan on religious grounds right after its independence, it chose to be a Secular country to assuage the fears of the minorities, historically, India always aspired to be a secular country. On the other hand, Afghanistan has always been an Islamic society and its ideals are deeply penetrated in the society and hence it chose to be a theocratic state, however, the society is divided along ethnic lines and hence minority rights have been safeguarded through consociational model. India could have adopted consociational model as like in Afghanistan but the limitations of consociation are well known, it can lead to further division of the society on religious lines. India despite being a federal structure, it has a strong center fearing the secessionist tendencies. Afghanistan had the same rationale while adopting for a unitary structure but however, the constitution did not provide for power percolation mechanism at the local level as has been done in India for the reasons explained in the paper.

Judiciary in India has been quite proactive in interpreting fundamental rights and is devising new methods for constitutionalism for safeguarding the rights of people and checking the power of the government. As referred in the paper, the judiciary of Afghanistan has its own challenges and is in its budding state, it would take time to arrive at its own ways to interpret the constitution progressively.

Conclusion

Having laid down the history of Afghanistan and its current political solutions, it is important for us to understand that the constitution is merely a bare text that can be brought to life only through positive judicial activism and the political will. In the case of Afghanistan, the country has been a war ground for super powers and is still ravaged by the interference of foreign forces. Instilling trust in the people is the need of the hour. Being one of the most recent constitutions, Afghanistan's constitution took birth amidst well laid constitutional principles and successful running of democracies, thus it has to import these foreign concepts and modify them so as to suit the requirements of the social, political, cultural and economic situation of the society. Constitutional morality has to be instilled in people through the enforcement of fundamental rights and principles of natural justice. This way, constitutionalism in the post conflict pluralist democracies can be one of the most important mechanisms to safeguard the rights and lives of people.

5

Afghanistan: Post Taliban Governance, Security, and U.S. Policy

BACKGROUND

Afghanistan has a history of a high degree of decentralization, and resistance to foreign invasion and occupation. Some have termed it the "graveyard of empires."

From Early History to the 19th Century

Alexander the Great conquered what is now Afghanistan in three years (330 B.C.E. to 327 B.C.E), although at significant cost and with significant difficulty, and requiring, among other steps, marriage to a resident of the conquered territory. For example, he was unable to fully pacify Bactria, an ancient region spanning what is now northern Afghanistan and parts of the neighboring Central Asian states. (A collection of valuable Bactrian gold was hidden from the Taliban when it was in power and emerged from the Taliban period unscathed.) From the third to the eighth century, A.D., Buddhism was the dominant religion in Afghanistan. At the end of the seventh century, Islam spread in Afghanistan when Arab invaders from the Umayyad Dynasty defeated the Persian empire of the Sassanians. In the 10th century, Muslim rulers called Samanids, from Bukhara (in what is now Uzbekistan), extended their influence into Afghanistan, and the complete conversion of Afghanistan to Islam occurred during the rule of the Gaznavids in the 11th century. They ruled over a vast empire based in what is now Ghazni province of Afghanistan.

In 1504, Babur, a descendent of the conquerors Tamarlane and Genghis Khan, took control of Kabul and then moved on to India, establishing the Mughal Empire. (Babur is buried in the Babur Gardens complex in Kabul, which has been refurbished with the help of the Agha Khan Foundation.) Throughout the 16th and 17th centuries, Afghanistan was fought over by the Mughal Empire and the Safavid Dynasty of Persia (now Iran), with the Safavids mostly controlling Herat and western Afghanistan, and the Mughals controlling Kabul and the east. A monarchy ruled by ethnic Pashtuns was founded in 1747 by Ahmad Shah Durrani. He was a senior officer in the army of Nadir Shah, ruler of Persia, when Nadir Shah was assassinated and Persian control over Afghanistan weakened.

A strong ruler, Dost Muhammad Khan, emerged in Kabul in 1826 and created concerns among Britain that the Afghans were threatening Britain's control of India; that fear led to a British decision in 1838 to intervene in Afghanistan, setting off the first Anglo-Afghan War (1838-1842). Nearly all of the 4,500-person British force was killed in that war. The second Anglo-Afghan War took place during 1878-1880.

Early 20th Century and Cold War Era

King Amanullah Khan (1919-1929) launched attacks on British forces in Afghanistan (Third Anglo-Afghan War) shortly after taking power and won complete independence from Britain as recognized in the Treaty of Rawalpindi (August 8, 1919). He was considered a secular modernizer presiding over a government in which all ethnic minorities participated. He was succeeded by King Mohammad Nadir Shah (1929-1933), and then by King Mohammad Zahir Shah. Zahir Shah's reign (1933-1973) is remembered fondly by many older Afghans for promulgating a constitution in 1964 that established a national legislature and promoting freedoms for women, including dropping a requirement that they cover their face and hair. In part, the countryside was secured during the King's time by local tribal militias called *arbokai.*

However, possibly believing that he could limit Soviet support for Communist factions in Afghanistan, Zahir Shah also built ties to the Soviet government by entering into a significant political and arms purchase relationship with the Soviet Union. The Soviets built large infrastructure projects in Afghanistan during Zahir Shah's time, such as the north-south Salang Pass/Tunnel and Bagram airfield.

This period was the height of the Cold War, and the United States sought to prevent Afghanistan from falling into the Soviet orbit. As Vice President, Richard Nixon visited Afghanistan in 1953, and President Eisenhower visited in 1959. President Kennedy hosted King Zahir Shah in 1963. The United States tried to use aid to counter Soviet influence, providing agricultural and other development assistance. Among the major U.S.-funded projects were large USAID-led irrigation and hydroelectric dam efforts in Helmand Province, including Kajaki Dam.

Afghanistan's slide into instability began in the 1970s, during the Nixon Administration, when the diametrically opposed Communist Party and Islamic movements grew in strength. While receiving medical treatment in Italy, Zahir Shah was overthrown by his cousin, Mohammad Daoud, a military leader who established a dictatorship with strong state involvement in the economy. Daoud was overthrown and killed in April 1978, during the Carter Administration, by People's Democratic Party of Afghanistan (PDPA, Communist party) military officers under the direction of two PDPA (Khalq, or "Masses" faction) leaders, Hafizullah Amin and Nur Mohammad Taraki, in what is called the *Saur* (April) Revolution. Taraki became president, but he was displaced in September 1979 by Amin. Both leaders drew their strength from rural ethnic Pashtuns and tried to impose radical socialist change on a traditional society, in part by redistributing land and bringing more women into government. The attempt at rapid modernization sparked rebellion by Islamic parties opposed to such moves.

Soviet Invasion and Occupation Period

The Soviet Union sent troops into Afghanistan on December 27, 1979, to prevent further gains by the Islamic militias, known as the *mujahedin* (Islamic fighters). Upon their invasion, the Soviets replaced Amin with another PDPA leader perceived as pliable, Babrak Karmal (Parcham, or "Banner" faction of the PDPA), who was part of the 1978 PDPA takeover but was exiled by Taraki and Amin.

Soviet occupation forces numbered about 120,000. They were assisted by Democratic Republic of Afghanistan (DRA) military forces of about 25,000-40,000, supplemented by about 20,000 paramilitary and tribal militia forces, including the PDPA-dominated organization called the *Sarandoy*. The combined Soviet and Afghan forces were never able to pacify the outlying areas of the country. DRA forces were consistently plagued by desertions and its effectiveness on behalf of the Soviets was limited. The *mujahedin* benefited from U.S. weapons and assistance, provided through the Central Intelligence Agency (CIA) in cooperation with Pakistan's Inter-Service Intelligence directorate (ISI).

THE SEVEN MAJOR "*MUJAHEDIN*" PARTIES AND THEIR ACTIVITIES

The mujahedin were also relatively well organized and coordinated by seven major parties that in early 1989 formed a Peshawar-based "Afghan Interim Government" (AIG). The seven party leaders and their parties—sometimes referred to as the "Peshawar 7"—were Mohammad Nabi Mohammadi (Islamic Revolutionary Movement of Afghanistan); Sibghatullah Mojaddedi (Afghan National Liberation Front); Gulbuddin Hikmatyar (Hezb-i-Islam—Gulbuddin, Islamic Party of Gulbuddin); Burhanuddin Rabbani (Islamic Society); Yunus Khalis (Hezb-i-Islam); Abd-i-Rab Rasul Sayyaf (Islamic Union for the Liberation of Afghanistan); and Pir Gaylani (National Islamic Front). Mohammadi and Khalis died of natural causes in 2002 and 2006, respectively, and Rabbani was killed in a September 20, 2011, assassination. The others are still active in Afghan politics and governance or, in the case of Hikmatyar, fighting the Afghan government.

The *mujahedin* weaponry included U.S.-supplied portable shoulder-fired anti-aircraft systems called "Stingers," which proved highly effective against Soviet aircraft. The United States decided in 1985 to provide these weapons to the mujahedin after substantial debate within the Reagan Administration and some in Congress over whether they could be used effectively and whether doing so would harm broader U.S.-Soviet relations. The *mujahedin* also hid and stored weaponry in a large network of natural and manmade tunnels and caves throughout Afghanistan. However, some warned that a post-Soviet power structure in Afghanistan could be adverse to U.S. interests because much of the covert aid was being channeled to the Islamist groups including those of Hikmatyar and Sayyaf.

Partly because of the effectiveness of the Stinger in shooting down Soviet helicopters and fixed wing aircraft, the Soviet Union's losses mounted—about 13,400 Soviet soldiers were killed in the war, according to Soviet figures—turning Soviet domestic opinion against the war. In 1986, after the reformist Mikhail Gorbachev became leader, the Soviets replaced Karmal with the director of Afghan intelligence, Najibullah Ahmedzai (known by his first name). Najibullah was a Ghilzai Pashtun, and was from the Parcham faction of the PDPA. Some Afghans say that some aspects of his governing style were admirable, particularly his appointment of a prime minister (Sultan Ali Keshtmand and others) to handle administrative duties and distribute power.

Geneva Accords (1988) and Soviet Withdrawal

On April 14, 1988, Gorbachev agreed to a U.N.-brokered accord (the Geneva Accords) requiring it to withdraw. The withdrawal was completed by February 15, 1989, leaving in place the weak Najibullah government. A warming of relations moved the United States and Soviet Union to try for a political settlement to the Afghan conflict, a trend accelerated by the 1991 collapse of the Soviet Union, which reduced Moscow's capacity for supporting communist regimes in the Third World. On September 13, 1991, Moscow and Washington agreed to a joint cutoff of military aid to the Afghan combatants as of January 1, 1992, which was implemented by all accounts.

The State Department has said that a total of about $3 billion in economic and covert military assistance was provided by the

U.S. to the Afghan *mujahedin* from 1980 until the end of the Soviet occupation in 1989. Press reports say the covert aid program grew from about $20 million per year in FY1980 to about $300 million per year during FY1986-FY1990. The Soviet pullout was viewed as a decisive U.S. "victory." The Soviet pullout caused a reduction in subsequent covert funding and U.S. assistance to Afghanistan remained at relatively low levels after the Soviet withdrawal. There was little support for a major U.S.-led effort to rebuild the economy and society of Afghanistan. The United States closed its embassy in Kabul in January 1989, as the Soviet Union was completing its pullout, and it remained so until the fall of the Taliban in 2001.

Despite the Soviet troop withdrawal in 1989, Najibullah still enjoyed Soviet financial and advisory support and Afghan forces beat back the first post-Soviet withdrawal*mujahedin* offensives—defying expectations that his government would immediately collapse after a Soviet withdrawal. However, military defections continued and his position weakened subsequently, particularly after the Soviets cut off financial and advisory support as of January 1, 2992 under the agreement with the United States discussed above. On March 18, 1992, Najibullah publicly agreed to step down once an interim government was formed. That announcement set off rebellions by Uzbek and Tajik militia commanders in northern Afghanistan—particularly Abdul Rashid Dostam, who joined prominent *mujahedin* commander Ahmad Shah Masoud of the Islamic Society, a largely Tajik party headed by Burhannudin Rabbani. Masoud had earned a reputation as a brilliant strategist by preventing the Soviets from conquering his power base in the Panjshir Valley north of Kabul. Najibullah fell, and the *mujahedin* regime began April 18, 1992.

THE *MUJAHEDIN* GOVERNMENT AND RISE OF THE TALIBAN

The fall of Najibullah exposed the differences among the *mujahedin* parties. The leader of one of the smaller parties (Afghan National Liberation Front), Islamic scholar Sibghatullah Mojadeddi, was president during April-May 1992. Under an agreement among the major parties, Rabbani became president in

June 1992 with agreement that he would serve until December 1994. He refused to step down at that time, saying that political authority would disintegrate without a clear successor. That decision was strongly opposed by other mujahedin leaders, including Gulbuddin Hikmatyar, a Pashtun, and leader of the Islamist conservative Hizb-e-Islam Gulbuddin *mujahedin*party. Hikmatyar and several allied factions began fighting to dislodge Rabbani. Rabbani reached an agreement for Hikmatyar to serve as Prime Minister, if Hikmatyar would cease the shelling Kabul that had destroyed much of the western part of the city. However, because of Hikmatyar's distrust of Rabbani, he never assumed a working prime ministerial role in Kabul.

In 1993-1994, Afghan Islamic clerics and students, mostly of rural, Pashtun origin, formed the Taliban movement. Many were former *mujahedin* who had become disillusioned with conflict among *mujahedin* parties and had moved into Pakistan to study in Islamic seminaries ("madrassas") mainly of the "Deobandi" school of Islam. Some say this interpretation of Islam is similar to the "Wahhabism" that is practiced in Saudi Arabia. Taliban practices were also consonant with conservative Pashtun tribal traditions. The Taliban's leader, Mullah Muhammad Umar, had been a fighter in Khalis's Hezb-i-Islam party during the anti-Soviet war—Khalis' party was generally considered moderate Islamist during the anti-Soviet war, but Khalis and his faction turned against the United States in the mid-1990s. Many of his fighters, such as Mullah Umar, followed Khalis' lead. Umar, a low-ranking Islamic cleric, lost an eye in the anti-Soviet war.

The Taliban viewed the Rabbani government as weak, corrupt, and anti-Pashtun, and the four years of civil war between the *mujahedin* groups (1992-1996) created popular support for the Taliban as able to deliver stability. With the help of defections, the Taliban peacefully took control of the southern city of Qandahar in November 1994. Upon that capture, Mullah Umar ordered the opening of the Qandahar shrine containing the purported cloak used by the Prophet Mohammad; he reportedly donned the purported cloak briefly in front of hundreds of followers. By February 1995, it was approaching Kabul, after which an 18-month stalemate ensued. In September 1995, the Taliban captured Herat province, bordering Iran, and imprisoned its governor, Ismail Khan, ally of Rabbani and Masoud, who later escaped and took refuge in Iran. In September 1996, new Taliban victories near Kabul led to the withdrawal of Rabbani and Masoud to the Panjshir Valley north of Kabul with most of their heavy weapons; the Taliban took control of Kabul on September 27, 1996. Taliban gunmen subsequently entered a U.N. facility in Kabul to seize Najibullah, his brother, and aides, and then hanged them.

TALIBAN RULE (SEPTEMBER 1996-NOVEMBER 2001)

The Taliban regime was led by Mullah Muhammad Umar, who held the title of Head of State and "Commander of the Faithful." He remained in the Taliban power base in Qandahar and almost never appeared in public, although he did occasionally receive high-level foreign officials. Al Qaeda leaders Osama bin Laden relocated from Sudan to Afghanistan, where he had been a recruiter of Arab fighters during the anti-Soviet war, in May 1996. He at first was located in territory in Nangarhar province controlled by Hezb-i-Islam of Yunus Khalis (Mullah Umar's party leader) but then had free reign in Afghanistan as the Taliban captured nearly all the territory in Afghanistan. Umar reportedly forged a political and personal bond with Bin Laden and refused U.S. demands to extradite him. Like Umar, most of the senior figures in the Taliban regime were Ghilzai Pashtuns, which predominate in eastern Afghanistan. They are rivals of the Durrani Pashtuns, who are predominant in the south.

The Taliban lost international and domestic support as it imposed strict adherence to Islamic customs in areas it controlled and employed harsh punishments, including executions. The Taliban authorized its "Ministry for the Promotion of Virtue and the Suppression of Vice" to use physical punishments to enforce strict Islamic practices, including bans on television, Western music, and dancing. It prohibited women from attending school or working outside the home, except in health care, and it publicly executed some women for adultery. In what many consider its most extreme action, and which some say was urged by Bin Laden, in March 2001 the Taliban blew up two large Buddha statues carved into hills above Bamiyan city, considering them idols.

U.S. Policy Toward the Taliban During Its Rule/Bin Laden Presence

The Clinton Administration opened talks with the Taliban after it captured Qandahar in 1994, and engaged the movement after it took power. However, the Administration was unable to moderate the Taliban's policies and relations worsened. The United States withheld recognition of Taliban as the legitimate government of Afghanistan, formally recognizing no faction as the government. The United Nations continued to seat representatives of the Rabbani government, not the Taliban. The State Department ordered the Afghan embassy in Washington, DC, closed in August 1997. U.N. Security Council Resolution 1193 (August 28, 1998) and 1214 (December 8, 1998) urged the Taliban to end discrimination against women. Women's rights groups urged the Clinton Administration not to recognize the Taliban government. In May 1999, the Senate-passed S.Res. 68 called on the President not to recognize an Afghan government that oppresses women.

The Taliban's hosting of Al Qaeda's leadership gradually became the Clinton Administration's overriding agenda item with Afghanistan. In April 1998, then-U.S. Ambassador to the United Nations Bill Richardson (along with Assistant Secretary of State Karl Inderfurth and NSC senior official Bruce Riedel) visited Afghanistan, but the Taliban refused to hand over Bin Laden. They did not meet Mullah Umar. After the August 7, 1998, Al Qaeda bombings of U.S. embassies in Kenya and Tanzania, the Clinton Administration began to strongly pressure the Taliban to extradite him, imposing U.S. sanctions on Taliban-controlled Afghanistan and achieving adoption of some U.N. sanctions as well. On August 20, 1998, as a response to the Africa embassy bombings, the United States fired cruise missiles at alleged Al Qaeda training camps in eastern Afghanistan, but Bin Laden was not hit. Some observers assert that the Administration missed several other opportunities to strike him, including a purported sighting of him by an unarmed Predator drone at a location called Tarnak Farm in Afghanistan in the fall of 2000. Clinton Administration officials said that domestic and international support for ousting the Taliban militarily was lacking.

The "Northern Alliance" Congeals

The Taliban's policies caused different Afghan factions to ally with the Tajik core of the anti-Taliban opposition—the ousted President Rabbani, Ahmad Shah Masoud, and their ally in the Herat area, Ismail Khan. Joining the Tajik factions in the broader "Northern Alliance" were Uzbek, Hazara Shiite, and even some Pashtun Islamist factions. Virtually all the figures mentioned remain key players in politics in Afghanistan, sometimes allied with and at other times adversaries of President Hamid Karzai. The Soviet occupation-era parties remain relatively intact informally, although they do not remain organized under those prior names. (Detail on these figures is in CRS Report RS21922, *Afghanistan: Politics, Elections, and Government Performance*, by Kenneth Katzman.)

Uzbeks/General Dostam. One major faction was the Uzbek militia (the Junbush-Melli, or National Islamic Movement of Afghanistan) of General Abdul Rashid Dostam. Frequently referred to by some Afghans as one of the "warlords" who gained power during the anti-Soviet war, Dostam first joined those seeking to oust Rabbani during his 1992-1996 presidency, but later joined him and the other Northern Alliance factions opposed to the Taliban.

Hazara Shiites. Members of Hazara tribes, mostly Shiite Muslims, are prominent in Bamiyan, Dai Kundi, and Ghazni provinces of central Afghanistan and have been the object of repression and disparagement by Afghan Pashtuns. The Hazaras have tended to serve in working class and domestic household jobs, although more recently they have been prominent in technology jobs in Kabul, raising their economic status. During the various Afghan wars, the main Hazara Shiite militia was Hizb-e-Wahdat (Unity Party, composed of eight groups). In 1995, the Taliban captured and killed Hizb-e-Wahdat's leader Abdul Ali Mazari. One of Karzai's vice president's Karim Khalili, is a Hazara. Another prominent Hazara faction leader, Mohammad Mohaqeq, is a Karzai critic.

Pashtun Islamists/Sayyaf. Some Pashtuns joined the Northern Alliance. Abd-i-Rab Rasul Sayyaf headed a Pashtun-dominated hardline Islamist *mujahedin*faction (Islamic Union for the Liberation of Afghanistan, *Ittihad Islami*) during the anti-Soviet war. Even though he is an Islamist conservative, Sayyaf viewed the Taliban as selling out Afghanistan to Al Qaeda. Sayyaf is politically close to Saudi Arabia, whose leaders perceived a domestic threat from bin Laden.

POLICY PRE-SEPTEMBER 11, 2001

Throughout 2001, but prior to the September 11 attacks, Bush Administration policy differed little from Clinton Administration policy: applying economic and political pressure on the Taliban while retaining some dialogue with it, and refusing to militarily assist the Northern Alliance. The September 11 Commission report said that, in the months prior to the September 11 attacks, Administration officials leaned toward providing such aid, as well as aiding anti-Taliban Pashtun. Additional covert options were reportedly under consideration. In accordance with U.N. Security Council Resolution 1333, in February 2001 the State Department ordered the Taliban representative office in New York closed, although Taliban representative Abdul Hakim Mujahid continued to operate informally. In March 2001, Administration officials received a Taliban envoy to discuss bilateral issues. In one significant departure from Clinton Administration policy, the Bush Administration stepped up engagement with Pakistan to try to reduce its support for the Taliban. At that time, there were widespread but unconfirmed allegations that Pakistani advisers were helping the Taliban in their fight against the Northern Alliance.

Even though the Northern Alliance was supplied with Iranian, Russian, and Indian financial and military support, the Northern Alliance nonetheless continued to lose ground to the Taliban after it lost Kabul in 1996. By the time of the September 11 attacks, the Taliban controlled at least 75% of the country, including almost all provincial capitals. The Alliance suffered a major setback on September 9, 2001 (two days before, and possibly a part of, the September 11 attacks), when Ahmad Shah Masoud was assassinated by Al Qaeda operatives posing as journalists. He was succeeded by one of his top lieutenants, Muhammad Fahim, a veteran Tajik figure but who lacked Masoud's charisma and undisputed authority.

September 11 Attacks and Operation Enduring Freedom

After the September 11 attacks, the Bush Administration decided to militarily overthrow the Taliban when it refused a final U.S. offer to extradite Bin Laden in order to avoid military action.

President Bush articulated a policy that equated those who harbor terrorists to terrorists themselves, and judged that a friendly regime in Kabul was needed to enable U.S. forces to search for Al Qaeda personnel there.

U.N. and Congressional Authorization for Use of Military Force (AUMF)

The Administration sought U.N. backing for military action, although the outcome was perhaps less clear cut than was sought. U.N. Security Council Resolution 1368 of September 12, 2001, said that the Council "expresses its readiness to take all necessary steps to respond (implying force) to the September 11 attacks." This was widely interpreted as a U.N. authorization for military action in response to the attacks, but it did not explicitly authorize Operation Enduring Freedom to oust the Taliban. Nor did the Resolution specifically reference Chapter VII of the U.N. Charter, which allows for responses to threats to international peace and security.

In Congress, S.J.Res. 23 (passed 98-0 in the Senate and with no objections in the House, P.L. 107-40, signed September 18, 2011), was somewhat more explicit than the U.N. Resolution, authorizing: "all necessary and appropriate force against those nations, organizations, or persons he determines planned, authorized, committed, or aided the terrorist attacks that occurred on September 11, 2001 *or harbored such organizations or persons*."

The War Begins

Major combat in Afghanistan (Operation Enduring Freedom, OEF) began on October 7, 2001. The U.S. effort initially consisted primarily of U.S. air-strikes on Taliban and Al Qaeda forces, facilitated by the cooperation between reported small numbers (about 1,000) of U.S. special operations forces and Central Intelligence Agency operatives. The purpose of these operations was to help the Northern Alliance and Pashtun anti-Taliban forces by directing U.S. air strikes on Taliban positions, for example on the Shomali plain that extends to Bagram Airfield; that airport marked the forward positions of the Northern Alliance. In late October 2001, about 1,300 Marines moved into Afghanistan to pressure the Taliban around Qandahar, but there were few pitched battles between U.S. and Taliban soldiers.

The Taliban regime unraveled rapidly after it lost Mazar-e-Sharif on November 9, 2001, to forces led by General Dostam, mentioned above. Northern Alliance forces—despite promises to then-Secretary of State Colin Powell that they would not enter Kabul—did so on November 12, 2001, to popular jubilation. The Taliban subsequently lost the south and east to U.S.-supported Pashtun leaders, including Hamid Karzai. The end of the Taliban regime is generally dated as December 9, 2001, when the Taliban and Mullah Umar fled Qandahar, leaving it under Pashtun tribal law.

Subsequently, U.S. and Afghan forces conducted "Operation Anaconda" in the Shah-i-Kot Valley south of Gardez (Paktia Province) during March 2-19, 2002, against 800 Al Qaeda and Taliban fighters. In March 2003, about 1,000 U.S. troops raided suspected Taliban or Al Qaeda fighters in villages around Qandahar (Operation Valiant Strike). On May 1, 2003, then-Secretary of Defense Rumsfeld announced an end to "major combat."

BEYOND 2014: LIKELY OUTCOMES AND SIZE OF RESIDUAL FORCE

Assessing that Afghan forces will continue to need direct military support after 2014 to prevent the Taliban from advancing, the United States and its NATO partners are attempting to formulate plans for a "residual force" that would remain in Afghanistan to continue to train and assist the ANSF and likely also conduct operations against high-value targets such as Al Qaeda. The residual force is intended to ensure sustainable stability until the Afghans can provide entirely for their own security.

Mainstream post-2014 options have been reported in various news stories. In November 2012, General Allen reportedly presented to the White House three options: 6,000, 10,000, or 20,000 forces—with decreasing levels of risk to U.S. gains associated as the number of troops increase with each option. The option providing for the fewest forces envisions mainly Special Operations forces remaining to help combat high-value targets. The mid-range option also provided for training of Afghan security forces. The largest option would provide for some continued U.S. patrols in highly contested areas. U.S. briefings at a February 21, 2013, NATO meeting in Brussels suggested that the Administration is leaning toward a post-2014 international force of approximately 8,000 to 12,000 trainers and mentors—of which about two-thirds would be U.S. forces and one third would be non-U.S. force contributions—plus a still unspecified number of mostly U.S. counterterrorism forces. This option comports with an August 2013 recommendation from former NATO commander Admiral James Stavridis for a residual force of 9,000 U.S. and 6,000 partner forces. U.S. officials assert that the residual force is to support the ANSF, and that it is not a "bridging force" to bear security responsibility until Afghan forces are more capable. There is continuing debate about whether any U.S. air assets remaining in Afghanistan in 2014 would support not only international troops but also the ANSF; this debate appears to take into account the ANSF deficiencies in aircraft and medical evacuation capabilities. Other reports say the United States will transfer to the ANSF mortars, long-range artillery, and unarmed remotely piloted vehicles.

Secretary of State Kerry stated on May 16, 2013, that President Obama will likely announce the size of the post-2014 U.S. force in late May or early June 2013. However, that announcement has been delayed, possibly because General Dunford said he wanted to assess the performance of the ANSF through the summer 2013 "fighting season." However, in press comments in July 2013, Gen. Dunford indicated the size of the post-2014 U.S. force needs to be determined by "late fall" of 2013 because of the planning process. The timing of the announcement could be dependent on finalization of the bilateral security agreement.

Some U.S. partner countries appear to be growing impatient about the U.S. post-2014 announcement because of the need to plan for post-2014 deployments. Germany announced in late April 2013 that it will keep about 800 forces in Afghanistan after 2014, mostly in the northern sector where Germany now leads the international contingent. At a June 4-5, 2013, NATO meeting, it was announced that Italy would also join a post-2014 force, continuing to lead in the western sector, and that Turkey is considering continuing its leadership in the Kabul area beyond 2014. That NATO meeting also reportedly decided that post-2014 NATO trainers would deploy in the northern, western, eastern, southern, and Kabul sectors. The United States and its partners reportedly are discussing retaining NATO leadership over the post-2014 international force under a mission name "Resolute Support."

CONTINGENCY ON THE BILATERAL SECURITY AGREEMENT

U.S. officials say the post-2014 U.S. deployment is contingent on finalizing a Bilateral Security Agreement (BSA) with the Afghan government that provides legal immunities for U.S. forces in Afghanistan (Status of Forces Agreement). On October 3, 2012, deputy SRAP James Warlick was named lead U.S. negotiator for the BSA; Afghan Ambassador to the United States Hakimi leads the talks for the Afghan side. The negotiations formally began on November 15, 2012, and Chairman of the Joint Chiefs of Staff Gen. Dempsey said in July 2013 that the United States wants an agreement to be in place by the end of October 2013. That date, according to U.S. officials, is intended to remove the BSA issue from Afghanistan's presidential election campaign, and to allow U.S. commanders ample time to plan for the residual force.

In recent months, the negotiations had appeared to be stalled by disagreements over the U.S. demand for legal immunities for U.S. troops, the authorities of U.S. troops, and President Hamid Karzai's demands for security guarantees against what Karzai sees as a potentially hostile threat from neighboring Pakistan. The stalling of the negotiations had led outside experts to assess that the Administration might, as happened in Iraq, decide to withdraw all U.S. troops from Afghanistan when the current international security mission concludes at the end of 2014 (known as the "zero option"). The zero option had been mentioned by Administration sources in press articles since mid-2013, possibly as a means of building U.S. negotiating leverage with Afghan leaders.

During October 11-12, 2013, Secretary of State John Kerry held intensive discussions in Kabul with President Karzai in an attempt to revive progress in the negotiations. At the conclusion of their meetings on October 12, Karzai and Kerry announced that they had resolved U.S.-Afghan differences on the key issues of U.S. operations authority and security guarantee. Karzai apparently relented on the demand that the United States protect Afghanistan from Pakistan, and the United States reportedly agreed to coordinate with the Afghan security forces on post-2014 anti-Al Qaeda operations in Afghanistan. Left open was the issue of legal immunities for U.S. troops in Afghanistan after 2014, which the United States asserts is a non-negotiable requirement if U.S. forces are to remain. Karzai stated that the decision on legal immunities would be placed before the Afghan National Assembly (parliament) and a special *loya jirga* - a traditional Afghan assembly composed of about 2,000 notables convened to consider major issues. That *loya jirga* is tentatively scheduled for November 19, 2013. However, the government selects many of the participants, and Karzai's tentative agreement with Kerry on the other outstanding major issues suggests that Karzai will lobby the *loya jirga*, probably successfully, to approve the legal immunity. A U.S.-Afghanistan BSA will likely serve as a model for similar agreements between Afghanistan and partner countries. U.S. forces currently operate in Afghanistan under "diplomatic notes" between the United States and the interim government of Afghanistan—primarily one that was exchanged in November 2002. The notes give the United States legal jurisdiction over U.S. personnel serving in Afghanistan.

Debate Over Mission Success At Likely Post-2014 Troop Levels

There is debate over how the ANSF will fare after 2014 with the levels of support currently receiving the most discussion (about 10,000 U.S. forces plus about 5,000 partner forces). According to some experts, this level of international support will succeed in encouraging the Taliban to seek a political settlement rather than face likely indefinite combat. Apparently factoring in a residual presence into their analysis, General Dempsey and General Dunford said in early 2013 that the Taliban will be a persistent, though not an "existential" threat, over the longer term.

However, some commanders and experts believe the relatively small residual force contemplated would enable the Taliban to make gains in the south and east and potentially unravel the Afghan security forces and government. On March 5, 2013, then Commander of U.S. Central Command General James Mattis told the Senate Armed Services Committee that he had recommended a total post-2014 force of about 20,000, of which 13,600 would be U.S. forces.

Whatever the level of post-2014 international forces, it is likely that, as international forces thin out sharply after 2014, local militias will re-form to deter or prevent Taliban gains. This was illustrated in a November 2012 meeting organized by Herat leader Ismail Khan, in which he reportedly began taking steps to reorganize his Soviet and Taliban-era militia. Vice President Muhammad Fahim has also discussed potentially reconstituting the Northern Alliance force in anticipation of the need to assist Afghan government forces against the Taliban. And, Uzbek leader Dostam, is also reportedly trying to reorganize his loyalists in northern Afghanistan. These and similar moves could spark ethnic and communal conflict from an all-out struggle for power and a reversion to Afghan rule by faction leaders rather than elected leaders.

Strategic Partnership Agreement

The BSA is being negotiated pursuant to the broader "Strategic Partnership Agreement" (SPA) signed by President Obama and President Karzai in Afghanistan on May 1, 2012. That broad agreement signaled that the United States is committed to Afghan stability and development for many years after the transition is complete. The SPA was completed after more than one year of negotiations that focused on resolution of two disagreements in particular— Afghan insistence on control over detention centers and a halt to or control over nighttime raids on insurgents by U.S. forces. The SPA agreement also demonstrated U.S.-Afghan ability to overcome public Afghan discomfort over such issues as the March 2011 burning of a Quran by a Florida pastor; the mistaken burning by U.S. soldiers of several Qurans on February 20, 2012; and the March 11, 2012, of 16 Afghans by a U.S. soldier, Sergeant Robert Bales, who was arrested and tried in the United States. On September 17, 2012, several hundred Afghans demonstrated near a U.S.-Afghan training facility east of Kabul city (Camp Phoenix) to protest a video made in the United States, "The Innocence of Muslims." About 40 Afghan police reportedly were wounded preventing the crowd from reaching the facility.

Other disputes were mostly, but not completely resolved, by the time the SPA was signed. The night raid issue was resolved in April 2012 when the United States agreed to give Afghans more control over night raids, including requiring an Afghan court warrant to hold any raid captives for more than 48 hours. The detainee issue was partly resolved on March 10, 2012, with a U.S. agreement to accelerate the transfer of imprisoned insurgents to Afghan control, to occur over six months. However, a dispute over the transfer to Afghan control of the detention center at Bagram Airfield lingered, particularly because the facility holds about 50 non-Afghans ("enduring security threats") that the United States believed must not be released. An initial agreement fell apart during the March 10, 2013, visit to Afghanistan by Defense Secretary Chuck Hagel, but subsequent talks produced an Afghan commitment to consult the United States on any releases of the enduring security threats, and the detainees at Bagram came under Afghan control on March 25, 2013. A related issue arose in March 2013 when Karzai demanded U.S. special forces withdraw from Wardak Province after he alleged that they were abusing Afghans there. An agreement was reached on March 20, 2013, under which the U.S. forces withdrew over several months.

The strategic partnership agreement represents a broad outline of the post-2014 relationship, with details to be filled in subsequently. It has a duration of 10 years. The major provisions include the following:

- A commitment to continue to foster U.S.-Afghan "close cooperation" to secure Afghanistan. This strongly implies, but does not state outright, that U.S. troops will remain in Afghanistan after 2014, and no troop numbers are mentioned in the document. The document provides for negotiations on the Bilateral Security Agreement.
- The U.S. administration will request appropriations to provide training and arms to the Afghan security forces. The agreement does not stipulate dollar amounts or which systems are to be provided.
- The United States will designate Afghanistan as a "Major Non-NATO Ally," a designation reserved for close U.S. allies. In keeping with that pledge, on July 7, 2012, then Secretary Clinton stopped in Afghanistan and announced that designation. It opens Afghanistan to receive (sale, donation) U.S. weaponry of the same level of sophistication as that sold to U.S. NATO allies, and facilitates provision of training and funds to leasing defense articles.
- There will be no "permanent" U.S. bases or the use of Afghan facilities for use against neighboring countries, but the agreement would apparently allow long-term U.S. use of Afghan facilities. Over the past several years, successive National Defense Authorization Acts have contained a provision explicitly prohibiting the U.S. establishment of permanent bases in Afghanistan.
- The Administration will request economic aid for Afghanistan for the duration of the agreement (2014-2024). No amounts were specified in the document. The Afghan government reportedly wanted a $2 billion per year commitment written into the agreement but the United States told Afghanistan that amounts can only be determined through the appropriations process.

In October 2011, Karzai called a *loya jirga* to endorse the concept of the SPA as well as his insistence on Afghan control over detentions and approval authority for U.S.-led night raids. A November 16-19, 2011, traditional *loya jirga* (the *jirga* was conducted not in accordance with the constitution and its views are therefore non-binding), consisting of about 2,030 delegates, gave Karzai the approvals he sought, both for the pact itself and his suggested conditions. The final SPA was ratified by the Afghanistan National Assembly on May 26, 2012, by a vote of 180-4.

The SPA replaced an earlier, more limited strategic partnership agreement established on May 23, 2005, when Karzai and President Bush issued a "joint declaration." The declaration provided for U.S. forces to have access to Afghan military facilities, in order to prosecute "the war against international terror and the struggle against violent extremism." Karzai's signing of the declaration was supported by the 1,000 Afghan representatives on May 8, 2005, at a consultative *jirga* in Kabul. The *jirga*supported an indefinite presence of international forces to maintain security but urged Karzai to delay a firm decision to request such a presence.

TRANSITION PILLAR: BUILDING AFGHAN FORCES AND ESTABLISHING RULE OF LAW

Key to the transition to Afghan lead—and the post-2014 future of Afghanistan—is the effectiveness of the Afghan National Security Forces (ANSF), consisting primarily of the Afghan National Army (ANA) and Afghan National Police (ANP). The forces have expanded considerably since 2002, but some experts doubt the ANSF's capability to secure Afghanistan after 2014. ANSF strengths and weaknesses, including performance ratings for its components, is contained in the semi-annual DOD reports on Afghanistan stability.

Among the concerns about the ANSF is that about 35% of the force does not re-enlist each year, meaning that about one-third of the force must be recruited to replenish its ranks. Many believe that the force has been expanded too quickly to allow for thorough vetting or for recruitment of the most qualified personnel. Incidents of ANSF attacks on coalition personnel increased during 2011-2012, causing reduced interaction between Afghan forces and their U.S.-led mentors. Many units also suffer from a deficiency of weaponry, spare parts, and fuel. The Special Inspector General for Afghanistan Reconstruction (SIGAR) reported in October 2012 that the Afghan government will likely prove incapable of sustaining ANSF installations after 2014, mainly because of a lack of skilled maintenance personnel.

U.S. commanders frequently note concerns about the ANSF's deficiency of logistical capabilities, such as airlift, medical evacuation, resupply, and other associated functions. It is these deficiencies that are a particular focus of U.S. planning for a residual support force after 2014. Some of the deficiency throughout the ANSF is due to illiteracy, which prompted an increasing focus on providing literacy training. To date, the large majority of the ANSF force has received literacy training and has at least first grade literacy.

U.S. forces, along with partner countries and contractors, train the ANSF and will likely continue to do so after 2014. In February 2010, the U.S.-run "Combined Security Transition Command-Afghanistan" (CSTC-A) that ran the training was subordinated to the broader NATO Training Mission—Afghanistan (NTM-A). CSTC-A's mission was reoriented to building the capacity of the Afghan Defense and Interior Ministries, and to provide resources to the ANSF.

Current and Post-2014 Size of the ANSF

On January 21, 2010, the joint U.N.-Afghan "Joint Coordination and Monitoring Board" (JCMB) agreed that, by October 2011, the ANA would expand to 171,600 and the ANP to about 134,000, (total ANSF of 305,600). Both forces reached that level by September 2011. In August 2011, a larger target size of 352,000 (195,000 ANA and 157,000 ANP) was set, to be reached by November 2012. The gross size of the force reached approximately that level by the end of September 2012, and remain at levels just below their targets. A higher target level of 378,000 was not adopted because of the concerns about the Afghan ability to sustain so large a force. About 1,700 women serve in the ANSF, of which about 1,370 are police.

In the run-up to the May 20-21, 2012, NATO summit in Chicago, which focused on long-term financial and military sustainment of the ANSF, there was initial agreement to reduce the total ANSF to 228,500 by 2017. However, based on assessments of the difficulty of securing Afghanistan, the February 21, 2013, NATO meeting tentatively reversed the decision to shrink the force, and it will stay at the 352,000 level until at least 2018.

ANSF Top Leadership/Ethnic and Factional Considerations

In the immediate aftermath of the 2001 ousting of the Taliban regime, Northern Alliance figures took key security positions and weighted recruitment for the new ANSF toward ethnic Tajiks. Many Pashtuns, in reaction, refused recruitment, but the naming of a Pashtun, Abdul Rahim Wardak, as Defense Minister in December 2004, mitigated that difficulty. The problem was further alleviated with better pay and more close involvement by U.S. forces, and that the force is ethnically integrated in each unit and representative. According to the July 2013 DOD report, the overall ANSF force continues to come into line. Tajiks are slightly overrepresented in the ANA (33.3% versus about 25% of the population) and Uzbeks are slightly underrepresented (6% versus 10% of the population). And, those Pashtuns who are in the force are disproportionately eastern Pashtuns (from the Ghilzai tribal confederations) rather than southern Pashtuns (mostly Durrani tribal confederations).

Until 2010, the chief of staff of the ANA was General Bismillah Khan, a Tajik and former Northern Alliance commander. He was replaced by a Pashtun, Lieutenant General Sher Mohammad Karimi. Khan then served as Interior Minister until his ouster by the National Assembly in August 2012; in that position, he reportedly promoted his Tajik allies to key Interior Ministry and ANP positions. In September 2012, Karzai appointed Khan as Defense Minister, and Khan has earned U.S. and partner country praise for his performance as Defense Minister, to date.

The same day he appointed Khan, Karzai appointed professional police commander Gen. Ghulam Mojtaba Patang as Interior Minister. Patang entered his position with high respect as the first professional officer to be appointed to the top police slot and the July 2013 DOD report credits Patang with appointing competent professionals throughout the Interior Ministry and ANP ranks. However, the National Assembly voted to remove him in July 2013 for failing to improve security along the Kabul-Qandahar highway. After seeking advice on the matter from the Afghan Supreme Court, Karzai replaced him on September 1, 2013 with Umar Daudzai, Karzai's former chief of staff, a Pashtun, who was serving as Ambassador to Pakistan. A highly respected Tajik figure, Kabul police chief Gen. Mohammad Ayub Salangi, was simultaneously appointed deputy Interior Minister.

Also in September 2012, Karzai named as intelligence director (National Directorate of Security, NDS) Asadullah Khalid, former Qandahar governor and a close Karzai ally, replacing Rehmatullah Nabil.

Khalid was wounded by a potential assassin in December 2012, but he resumed his duties after undergoing several months of treatment in the United States. His predecessor, Nabil, was returned to the post on September 1, 2013.

ANSF Funding

On the assumption that the post-2014 ANSF force would shrink to 228,000, it was determined that sustaining a force that size would cost $4.1 billion annually. The United States pledged $2.3 billion yearly; the Afghan government pledged $500 million yearly; and allied contributions constituted the remaining $1.3 billion. The Afghan contribution was to rise steadily until 2024, at which time Afghanistan is expected to fund its own security needs. However, the apparent decision to keep the ANSF force at 352,000 necessitates revised funding levels of about $6 billion per year. Donor pledges to fund the force at that level have not been announced to date.

Even the $4.1 billion figure was considered difficult to raise. The GAO estimated in February 2013 that there was a $600 million per year discrepancy between allied donor pledges and the $1.3 billion requirement.

The specific known yearly pledges have included Germany ($190 million per year), Britain ($110 million per year), and Australia ($100 million per year). Other countries that are confirmed to have made pledges, but of unspecified amounts, include Denmark, Italy, Estonia, and the Netherlands. The Special Inspector General for Afghanistan Reconstruction (SIGAR) issued an audit in October

2012 saying the Afghan government will have major difficulty meeting its obligations to fund the force as donor countries wind down their involvement. According to a SIGAR audit (13-4), CSTC-A plans to provide about $1 billion directly to the Afghan government during 2013-2019 to pay for fuel for the ANSF.

The U.S. costs to train and equip the ANSF are provided in the aid table at the end of this paper. As of FY2005, the security forces funding has been DOD funds, not State Department funds (Foreign Military Financing, FMF).

NATO Trust Fund for the ANA

In 2007 ISAF set up a trust fund for donor contributions to fund the transportation of equipment donated to and the training of the ANA; the mandate was expanded in 2009 to include sustainment costs. In November 2010 a further expansion was agreed on to support literacy training for the ANA. As of March 2013, donor contributions and pledges to the ANA Trust Fund total about $700 million. U.S. funding for the ANA is provided separately, not through this fund.

Law and Order Trust Fund for the ANP

There is also a separate "Law and Order Trust Fund for Afghanistan" (LOTFA), run by the U.N. Development Program (UNDP), which is used to pay the salaries of the ANP and other police-related functions. The United States donates to that fund, for the purpose of paying ANP salaries and food costs. From 2002-2012, donors contributed $2.75 billion to the Fund, of which the United States contributed about $1 billion. Japan's 2009 pledge to pay the expenses of the Afghan police for at least six months (about $125 million for each six month period) is implemented through the LOTF. The EU pledged $175 million for the fund from January 2011-March 2013.

In May 2012, there were reports of misfeasance at the fund. UNDP began to investigate the allegations and immediately terminated the contracts of three personnel and placed two others on administrative leave. UNDP is continuing to investigate the issue.

Other Bilateral Donations

The DOD reports discuss other bilateral donations to the ANSF, both in funds and in arms and equipment donations. There is a "NATO Equipment Donation Program," through which donor countries supply the ANSF with equipment. Since 2002, about $2.9 billion in assistance to the ANSF has come from these sources. As an example, in October 2011, Croatia and Slovenia donated a total of over 20,000 AK-47 assault rifles to the ANP. Australia contributed $40 million to relocate the ANA's 205th Corps, and South Korea contributed $30 million for medical and communications equipment.

There is also a NATO-Russia Council Helicopter Maintenance Trust Fund. Launched in March 2011, this fund provides maintenance and repair capacity to the Afghan Air Force helicopter fleet, much of which is Russian-made.

THE AFGHAN NATIONAL ARMY (ANA)

The Afghan National Army has been built "from scratch" since 2002—it is not a direct continuation—or enhanced version—of the national army that existed from the 1880s until the Taliban era. That army disintegrated entirely during the 1992-1996 *mujahedin* civil war and the 1996-2001 Taliban period. Some officers who served prior to the Taliban have joined the ANA.

U.S. and allied officers say that the ANA is becoming a major force in stabilizing the country and a national symbol. The ANA now leads about 80%-90% of all combat operations, and it leads operations in 261 of Afghanistan's 364 districts. It plans and conducts some combat operations completely on its own, with no U.S. or international input. The commando forces of the ANA, trained by U.S. Special Operations Forces, and numbering about 5,300, are considered well-trained and are taking the lead in some operations against high-value targets.

There is a problem of absenteeism within the ANA because soldiers do not serve in their provinces of residence. Many in the ANA take long trips to their home towns to remit funds to their families, and often then return to the ANA after a long absence. However, that problem has eased somewhat in recent years because

98% of the ANA is now paid electronically, according to U.S. officials. The FY2005 foreign aid appropriation (P.L. 108-447) required that ANA recruits be vetted for terrorism, human rights violations, and drug trafficking.

To assist its performance, the United States is attempting to better equip the ANA. Approximately $2.7 billion worth of vehicles, weapons, equipment, and aircraft were provided during August 2011-March 2012. The United States is also helping the ANSF build up an indigenous weapons production capability. However, in line with U.S. efforts to cut costs for the ANSF, the Defense Department reportedly plans to shift in FY2013 from providing new equipment to maintaining existing equipment.

The United States has built five ANA bases: Herat (Corps 207), Gardez (Corps 203), Qandahar (Corps 205), Mazar-e-Sharif (Corps 209), and Kabul (Division HQ, Corps 201, Air Corps). Coalition officers conduct heavy weapons training for a heavy brigade as part of the "Kabul Corps," based in Pol-e-Charki, east of Kabul. U.S. funds are being used to construct a new Defense Ministry headquarters in Kabul at a cost of about $92 million.

Afghan Air Force

Equipment, maintenance, and logistical difficulties continue to plague the Afghan Air Force, and it remains mostly a support force for ground operations rather than a combat-oriented force. However, the Afghan Air Force has been able to make ANA units nearly self-sufficient in airlift. The force is a carryover from the Afghan Air Force that existed prior to the Soviet invasion, and is expanding gradually after its equipment was virtually eliminated in the 2001-2002 U.S. combat against the Taliban regime. It has about 6,300 personnel of a target size of about 8,000 by 2016. There are five female Afghan Air Force personnel; four arrived in the United States in July 2011 for training as military helicopter pilots.

The Air Force has about 100 aircraft including gunship, attack, and transport helicopters—of a planned fleet of 140 aircraft. Because the Afghan Air Force has familiarity with Russian helicopters and other equipment, the post-2014 Afghan Air Force is planned to have 86 Mi-17 helicopters. The force has about 60 of them as of

August 2013. Defense Department officials say the United States is planning to buy the force another 30 Mi-17 helicopters, via the Russian state-owned Rosoboronexport arms sales agency at a cost of about $572 million and delivery by the end of 2014. However, separate House and Senate letters to the Administration, with a total of nearly 100 Member signers, call on the Defense Department to cancel the purchase because Rosoboronexport is the top supplier to the government of President Bashar Al Assad of Syria.

Among other U.S.-funded purchases, the Brazilian firm Embraer has been contracted by DOD to provide 20 Super Tucano turboprop aircraft to the force. U.S. plans do not include supply of fixed-wing combat aircraft such as F-16s, which Afghanistan wants as part of a broader request for the United States to augment Afghan air capabilities, according to U.S. military officials. There is a concern that Afghanistan will not soon have the capability to sustain operations of an aircraft as sophisticated as the F-16.

Afghanistan also is seeking the return of 26 aircraft, including some MiG-2s that were flown to safety in Pakistan and Uzbekistan during the past conflicts in Afghanistan. In 2010, Russia and Germany supplied MI-8 helicopters to the Afghan Air Force.

Afghan National Police (ANP)

U.S. and Afghan officials believe that building up a credible and capable national police force is at least as important to combating the insurgency as building the ANA. The DOD reports on Afghanistan contain substantial detail on U.S.-led efforts to continue what it says are "significant strides [that] have been made in professionalizing the ANP." However, many outside assessments of the ANP are disparaging, asserting that there is rampant corruption to the point where citizens mistrust and fear the ANP. Among other criticisms are a desertion rate far higher than that of the ANA; substantial illiteracy; involvement in local factional or ethnic disputes because the ANP works in the communities its personnel come from; and widespread use of drugs. It is this view that has led to consideration of stepped up efforts to promote local security solutions. About 1,300 ANP are women.

The United States and Afghanistan have worked to correct longstanding deficiencies. Some U.S. commanders credit a November 2009 doubling of police salaries (to $240 per month for service in high combat areas), and the streamlining and improvement of the payments system for the ANP, with reducing the solicitation of bribes by the ANP. The raise also stimulated an eightfold increase in recruitment. Others note the success, thus far, of efforts to pay police directly (and avoid skimming by commanders) through cell phone-based banking relationships (E-Paisa, run by Roshan cell network).

The ANP is increasingly being provided with heavy weapons and now have about 5,000 armored vehicles countrywide. Still, most police units lack adequate ammunition and vehicles. In some cases, equipment requisitioned by their commanders is being sold and the funds pocketed by the police officers.

The U.S. police training effort was first led by State Department/INL, but DOD took over the lead in police training in April 2005. A number of early support programs, such as the auxiliary police program attempted during 2005, was discarded as ineffective. It was replaced during 2007-2011 with the *"focused district development"* program in which a district police force was taken out and retrained, its duties temporarily performed by more highly trained police (Afghan National Civil Order Police, or ANCOP), and then reinserted after the training. However, the ANCOP officers were subsequently used mostly to staff new checkpoints that are better securing the most restive districts. Police training includes instruction in human rights principles and democratic policing concepts, and the State Department human rights report on Afghanistan, referenced above, says the government and observers are increasingly monitoring the police force to prevent abuses.

Supplements to the National Police: Afghan Local Police (ALP) and Other Local Forces

In 2008, the failure of several police training efforts led to a decision to develop local forces to protect their communities. Until then, U.S. military commanders opposed assisting local militias anywhere in Afghanistan for fear of re-creating militias that commit abuses and administer arbitrary justice. However, the urgent security needs in Afghanistan caused General Petraeus and his successors to expand local security experiments, based on successful experiences in Iraq and after designing mechanisms to place them firmly under Afghan government (mainly Ministry of Interior) control. Among these initiatives are:

- *Village Stability Operations/Afghan Local Police (ALP).* The Village Stability Operations concept began in February 2010 in Arghandab district of Qandahar Province. U.S. Special Operations Forces organized about 25 villagers into an armed neighborhood watch group, and the program was credited by U.S. commanders as bringing normal life back to the district. The pilot program was expanded and formalized into a joint Afghan-U.S. Special Operations effort in which 12 person teams from these forces live in communities to help improve governance, security, and development.
- An outgrowth of the Village Stability Operations is the Afghan Local Police (ALP) program in which the U.S. Special Operations Forces conducting the Village Stability Operations set up and train local security organs of about 300 members each. These local units are under the control of district police chiefs and each fighter is vetted by a local shura as well as Afghan intelligence. There are about 23,000 ALP operating in nearly 100 districts. A total of 169 districts have been approved for the program, and there are expected to be 30,000 ALP on duty by December 2015. However, the ALP program, and associated and preceding such programs, were heavily criticized in a September 12, 2011, Human Rights Watch report citing wide-scale human rights abuses (killings, rapes, arbitrary detentions, and land grabs) committed by the recruits. The report triggered a U.S. military investigation that substantiated many of those findings, although not the most serious of the allegations. In May 2012, Karzai ordered one ALP unit in Konduz disbanded because of its alleged involvement in a rape there. ALP personnel reportedly were responsible for some of the insider attacks in 2012.

- The ALP initiative was also an adaptation of another program, begun in 2008, termed the "Afghan Provincial Protection Program" (APPP, commonly called "AP3"), funded with DOD (CERP) funds. The APPP got underway in Wardak Province (Jalrez district) in early 2009 and 100 local security personnel "graduated" in May 2009. It was subsequently expanded to 1,200 personnel. U.S. commanders said no U.S. weapons were supplied to the militias, but the Afghan government provided weapons (Kalashnikov rifles) to the recruits, possibly using U.S. funds. Participants in the program are given $200 per month. General Petraeus showcased Wardak in August 2010 as an example of the success of the APPP and similar efforts, but the program was largely replaced by the ALP program. And, U.S. Special Forces pulled out of Wardak pursuant to Karzai's February 2013 demand that they do so.
- *Afghan Public Protection Force.* This force, which operates as a "state-owned enterprise" (a business) but under the supervision of the Ministry of Interior, guards sites and convoys. It was formed to implement Karzai's August 17, 2010, decree (No. 62) that private security contractor forces be disbanded and their functions performed by official Afghan government forces by March 20, 2012. That deadline was extended to March 2013 because of the slow pace of standing up the new protection force, and some development organizations continued to use locally hired guard forces. The unit has begun operations to secure supply convoys and sites, and now numbers about 17,000 personnel guarding nearly 150 sites. General Patang, was in charge of building this force prior to his September 2012 Interior Minister appointment. Observers reported in late August 2013 that the APPF was nearly insolvent because of corruption and mismanagement.

The local security experiments to date resemble but technically are not *arbokai,* which are private tribal militias. Some believe that the arbokai concept should be revived as a means of securing

Afghanistan, as the *arbokai* did during the reign of Zahir Shah and in prior pre-Communist eras. Reports persist that some tribal groupings have formed arbokai without specific authorization.

The local security programs somewhat reverse the 2002-2007 efforts to disarm local sources of armed force. And, as noted in several DOD reports on Afghan stability, there have sometimes been clashes and disputes between the local security units and the ANSF units, particularly in cases where the units are of different ethnicities. These are the types of difficulties that prompted earlier efforts to disarm local militia forces.

DDR. The main program, run by UNAMA, was called the "DDR" program—Disarmament, Demobilization, and Reintegration—and it formally concluded on June 30, 2006. The program got off to a slow start because the Afghan Defense Ministry did not reduce the percentage of Tajiks in senior positions by a July 1, 2003, target date, dampening Pashtun recruitment. In September 2003, Karzai replaced 22 senior Tajiks in the Defense Ministry officials with Pashtuns, Uzbeks, and Hazaras, enabling DDR to proceed. The major donor for the program was Japan, which contributed about $140 million. Figures for collected weapons are in and U.S. spending on the programs are in the U.S. aid tables later in the report.

The DDR program was initially expected to demobilize 100,000 fighters, although that figure was later reduced. Of those demobilized, 55,800 former fighters exercised reintegration options provided by the program: starting small businesses, farming, and other options. Some studies criticized the DDR program for failing to prevent a certain amount of rearmament of militiamen or stockpiling of weapons and for the rehiring of some militiamen. Part of the DDR program was the collection and cantonment of militia weapons, but generally only poor-quality weapons were collected. As noted, there are indications that some faction leaders may be seeking to revive militias, fearing a Taliban comeback after the international security mission ends in 2014.

DIAG. Since June 11, 2005, the disarmament effort has emphasized another program called "DIAG"—Disbandment of Illegal Armed Groups. It is run by the Afghan Disarmament and

Reintegration Commission, headed by Vice President Khalili. Under the DIAG, no payments are available to fighters, and the program depends on persuasion rather than use of force against the illegal groups. DIAG has not been as well funded as was DDR: it has received $11 million in operating funds. As an incentive for compliance, Japan and other donors have made available $35 million for development projects where illegal groups have disbanded. These incentives were intended to accomplish the disarmament of a pool of as many as 150,000 members of 1,800 different "illegal armed groups": militiamen that were not part of recognized local forces (Afghan Military Forces, AMF) and were never on the rolls of the Defense Ministry. These goals were not met by the December 2007 target date in part because armed groups in the south said they need to remain armed against the Taliban. UNAMA reported in a March 9, 2011, report that 100 out of 140 districts planned for DIAG are considered "DIAG compliant."

Rule of Law/Criminal Justice Sector

Many experts believe that an effective justice sector is vital to Afghan governance. Some of the criticisms and allegations of corruption at all levels of the Afghan bureaucracy have been discussed throughout this report. U.S. justice sector programs generally focus on promoting rule of law and building capacity of the judicial system, including police training and court construction. The rule of law issue is covered in CRS Report RS21922, *Afghanistan: Politics, Elections, and Government Performance*, and CRS Report R41484, *Afghanistan: U.S. Rule of Law and Justice Sector Assistance.*

Policy Component: Provincial Reconstruction Teams (PRTs)

U.S. and partner officials have praised the effectiveness of "Provincial Reconstruction Teams" (PRTs)—enclaves of U.S. or partner forces and civilian officials that provide safe havens for international aid workers to help with reconstruction and to extend the writ of the Kabul government. The PRTs, the concept for which was announced in December 2002, have performed activities ranging from resolving local disputes to coordinating local reconstruction projects, although most U.S.-run PRTs and most PRTs in combat-heavy areas focus on counter-insurgency. Many of the additional U.S. civilian officials deployed to Afghanistan during 2009 and 2010 were based at PRTs, which have facilities, vehicles, and security. Some aid agencies say they felt more secure since the PRT program began, but several relief groups did not want to associate with military forces because doing so might taint their perceived neutrality.

Virtually all the PRTs, were placed under the ISAF mission. Each PRT operated by the United States has U.S. forces; DOD civil affairs officers; representatives of USAID, State Department, and other agencies; and Afghan government (Interior Ministry) personnel. Most PRTs, including those run by partner forces, have personnel to train Afghan security forces. USAID officers assigned to the PRTs administer PRT reconstruction projects. USAID spending on PRT projects is in the table at the end of this report.

Despite the benefits, President Karzai criticized the PRTs as holding back Afghan capacity-building and repeatedly called for their abolition as "parallel governing structures." USAID observers backed some of the criticism, saying that there has been little Afghan input into PRT development project decision-making or as contractors for PRT-funded construction. To address some of this criticism, during 2008-2012 some donor countries enhanced the civilian component of the PRTs and tried to change their image from military institutions. The State Department sought to "civilianize" U.S.-run PRTs by assuming a larger role for State Dept. and USAID development and governance experts at the PRTs. In 2006, the PRT in the Panjshir Valley became the first U.S.-led PRT to be State Department led. As noted, in March 2009, the Netherlands converted its PRT to civilian lead, although that alteration ceased after the assumption of U.S. and Australian PRT command in July 2010.

The declaration of the May 20-21, 2012, NATO summit in Chicago expresses agreement to phase out the PRTs by the end of 2014. Karzai's July 26, 2012, administrative reforms called on the Afghan government to beginning planning to assume their functions. As of August 2013, numerous PRTs have already closed.

Related U.S.-led structures such as District Support Teams (DSTs), which help district officials provide government services, are to close by the end of 2014 as well.

COOPERATION WITH ALLIES/MANAGING THE 2014 EXIT

Partner forces have been key to the U.S. mission in Afghanistan. Since 2006, the vast bulk of all U.S. troops in Afghanistan have served under the umbrella of the NATO-led "International Security Assistance Force" (ISAF). ISAF consists of all 28 NATO members states plus partner countries—a total of 50 countries including the United States. Since the transition to Afghan security leadership began in July 2011, U.S. officials have attempted, with some success, to prevent a "rush to the exits" by partner forces. As of September 2013, about 2,000 international troops, including U.S. forces, are leaving Afghanistan each week. Partner drawdowns have occurred at roughly the same rate and proportion as the U.S. drawdown, even though the European governments, in particular, have been under pressure from their publics and parliaments to end or reduce their military involvement in Afghanistan. Among previous setbacks to the U.S. partner recruitment effort, during 2010 and 2011, the Netherlands and Canada, respectively, ended their combat missions, although they continue to furnish 500 and 950 trainers for the ANSF, respectively. Partner forces that continue to bear the brunt of combat in Afghanistan include Britain, Canada, Poland, France, Denmark, Romania, and Australia. Romania reportedly has also offered use of its facilities to withdraw personnel and equipment as part of the international drawdown in 2014.

Still, some partner countries have already withdrawn or announced withdrawals.

- President Francois Hollande, inaugurated in May 2012, reiterated at the May 2021 NATO summit in Chicago that he would pull French combat troops out by the end of 2012, a year earlier than the time frame of former President Sarkozy. France formally ended its combat mission in November 2012, although some French troops remain to train the ANSF.
- Britain withdrew 500 of its force in 2012, and is removing about 3,800 forces in 2013. British forces have been deployed

mostly in Helmand, and some forces periodically have gone back into Helmand to deal with specific security setbacks. The remainder of the contingent is to remain until the end of 2014. In September 2012, British officials say they will likely keep some trainers in Afghanistan after 2014.

- In October 2012, Germany capped its troop contribution at 4,400 for 2013 and 3,300 for 2014, while augmenting its combat helicopter force to partially compensate for the decreased ground. Germany announced in April 2013 that it would keep about 800 forces in Afghanistan after 2014, mostly in the north.
- At the NATO meeting of June 4-5, 2013, Italy pledged to keep trainers and advisors after 2014, although no numbers were announced.
- Denmark withdrew 120 troops by the end of 2012, but continues development aid and ANSF training contributions.
- Poland said in March 2012 that it would not withdraw forces before the end of 2014. However, in August 2013 it said it would remove 1,000 of its forces in October 2013, leaving a small contingent in place to train the ANSF.
- Belgium removed 300 personnel from Kabul Airport at the end of 2012.
- Turkey is to redeploy 200-300 personnel from Kabul by the end of 2013 but reportedly is considering remaining in the Kabul sector after 2014.
- Australia announced in April 2013 that it will withdraw most of its troops by the end of 2013 and will close down its bases in Uruzgan Province.
- New Zealand's troops in Bamiyan Province withdrew by April 5, 2013, and its PRT has closed. It is keeping 27 military personnel in Afghanistan as trainers at least until the 2014 transition.
- In early 2013, South Korea reduced its force in Parwan Province from 400 to 350 personnel, with the remainder to stay until the end of 2014.

- Georgia said in November 2012 it had doubled its troops in Afghanistan to about 1,570. The announcement was likely intended to support its bid to join NATO.

The International Security Assistance Force (ISAF) was created by the Bonn Agreement and U.N. Security Council Resolution 1386, initially limited to Kabul. In October 2003, after Germany agreed to contribute 450 military personnel to expand ISAF into the city of Konduz, ISAF contributors endorsed expanding its presence to several other cities, contingent on formal U.N. approval—which came on October 14, 2003, in U.N. Security Council Resolution 1510. In August 2003, NATO took over command of ISAF— previously the ISAF command rotated among donor forces including Turkey and Britain.

NATO/ISAF's responsibilities broadened significantly in 2004 with NATO/ISAF's assumption of security responsibility for northern and western Afghanistan (Stage 1, Regional Command North, in 2004 and Stage 2, Regional Command West, in 2005, respectively). The transition process continued on July 3 1, 2006, with the formal handover of the security mission in southern Afghanistan to NATO/ISAF control. As part of this "Stage 3," a British/Canadian/Dutch-led "Regional Command South" (RC-S) was formed. Britain is the lead force in Helmand; Canada is lead in Qandahar, and the Netherlands was lead in Uruzgan until its departure in July 2010; the three rotated the command of RC-S. "Stage 4," the assumption of NATO/ISAF command of peacekeeping in 14 provinces of eastern Afghanistan (and thus all of Afghanistan), was completed on October 5, 2006. As part of the completion of the NATO/ISAF takeover, the United States put about half the U.S. troops then operating in Afghanistan under NATO/ISAF in "Regional Command East" (RC-E).

The ISAF mission was renewed (until October 13, 2012) by U.N. Security Council Resolution 201 1 (October 12, 201 1), which reiterated previous resolutions' support for the Operation Enduring Freedom mission. Resolution 2069 of October 10, 2012, renewed the mandate for another full year (until October 1 1, 2014). That will likely be the last renewal until the ISAF mission ends at the end of 2014. Some countries, such as Germany and Russia (not an

ISAF member), want a U.N. mandate to authorize international forces to remain in Afghanistan after 2014. Tables at the end of this report list contributing forces, areas of operations, and their Provincial Reconstruction Teams.

Major Contingent Developments During the U.S. "Surge"

U.S. partners note that they have repeatedly answered U.S. calls to support the mission. In concert with the U.S. surge in early 2009, additional pledges came through at the April 3-4, 2009, NATO summit. Other force pledges were announced in conjunction with the January 28, 2010, conference on Afghanistan in London. Among major pledges that supported the U.S. surge:

- July 2009: South Korea announced it would increase its aid contribution to Afghanistan by about $20 million, in part to expand the hospital capabilities at Bagram Air Base. In July 2010, it returned about 150 engineers to Afghanistan for development missions, protected by 400 South Korean forces, to Parwan Province.
- November 10, 2009: Ahead of President Obama's visit to Asia, Japan announced a pledge of $5 billion over the next five years for Afghanistan civilian development, although it suspended its naval refueling mission. Japan has been covering about half of the $250 million yearly salary costs of the ANP.
- December 2009-January 2010 (London conference): A total of about 9,000 forces were pledged (including retaining 2,000 sent for the August 2009 election who were due to rotate out). Several countries pledged police trainers.

POTENTIAL POSITIVES: REINTEGRATION AND RECONCILIATION WITH INSURGENTS

Some believe that there are substantial chances for a political settlement between insurgent leaders and the Afghan government and/or the reintegration of insurgent fighters into society. These concepts inevitably involve compromises that might produce backsliding on human rights; most insurgents are highly conservative Islamists who seek strict limitations on women's rights.

Many leaders of ethnic minorities believe that reconciliation and reintegration might further Pashtun political strength within Afghanistan, and enhance Pakistani influence. The United States and the Afghan government stipulate that any settlement require insurgent leaders, as an outcome, to (1) cease fighting, (2) accept the Afghan constitution, and (3) sever any ties to Al Qaeda or other terrorist groups.

Reintegration

The concept of providing incentives to persuade insurgents to surrender and reenter their communities has received at least some U.S. and Afghan attention since 2002. The elements included in a formal reintegration plan drafted by the Afghan government and adopted by a "peace *loya jirga*" during June 2-4, 2010, included providing surrendering fighters with jobs, amnesty, protection, and an opportunity to be part of the security architecture for their communities. Later in June 2010, President Karzai issued a decree to implement the plan, which includes efforts by Afghan local leaders to convince insurgents to reintegrate.

According to the July 2013 DOD report, about 6,300 fighters have been reintegrated. A majority of those reintegrated are from the north and west, with growing participation from militants in the more violent south and east. Some observers say there have been cases in which reintegrated fighters have committed human rights abuses against women and others, suggesting that the reintegration process might have unintended consequences.

The reintegration effort received formal international backing at the July 20, 2010, Kabul Conference. Britain, Japan, and several other countries, including the United States, have announced a total of about $235 million in donations to a fund to support the reintegration process, of which $134 million has been received. The U.S. contribution has been about $100 million (CERP funds), of which $50 million was formally pledged in April 2011. Of that latter pledge, $20 million has been spent as of late-March 2013, according to the DOD report.

Previous efforts had marginal success. A "Program for Strengthening Peace and Reconciliation" (referred to in Afghanistan by its Pashto acronym "PTS") operated during 2003-2008, headed by then *Meshrano Jirga* speaker Sibghatullah Mojadeddi and Vice President Karim Khalili, and overseen by Karzai's National Security Council. The program persuaded 9,000 Taliban figures and commanders to renounce violence and join the political process, but made little impact on the tenacity or strength of the insurgency.

Reconciliation With Militant Leaders

A related U.S. and Afghan initiative is to reach a conflict-ending settlement with the Taliban. The Obama Administration initially withheld endorsement of the concept, fearing it might result in the incorporation into the Afghan political system of insurgent leaders who retain ties to Al Qaeda and would roll back freedoms. The minority communities in the north, women, intellectuals, and others remain skeptical that their freedoms can be preserved if there is a political settlement with the Taliban—a settlement that might involve Taliban figures obtaining ministerial posts, seats in parliament, or even control over territory. Then Secretary of State Clinton said in India on July 20, 2011, that any settlement must not result in and undoing of "the progress that has been made [by women and ethnic minorities] in the past decade." To respond to those fears, Afghan and U.S. officials say that the outcome—not precondition—of a settlement would require the Taliban to drop demands that a new, "Islamic" constitution be adopted and Islamic law be imposed. On the other hand, Afghan officials have not completely ruled out amending the constitution to incorporate more Islamic tenets as part of a settlement with the Taliban.

An "Afghan High Peace Council" (HPC) intended to oversee the settlement process was established on September 5, 2010. Former President and Northern Alliance political leader Burhanuddin Rabbani was appointed by Karzai to head it, largely to gain Tajik and other Northern Alliance support for the concept. On September 20, 2011, Rabbani was assassinated by a Taliban infiltrator posing as an intermediary; on April 14, 2012, the HPC voted his son, Salahuddin, as his replacement.

During 2011, informal meetings among U.S., Taliban, and Afghan representatives proliferated, particularly in the form of

U.S. meetings with Tayeb Agha, an aide to Mullah Umar. In December 2011, U.S. officials pursued confidence-building measures under which the Taliban would open a political office in Qatar; the United States would transfer five senior Taliban captives from the Guantanamo detention facility to a form of house arrest in Qatar; and the Taliban would release the one U.S. prisoner of war, it holds, Bowe Bergdahl. (A release of Taliban captives would require U.S. congressional notification.) The Taliban figures to be released to Qatar include some, such as Mullah Mohammad Fazl who were major figures in the Taliban regime (Fazl was deputy defense minister). The United States also demanded a public Taliban statement severing its ties to Al Qaeda or other terrorist groups.

The confidence-building measures were not implemented, and U.S.-Taliban talks broke off in March 2012 reportedly over Qatar's failure to fully assure the United States that released detainees would be able to escape custody. The joint statement of President Karzai and President Obama on January 11, 2013 stated support for the formal opening of a Taliban office in Qatar. Karzai visited Qatar during March 30-31, 2013, and again on June 9, 2013, to discuss the opening of the office and to press his insistence that talks with the Taliban be channeled through the HPC and not remain a U.S.-Taliban channel only.

Taliban Office and Subsequent Developments. On June 18, 2013, with U.S. and Qatari concurrence, the Taliban formally opened its political office in Qatar, simultaneously issuing a statement refusing future ties to international terrorist groups and expressing willingness to eventually transition to Afghan government-Taliban talks. However, the Taliban violated reported understandings with the United States and Qatar by raising a flag of the former Taliban regime and calling the facility the office of the "Islamic Emirate" of Afghanistan—the name the Taliban regime gave for Afghanistan during its rule. These actions caused President Karzai to temporarily break off BSA talks with the United States and prompted U.S. officials, through Qatar, to compel the Taliban to remove the offending symbols. Still, possibly due to Taliban indecision on moving forward on the confidence-building measures, SRAP Dobbins did not meet with the Taliban negotiators after the office opened. The office reportedly closed in mid-July 2013, although the Taliban officials are said to remain in Qatar to hold discussions with foreign officials there.

Aside from the U.S.-Taliban discussions, there have been exchanges between Taliban representatives and the Afghan government. Some Afghan officials have at times expressed optimism the talks will yield a settlement eventually, particularly if the Afghan government provides assurances of security for Taliban leaders who reconcile. In June 2012, Afghan government officials and Taliban representatives held talks at two meetings—one in Paris, and one an academic conference in Kyoto, Japan, on reconciliation issues.

At the Kyoto meeting, the Afghan government was represented by Mohammad Stanekzai, a member of the High Peace Council, and the Taliban was represented by Qari Din Mohammad, a member of the Taliban political council who had traveled from Qatar. The Kyoto meeting appeared to represent an acceptance by the Taliban of direct talks with Afghan government officials. Potentially even more significant meetings took place between senior Taliban figures and members of the Northern Alliance faction in France (December 20-21, 2012), and then between the Northern Alliance and the HIG faction in mid-March 2013. The meeting in France reportedly included submission by the Taliban of a political platform that signaled acceptance of some aspects of human rights and women's rights provisions of the current constitution. An end-of-Ramadan statement by Mullah Omar in early August 2013 said the Taliban no longer seeks a monopoly of power but rather an "inclusive" government, and backs modern education. On the other hand, the statement said the movement would not participate in the 2014 Afghan elections at all.

Role of Pakistan. Pakistan has also become more supportive of the reconciliation process. In February 2012, Pakistani leaders, for the first time, publicly encouraged Taliban leaders to negotiate a settlement to the conflict. Following a mid-November 2012, visit to Pakistan by Rabbani and other High Peace Council members, Pakistan released at least 18 high-ranking Taliban figures who favor reconciliation, and it released another eight in December 2012. Karzai visited Pakistan during August 26-27, 2013 and, ten days later, Pakistan released seven moderate senior Taliban figures. On September 22, 2013, it released from prison the highest profile Taliban figure in detention, Mullah Abdul Ghani Bradar, who had been arrested by Pakistan in February 2010, purportedly to halt talks between Bradar and Afghan intermediaries. Bradar reportedly remains under house arrest or close surveillance in Pakistan. Earlier, in August 2012, Pakistan had allowed Afghan officials to hold talks with the incarcerated Bradar. Afghan officials are said to want him to open a Taliban office in Saudi Arabia or Turkey. On the other hand, Pakistani clerics withdrew from participating in a planned joint conference in March 2013 with Afghan clerics.

Previous talks have taken place primarily in Saudi Arabia and UAE. Press reports said that Afghan officials, including Karzai's brother, Qayyum; Arsala Rahmani, a former Taliban official who reconciled but was assassinated in May 2012; and the former Taliban Ambassador to Pakistan, Abdul Salam Zaeef, who purportedly is in touch with Umar's inner circle. These same Taliban representatives may be involved in the ongoing talks referred to above. Some Taliban sympathizers reportedly attended the June 2-4, 2010, consultative peace jirga.

Removing Taliban Figures From U.N. Sanctions Lists. A key Taliban demand in negotiations is the removal of the names of some Taliban figures from U.N. lists of terrorists. These lists were established pursuant to Resolution 1267 and Resolution 1333 (October 15, 1999, and December 19, 2000, both pre-September 11 sanctions against the Taliban and Al Qaeda) and Resolution 1390 (January 16, 2002). The Afghan government has submitted a list of 50 Taliban figures it wants taken off the list, which includes about 140 Taliban-related persons or entities. On January 26, 2010, Russia, previously a hold-out against such a process, dropped opposition to removing five Taliban-era figures from these sanctions lists, paving the way for their de-listing: those removed included Taliban-era foreign minister Wakil Mutawwakil and representative to the United States Abdul Hakim Mujahid. Mujahid is now deputy chair of the High Peace Council.

On June 17, 2011, in concert with U.S. confirmations of talks with Taliban figures, the U.N. Security Council adopted Resolution 1988 and 1989. The resolutions drew a separation between the Taliban and Al Qaeda with regard to the sanctions. However, a decision on whether to remove the 50 Taliban figures from the list, as suggested by Afghanistan, was deferred. On July 21, 2011, 14 Taliban figures were removed from the "1267" sanctions list; among them were four members of the High Peace Council (including Arsala Rahmani, mentioned above).

REGIONAL DIMENSION

The Obama Administration is promoting Afghanistan's integration into regional security and economic organizations and patterns, and attempting to deter Afghanistan's neighbors from meddling there to secure their own interests in a post-2014 Afghanistan. The Administration is emphasizing development of a Central Asia-South Asia trading hub—part of a "New Silk Road" (NSR)—in an effort to keep Afghanistan stable and economically vibrant as donors wind down their involvement.

The Administration obtained pledges from Afghanistan's neighbors to non-interference in Afghanistan at an international meeting on Afghanistan in Istanbul on November 2, 2011 ("Istanbul Declaration"), and again at the December 5, 2011, Bonn Conference on Afghanistan (the 10th anniversary of the Bonn Conference that formed the post-Taliban government). The latter meeting was attended by high-level representatives from 85 countries and 15 international organizations. As a follow-up to the Istanbul Declaration, confidence-building measures to be taken by Afghanistan's neighbors, were discussed at a Kabul ministerial conference on June 14, 2012. At that meeting, also known as the "Heart of Asia" ministerial conference, Afghanistan hosted 14 other countries from the region, as well as 14 supporting countries and 11 regional and international organizations. The assembled nations and organizations agreed to jointly fight terrorism and drug trafficking, and pursue economic development. A subsequent Heart of Asia meeting was held in April 2013 in Kazakhstan.

Prior to the recent efforts, Afghanistan has been slowly integrated into regional security and economic organizations. In

November 2005, Afghanistan joined the South Asian Association for Regional Cooperation (SAARC), and, in June 2012, Afghanistan was granted full observer status in the Shanghai Cooperation Organization (SCO), a security coordination body that includes Russia, China, Uzbekistan, Tajikistan, Kazakhstan, and Kyrgyzstan. There was extensive discussion of greater SCO country involvement in Afghanistan after the 2014 transition during the June 6-7, 2012, meeting of the group in Beijing, which Karzai attended. U.S. officials have also sought to enlist both regional and greater international support for Afghanistan through the still-expanding 50-nation "International Contact Group."

Several regional meeting series have been established involving Afghanistan, including:

- Summit meetings between Afghanistan, Pakistan, and Turkey; and between Iran, Afghanistan, and Pakistan. The latest Iran-Afghanistan-Pakistan meeting took place in Islamabad on February 16-17, 2012, but this series ended in mid-2012 after Afghanistan signed the SPA with the United States, which Iran strongly opposed. Britain hosted an Afghanistan-Pakistan meeting in February 2013.
- Turkey and UNAMA co-chair a "Regional Working Group" initiative, which organized the November 2, 2011, Istanbul meeting mentioned above. UNAMA also leads a "Kabul Silk Road" initiative to promote regional cooperation on Afghanistan.
- Russia has assembled several "quadrilateral summits" among it, Pakistan, Afghanistan, and Tajikistan, to focus on counter-narcotics and anti-smuggling.
- Another effort is the Regional Economic Cooperation Conference (RECCA) on Afghanistan, which was launched in 2005. It held its fifth meeting in Tajikistan on March 26-27, 2012.

Afghan and Regional Facilities Used for Operations in and Supply Lines to Afghanistan

Bagram Air Base: 50 miles north of Kabul, the operational hub of U.S. forces in Afghanistan, and base for CJTF-82. At least 2,000

U.S. military personnel are based there. Handles many of the I50+ U.S. aircraft (including helicopters) in country. Hospital constructed, one of the first permanent structures there. FY2005 supplemental (P.L. 109-13) provided about $52 million for various projects to upgrade facilities at Bagram, including a control tower and an operations center, and the FY2006 supplemental appropriation (P.L. I09-234) provided $20 million for military construction there. NATO also using the base and sharing operational costs. Bagram can be accessed directly by U.S. military flights following April 20I0 agreement by Kazakhstan to allow overflights of U.S. lethal equipment.

Qandahar Air Field: Just outside Qandahar, the hub of military operations in the south. Turned over from U.S. to NATO/ISAF control in late 2006 in conjunction with NATO assumption of peacekeeping responsibilities. Enhanced (along with other facilities in the south) at cost of $1.3 billion to accommodate influx of U.S. combat forces in the south.

Shindand Air Base: In Farah province, about 20 miles from Iran border. Used by U.S. forces and combat aircraft since October 2004, after the dismissal of Herat governor Ismail Khan, who controlled it.

Peter Ganci Base: Manas, Kyrgyzstan: Used by 1,200 U.S. military personnel as well as refueling and cargo aircraft for shipments into Afghanistan.

Leadership of Kyrgyzstan changed in April 2005 in an uprising against President Askar Akayev and again in April 20I0 against Kurmanbek Bakiyev. Previous Kyrgyz governments demanded the U.S. vacate the base but subsequently agreed to allow continued use in exchange for large increase in U.S. payments for its use (to $60 million per year currently. Defense Secretary Panetta visited in March 2012 to launch talks on extending U.S. use of the facility beyond 2014. Kyrzyz parliament voted in June 2013 not to extend the U.S. lease beyond 2014.

Incirlik Air Base, Turkey: About 2,100 U.S. military personnel there; U.S. aircraft supply U.S. forces in Iraq and Afghanistan. U.S. use repeatedly extended for one year intervals by Turkey.

Al Dhafra, UAE: Air base used by about 1,800 U.S. military personnel, to supply U.S. forces and related transport into Iraq and Afghanistan.

Al Udeid Air Base, Qatar: Largest air facility used by U.S. in region. Houses central air operations coordination center for U.S. missions in Iraq and Afghanistan; also houses CENTCOM forward headquarters. About 5,000 U.S. personnel in Qatar.

Naval Support Facility, Bahrain: U.S. naval command headquarters for OEF anti-smuggling, anti-terrorism, and anti-proliferation naval search missions, and Iraq-related naval operations (oil platform protection) in the Persian Gulf and Arabian Sea. About 5,000 U.S. military personnel there.

Karsi-Khanabad Air Base, Uzbekistan: Not used by U.S. since September 2005 following U.S.-Uzbek dispute over May 2005 Uzbek crackdown on unrest in Andijon. Once housed about I,750 U.S. military personnel (900 Air Force, 400 Army, and 450 civilian) supplying Afghanistan. U.S. relations with Uzbekistan have improved since 2009, but there is still no U.S. use of the air base. Some U.S. shipments began in February 2009 through Navoi airfield in central Uzbekistan, and U.S. signed agreement with Uzbekistan on April 4, 2009, allowing nonlethal supplies for the Afghanistan war. Goods are shipped to Latvia and Georgia, some transits Russia by rail, then to Uzbekistan.

Tajikistan: Some use of air bases and other facilities by coalition partners, including France, and emergency use by U.S. India also uses bases under separate agreement. New supply lines to Afghanistan established in February 2009 ("northern route") make some use of Tajikistan.

Pakistan: Most U.S. supplies have flowed through Pakistan, but increased use is being made through the Northern Distribution Network. Heavy equipment docks in Karachi and is escorted by security contractors to the Khyber Pass crossing.

Russia: Allows non-lethal equipment to transit Russia by rail. In March 2012, expressed willingness to allow use of an airfield to move goods to Afghanistan. Still does not allow lethal aid to transit and may reduce cooperation after 2014 if the U.N. mandate for international forces ends.

PAKISTAN/PAKISTAN-AFGHANISTAN BORDER

The Afghanistan neighbor that is considered most crucial to Afghanistan's future is Pakistan. DOD reports on Afghanistan's stability repeatedly identify Afghan militant safe haven in Pakistan as among the largest threats to Afghan stability after 2014. Pakistan's goal is that Afghanistan, at the very least, not align with rival India, and, at best, provide Pakistan strategic depth against India. Pakistan says India is using its Embassy and four consulates in Afghanistan (Pakistan says India has nine consulates) to recruit anti-Pakistan insurgents, and that India is using its aid programs only to build influence there. Pakistan's goal in allowing some groups, such as the Haqqani Network, relative safehaven may be to develop leverage with Afghanistan to support Pakistan's policies. At the same time, Pakistan's releases of major pragmatic Afghan Taliban figures since November 2012 could signal that Pakistan has assessed that perpetual instability in Afghanistan would rebound to Pakistan's detriment.

Afghanistan-Pakistan relations continue to fluctuate. Many Afghans fondly remember Pakistan's role as the hub for U.S. backing of the *mujahedin* that forced the Soviet withdrawal in 1988-1989. Later, many Afghans came to resent Pakistan as the most public defender of the Taliban movement when it was in power; it was one of only three countries to formally recognize the Taliban as the legitimate government (Saudi Arabia and the United Arab Emirates are the others.) Anti-Pakistan sentiment is particularly strong among the Tajiks and other non-Pashtuns.

After military leader President Pervez Musharraf left office in 2008, relations improved. Karzai attended the September 9, 2008, inauguration of civilian President Asif Zardari, and Zardari visited Kabul on January 9, 2009 to sign a joint declaration against terrorism. A September 2010 meeting between them reaffirmed this declaration. Afghan and Pakistani ministers jointly visited Washington, DC, during late February 2009, to participate in the first Obama Administration strategic review, and Karzai and Zardari conducted a joint visit to Washington, DC, in May 2009.

The September 2011 insurgent attacks on the U.S. Embassy and the killing of former President Rabbani caused another reversal.

Largely as a response, Karzai, on October 5, 2011, signed a significant trade and security pact with India. Subsequently relations improved in 2012 as Pakistan signaled more cooperation in stabilizing Afghanistan, but deteriorated again after a February 2013 meeting in Britain in which Pakistan demanded that Afghanistan scale back relations with India and sign a strategic agreement with Pakistan that includes Pakistani training for the ANSF. In early May 2013, border forces of the two countries clashed, killing some border police officers from each side. There also are rival efforts to undertake military construction at contested points along the border.

The clashes occurred just prior to Pakistan's elections that brought Nawaz Sharif back into office as Prime Minister; he is close to Saudi Arabia and Islamist factions and could potentially be helpful in persuading the Taliban to reconcile with the Afghan government. The Sharif government appears to have brightened prospects for Afghanistan-Pakistan relations with the sending of a high level envoy, foreign policy advisor Sartaj Aziz, to Afghanistan, and the subsequent announcement (July 23) that Karzai had accepted Pakistan's invitation to visit. Karzai's visit occurred during August 26-7, 2013 and produced some eventual results in September 2013 when Pakistan released several moderate Taliban figures, including Mullah Bradar.

International Border Question. The border clashes could have been a product of the differences between and Afghanistan and Pakistan over their border. Pakistan wants the government of Afghanistan to formally recognize as the border the "Durand Line," a border agreement reached between Britain (signed by Sir Henry Mortimer Durand) and then Afghan leader Amir Abdul Rahman Khan in 1893, separating Afghanistan from what was then British-controlled India (later Pakistan after the 1947 partition). The border is recognized by the United Nations, but Afghanistan continues to indicate that the border was drawn unfairly to separate Pashtun tribes and should be renegotiated. Afghan leaders bridled at October 21, 2012, comments by then SRAP Grossman that U.S. "policy is that border is the international border," even though that comment reflected a longstanding U.S. position. As of October

2002, about 1.75 million Afghan refugees have returned from Pakistan since the Taliban fell, but as many as 3 million might still remain in Pakistan.

Afghanistan-Pakistan Transit Trade Agreement (APTTA). U.S. efforts to persuade Pakistan to forge a "transit trade" agreement with Afghanistan bore success with the signature of a trade agreement between the two on July 18, 2010. The agreement allows for easier exportation via Pakistan of Afghan products, which are mostly agricultural products that depend on rapid transit and are key to Afghanistan's economy. On June 12, 2011, in the context of a Karzai visit to Islamabad, both countries began full implementation of the agreement. It is expected to greatly expand the $2 billion in trade per year the two countries were doing prior to the agreement. The agreement represented a success for the Canada-sponsored "Dubai Process" of talks between Afghanistan and Pakistan on modernizing border crossings, new roads, and a comprehensive border management strategy to meet IMF benchmarks. A drawback to the agreement is that Afghan trucks, under the agreement, are not permitted to take back cargo from India after dropping off goods there. The Afghanistan-Pakistan trade agreement followed agreements to send more Afghan graduate students to study in Pakistan, and a June 2010 Afghan agreement to send small numbers of ANA officers to undergo training in Pakistan.

U.S.-PAKISTANI COOPERATION ON AFGHANISTAN

The U.S. military effort in Afghanistan has depended on cooperation from Pakistan. That cooperation has generally survived occasional U.S.-Pakistan strains but has also had periods of tension. The May 1, 2011, U.S. raid that killed Osama bin Laden in Pakistan added to pre-existing strains caused by Pakistan's refusal to crack down on the Haqqani network. Relations worsened further after a November 26, 2011, incident in which a U.S. airstrike killed 24 Pakistani soldiers, and Pakistan responded by closing border crossings, suspending participation in the border coordination centers, and boycotting the, December 2011 Bonn Conference. President Obama declined to hold a formal meeting with President Zardari during the May 20-21, 2012, NATO summit in Chicago, but then Secretary of State Clinton's July 2, 2012, expression of remorse for the 24 Pakistani soldier deaths led Pakistan to reopen the border crossings.

In the several years after the September 11, 2001, attacks, Pakistani cooperation against Al Qaeda was considered by U.S. officials to be relatively consistent and effective. Pakistan arrested over 700 Al Qaeda figures after the September 11 attacks. Pakistan allowed U.S. access to Pakistani airspace, some ports, and some airfields for OEF. Others say Musharraf acted against Al Qaeda only when it threatened him directly; for example, after the December 2003 assassination attempts against him.

In April 2008, in an extension of the work of the Tripartite Commission (Afghanistan, Pakistan, and ISAF, in which military leaders of these entities meet on both sides of the border), the three countries agreed to set up five "border coordination centers" (BCCs) which include networks of radar nodes to give liaison officers a common view of the border area. These centers build on an agreement in May 2007 to share intelligence on extremists' movements. Four have been established to date, including one near the Torkham Gate at the Khyber Pass, but all four are on the Afghan side of the border. Pakistan has not fulfilled its May 2009 pledge to establish one on the Pakistani side of the border.

Iran

As an immediate goal, Iran seeks to deny the United States the use of Afghanistan as a base from which to pressure or attack Iran, to the point where Iran strenuously sought to scuttle the May 1, 2012, U.S.-Afghanistan SPA. As a longer term objective, Iran seeks to exert its historic influence over western Afghanistan, which was once part of the Persian empire, and to protect Afghanistan's Shiite and other Persian-speaking minorities. Most experts appear to see Iran as a relatively marginal player, particularly compared to Pakistan, while others believe Tehran is able to mobilize large numbers of Afghans, particularly in the west, to support its policies. The United States will attempt to better gauge Tehran's influence through the "Iran watch" diplomatic position at the U.S. consulate in Herat established in early 2013.

The Obama Administration initially saw Iran as potentially helpful to its strategy for Afghanistan. Iran was invited to the U.N.-led meeting on Afghanistan at the Hague on March 31, 2009, and then SRAP Holbrooke gave Iran's delegation leader a letter on several outstanding human rights cases involving Iranian-Americans. At the meeting, Iran pledged cooperation on combating Afghan narcotics and in helping economic development in Afghanistan—both policies Iran is pursuing to a large degree. The United States supported Iran's attendance of the October 18, 2010 meeting of the International Contact Group on Afghanistan, held in Rome. Earlier, the United States and Iran took similar positions at a U.N. meeting in Geneva in February 2010 that discussed drug trafficking across the Afghan border. Iran did not attend the January 28, 2010, international meeting in London, but it did attend the July 28, 2010, international meeting in Kabul. As a member of the OIC, an Iranian representative attended the March 3, 2011, Contact Group meeting at OIC headquarters in Jeddah. Iran attended the region-led international meeting in Istanbul on November 2, 2011, the December 5, 2011, Bonn Conference, and the Tokyo donors' conference on July 8, 2012.

Bilateral Government-to-Government Relations

Iran has had some success in building ties to the Afghan government, despite that government's heavy reliance on U.S. support and despite Iran's aid to Taliban and other militants. Karzai has, at times, called Iran a "friend" of Afghanistan; and there were regular bilateral and multilateral meetings between Karzai and then Iranian President Mahmoud Ahmadinejad. Karzai has repeatedly said that Afghanistan must not become an arena for the broader competition and disputes between the United States and Iran. In June 2011, Iran's then Defense Minister, Ahmad Vahidi, visited Kabul to sign a bilateral border security agreement. In October 2010 when Karzai acknowledged accepting about $2 million per year in cash payments from Iran. Afghan officials say Iran ceased the payments after the Karzai government went ahead with the SPA with the United States in May 2012.

The basis for the relationship is that many Afghans appreciate Iran's aid for efforts to try to oust the Taliban regime when it was in power. Iran saw the Taliban regime, which ruled during 19962001, as a threat to its interests in Afghanistan, especially after Taliban forces captured Herat in September 1995. Iran subsequently drew even closer to the ethnic minority-dominated Northern Alliance than previously, providing its groups with fuel, funds, and ammunition. In September 1998, Iranian and Taliban forces nearly came into direct conflict when Iran discovered that nine of its diplomats were killed in the course of the Taliban's offensive in northern Afghanistan. Iran massed forces at the border and threatened military action, but the crisis cooled without a major clash, possibly out of fear that Pakistan would intervene on behalf of the Taliban. Iran offered search and rescue assistance in Afghanistan during the U.S.-led war to topple the Taliban, and it also allowed U.S. humanitarian aid to the Afghan people to transit Iran. Iran helped construct Afghanistan's first post-Taliban government, in cooperation with the United States—at the December 2001 "Bonn Conference." In February 2002, Iran expelled Karzai-opponent Gulbuddin Hikmatyar, but it did not arrest him.

At other times, Afghanistan and Iran have had disputes over Iran's efforts to expel Afghan refugees. There are 1 million registered Afghan refugees in Iran, and about 1.4 million Afghan migrants (non-refugees) living there. A crisis erupted in May 2007 when Iran expelled about 50,000 into Afghanistan. About 300,000 Afghan refugees have returned from Iran since the Taliban fell.

Iranian Assistance to Afghan Militants and to Pro-Iranian Groups and Regions

Despite its relations with the Afghan government, Iran, perhaps attempting to demonstrate that it can cause U.S. combat deaths in Afghanistan, is allegedly arming militants there. The State Department report on international terrorism for 2012, released May 30, 2013, repeats language in prior reports that the Qods Force of the Islamic Revolutionary Guard Corps of Iran provides training to the Taliban on small unit tactics, small arms, explosives, and indirect weapons fire, and that it has shipped arms to militants in Qandahar. This phrasing implies that Iran is arming Pashtun Taliban militants in the core of the combat zone in Afghanistan. Weapons provided, according to the State Department report, include mortars, 107mm rockets, rocket-propelled grenades, and plastic explosives. On March 9, 2011, NATO said it had seized 48 Iranian-made rockets in Nimruz Province, bound for Afghan militants; the 122mm rockets, have a range (13 miles) greater than those previously provided by Iran. On August 3, 2010, the Treasury Department, acting under Executive Order 13224, named two Qods Force officers as terrorism supporting entities, freezing any U.S.-based assets: Hossein Musavi, Commander of the Qods Force Ansar Corps (the Qods unit involved in Afghanistan), and Hasan Mortezavi, a Qods officer responsible for providing funds and materiel to the Taliban, according to the Treasury Department.

Iran reportedly has allowed a Taliban office to open in Iran, and a high-level Taliban delegation traveled from Qatar to Iran in early June 2013 (prior to the opening of the Taliban office there) for meetings with Iranian officials. While some see the contacts as Iranian support of the insurgency, others see it as an effort to exert some influence over reconciliation efforts. Iran previously allowed Taliban figures to attend conferences in Iran that were attended by Afghan figures, including the late High Peace Council head Burhanuddin Rabbani.

6

Post Taliban Governance-Building Efforts

The George W. Bush Administration argued that the U.S. departure from the region after the 1989 Soviet pullout allowed Afghanistan to degenerate into chaos, and that this pattern not be repeated after the defeat of the Taliban. The Bush Administration and international partners of the United States decided to try to dismantle local security structures and try to build a relatively strong, democratic, Afghan central government and develop Afghanistan economically. The effort, which many outside experts described as "nation-building," was supported by the United Nations, international institutions, and U.S. partners.

The Obama Administration's strategy review in late 2009 initially narrowed official U.S. goals to preventing terrorism safe haven in Afghanistan, but policy in some ways expanded the preexisting nation-building effort. No matter how the U.S. mission has been defined, building the capacity of and reforming Afghan governance have been consistently judged to be key to the success of U.S. policy. This has been stated explicitly in each Obama Administration policy review, strategy statement, and report on progress in Afghanistan, as well as all major international conferences on Afghanistan, including the NATO summit in Chicago during May 20-21, 2012, and the Tokyo donors' conference on July 8, 2012.

The conclusion of virtually every Administration and outside assessment has been that Afghan central governmental capacity and effectiveness has increased, but that local governance remains weak and all levels of government are plagued by governmental corruption. U.S. assessments say that the deficiencies in governance could jeopardize stability after the 2014 transition. Table 1 briefly depicts the process and events that led to the formation of the post-Taliban government of Afghanistan.

Interim Administration: Formed by Bonn Agreement. Headed by Hamid Karzai, an ethnic Pashtun, but key security positions dominated by mostly minority "Northern Alliance." Karzai reaffirmed as leader by June 2002 "emergency *loya jirga*." (A *jirga* is a traditional Afghan assembly.)

Constitution: Approved by January 2004 "Constitutional *Loya Jirga*" (CLJ). Set up strong presidency, a rebuke to Northern Alliance that wanted prime ministership to balance presidential power, but gave parliament significant powers to compensate. Gives men and women equal rights under the law, allows for political parties as long as they are not "un-Islamic;" allows for court rulings according to Hanafi (Sunni) Islam. Set out electoral roadmap for simultaneous (if possible) presidential, provincial, and district elections by June 2004. Named ex-King Zahir Shah to non-hereditary position of "Father of the Nation;" he died July 23, 2007.

Presidential Election: Elections for president and two vice presidents, for five-year term, held October 9, 2004. Turnout was 80% of 10.5 million registered. Karzai and running mates (Ahmad Zia Masoud, a Tajik and brother of legendary *mujahedin* commander Ahmad Shah Masoud, who was assassinated by Al Qaeda two days before the September 11 attacks, and Karim Khalili, a Hazara) elected with 55% against 16 opponents. Second highest vote getter, Northern Alliance figure (and Education Minister) Yunus Qanooni (16%). One female ran. Funding: $90 million from donors, including $40 million from U.S. (FY2004, P.L. 108-106).

Parliamentary Elections: Elections held September 18, 2005, on "Single Non-Transferable Vote" System; candidates stood as individuals, not in party list. Parliament consists of a 249 elected lower house (*Wolesi Jirga,* House of the People) and a selected 102 seat upper house (*Meshrano Jirga,* House of Elders). 2,815 candidates for *Wolesi Jirga,* including 347 women. Turnout was 57% (6.8 million voters) of 12.5 million registered. Upper house is appointed by Karzai (34 seats, half of which are to be women), and by the provincial councils (68 seats). When district councils are elected, they will appoint 34 of the seats. Funded by $ 160 million in international aid, including $45 million from U.S. (FY2005 supplemental, P.L. 109-13).

First Provincial Elections/ District Elections: Provincial elections held September 18, 2005, simultaneous with parliamentary elections. Exact powers vague, but now taking lead in deciding local reconstruction Provincial council sizes range from 9 to the 29 seats on the Kabul provincial council. Total seats are 420, of which 121 held by women. 13,185 candidates, including 279 women. District elections not held due to complexity and potential tensions of drawing district boundaries.

Second Presidential/Provincial Elections: Presidential and provincial elections were held August 20, 2009, but required a runoff because no candidate received over 50% in certified results issued October 20. Second round not held because Dr. Abdullah pulled out of runoff. Election costs: $300 million.

Second Parliamentary Elections: Originally set for May 22, 2010; held September 18, 2010. Results disputed, but agreement reached for Karzai to inaugurate new lower house on January 26, 201 1. 70 women elected, two more than quota. Speaker selected on February 27, Abdul Raouf Ibrahimi, an ethnic Uzbek. Special tribunal set up to investigate results and on June 23 ruled that 62 results be altered, but crisis eased on August 11, 2011, when Karzai announced that only the election bodies have standing to overturn results and Independent Election Commission unseated only nine lower house winners. For the upper house, 68 seats council are appointed to four-year terms by the elected provincial councils in each of Afghanistan's 34 provinces, and remain in office. Karzai made his 34 appointments on February 19, 2011. The speaker of that body is Muslim Yaar (a Pashtun).

Third Presidential/Provincial Election: To be held on April 5, 2014. Needed election laws have been passed by the National Assembly and signed by Karzai, who cannot run again. Twenty six slates filed for the presidential race, and ten were approved by the election commission. Major slates include that of Islamic conservative Abd-i-Rab Rasul Sayyaf, Foreign Minister Zalmay Rassoul, Karzai's brother Qayyum, and Northern Alliance opposition leader Dr. Abdullah.

U.S. AND INTERNATIONAL CIVILIAN POLICY STRUCTURE

Building the capacity of the Afghan government, and helping it develop economically, is primarily the purview of U.S. and international civilian officials and institutions. In line with the prioritization of Afghanistan policy, in February 2009, the Administration set up the position of appointed "Special Representative for Afghanistan and Pakistan" (SRAP), occupied first by Ambassador Richard Holbrooke, reporting to Secretary of State Clinton. Holbrooke died on December 13, 2010, and that office at the State Department was led during February 2011-November 2012 by Ambassador Marc Grossman. In May 2013, Secretary of State John Kerry replaced him with Ambassador James Dobbins. The SRAP office is likely to be retained until the end of the transition in 2014.

At the U.S. Embassy in Kabul, Ambassador Ryan Crocker was succeeded by James Cunningham, formerly the "deputy Ambassador" in July 2012. There are high-ranking officials who manage U.S. economic assistance and Embassy operations, and coordinate U.S. rule of law programs. Some U.S. civilian and coalition military personnel are assigned as advisors to Afghan ministries. Some Afghan groups want the United States to name a high level coordinator at the Embassy for the 2014 presidential elections, as there was in 2009, to try to ensure election fairness.

The U.S. Embassy has progressively expanded its personnel and facilities to accommodate the additional civilian hires and Foreign Service officers who have been posted to Afghanistan since 2009 as mentors and advisers to the Afghan government. U.S. officials say there are more than 1,300 U.S. civilian officials in Afghanistan up from only about 400 in early 2009. Of these at least 400 serve outside Kabul to help build governance at the provincial and district levels. That is up from 67 outside Kabul in 2009. However, the State Department is planning for a 20%

reduction in staff by the completion of the transition in 2014. The State Department request for ongoing Diplomatic and Consular programs in Afghanistan for FY2014 is $708 million less than amounts provided for those functions in FY2012.

On February 7, 2010, in an effort to improve civilian coordination between the United States, its foreign partners, and the Afghan government, the powers of the NATO "Senior Civilian Representative" in Afghanistan were enhanced as UK Ambassador Mark Sedwill took office. This office works with U.S. military officials, officials of partner countries, and the special U.N. Assistance Mission-Afghanistan. In April 2011 Sedwill was replaced by the former British Ambassador to Iran, Sir Simon Gass, who in turn was replaced in June 2013 by Dutch senior diplomat Maurits Jochems.

Afghan Ambassador to the United States Sayed Tayib Jawad served as Ambassador from 2004 until his recall in August 2010. Then deputy Foreign Minister Eklil Hakimi replaced him on February 23, 2011. Hakimi is Afghanistan's chief negotiator of the Bilateral Security Agreement.

Consulate Established in Herat and Others Planned

As the military aspect of U.S. involvement in Afghanistan winds down, the Administration has sought to "normalize" its presence in Afghanistan. The State Department is currently planning to assume the lead role in Afghanistan, as it did in Iraq. In June 2010, Deputy Secretary of State William Burns formally inaugurated a U.S. consulate in Herat. The State Department spent about $80 million on a facility in Mazar-e-Sharif that was slated to open as a U.S. consulate in April 2012, but the site was abandoned because of concerns about the security of the facility. A U.S. consulate there is considered an important signal of U.S. interest in engagement with the Tajik and Uzbek minorities of Afghanistan. Alternative locations are being considered, and consulates are planned for the maj or cities of Qandahar and Jalalabad by the end of 2014. A significant insurgent attack on the Herat consulate in mid-September 2013 could stall or delay those plans, even though no U.S. diplomats were hurt in the attack. The tables at the end of this report include U.S. funding for State Department and USAID operations, including Embassy construction and running the "Embassy air wing," a fleet of twin-engine turboprops that ferry U.S. officials and contractors around Afghanistan.

SECURITY POLICY: TRANSITION, AND BEYOND

The Obama Administration policy goal is to prevent Afghanistan from again becoming a safe haven for terrorist organizations. The Administration has defined that goal as enabling the Afghan government and security forces to defend the country and govern effectively and transparently. Under an agreement announced after a meeting between President Obama and President Karzai in Washington, DC, on January 11, 2013, the U.S. security mission was to change from combat leadership to a "support" role by the end of June 2013. That transition was announced on June 18, 2013. Even with Afghan forces now in the lead, many of the pillars of U.S. and NATO security strategy will remain intact at least until the end of 2014 and possibly, to some extent, beyond that. The United States remains partnered with 49 other countries and the Afghan government and security forces. On February 10, 2013, Marine General Joseph Dunford succeeded Lieutenant General John Allen as top U.S. and NATO commander in Afghanistan.

Who Is "The Enemy"? Taliban, Haqqani, Al Qaeda, and Others

Security in Afghanistan is challenged by several armed groups, loosely allied with each other. There is not agreement about the relative strength of insurgents in the areas where they operate.

Groups: The Taliban/"Quetta Shura Taliban"(QST)

The core insurgent faction in Afghanistan remains the Taliban movement, much of which remains at least nominally loyal to Mullah Muhammad Umar, leader of the Taliban regime during 19962001. Although press reports say even many of his top aides do not see him regularly, he and those subordinates reportedly still operate from Pakistan, probably the city of Quetta but possibly also Karachi. This accounts for the term usually applied to Umar and his aides: "Quetta Shura Taliban" (QST). In recent years, Umar has lost some of this top aides and commanders to U.S.-led military action or Pakistan arrests, including Mullah Dadullah, Mullah Obeidullah Akhund, and Mullah Usmani.

Some of Umar's inner circle has remained intact, and the release by Pakistan of several top Taliban figures close to Umar has helped him restore the leadership circle. Mullah Abdul Ghani Bradar, was arrested by Pakistan in February 2010 for purportedly trying to engage in negotiations with the Afghan government without Pakistani concurrence; he was released to house arrest/close surveillance in September 2013. Other pragmatists around Umar include Akhtar Mohammad Mansoor, a logistics expert and head of the Taliban's senior *shura* council; Shahabuddin Delawar; Noorudin Turabi; and several other figures released by Pakistan since late 2012. Umar and the pragmatists reportedly blame their past association with Al Qaeda for their loss of power. Signals of Mullah Umar's potential for compromise have been several statements, including one on the 10th anniversary of the September 11 attacks, acknowledging there have been some settlement talks; and another on October 24, 2012, that the Taliban does not seek to regain a monopoly of power.

The pragmatists are facing debate from younger and reputedly hardline, anti-compromise leaders such as Mullah Najibullah (a.k.a. Umar Khatab) and Mullah Abdul Qayyum Zakir. Zakir, a U.S. detainee in Guantanamo Bay, Cuba until 2007, is the top military commander of the Taliban and purportedly believes outright Taliban victory is possible after 2014. The Taliban has several official spokespersons, including Qari Yusuf Ahmadi and Zabiullah Mujahid. It operates a clandestine radio station, "Voice of Shariat" and publishes videos.

Al Qaeda/Bin Laden

U.S. officials have long considered Al Qaeda to have been largely expelled from Afghanistan itself, characterizing Al Qaeda militants in Afghanistan as facilitators of militant incursions into Afghanistan rather than active fighters. U.S. officials put the number of Al Qaeda fighters in Afghanistan at between 50-100, who operate mostly in provinces of eastern Afghanistan such as Kunar. Some of these fighters belong to Al Qaeda affiliates such as the Islamic Movement of Uzbekistan (IMU), which is active in Faryab and Konduz provinces.

Until the death of Bin Laden at the hands of a U.S. Special Operations Force raid on May 1, 2011, there had been frustration within the U.S. government with the search for Al Qaeda's top leaders. In December 2001, in the course of the post-September 11 major combat effort, U.S. Special Operations Forces and CIA operatives reportedly narrowed Osama Bin Laden's location to the Tora Bora mountains in Nangarhar Province (30 miles west of the Khyber Pass), but Afghan militia fighters surrounding the area did not prevent his escape into Pakistan. Some U.S. officials later publicly questioned the U.S. decision to rely mainly on Afghan forces in this engagement.

U.S. efforts to find Al Qaeda leaders reportedly focus on his close ally Ayman al-Zawahiri, who is also presumed to be on the Pakistani side of the border and who was named new leader of Al Qaeda in June 2011. CNN reported October 18, 2010, that assessments from the U.S.-led coalition said Zawahiri was likely in a settled area, and not in a remote area. A U.S. strike reportedly missed Zawahiri by a few hours in the village of Damadola, Pakistan, in January 2006. Many observers say that Zawahiri is increasingly focused on taking political advantage of the Arab uprisings, particularly in Egypt where a Muslim Brotherhood leader, Mohammad Morsi, became president but then was ousted by the Egyptian military in July 2013. Other senior Al Qaeda leaders are said to be in Iran, including Sayf al Adl, although another figure, Sulayman Abu Ghaith, son-in-law of bin Laden, was expelled by Iran in March 2013. The United States has called on Iran to arrest and submit any Al Qaeda operatives to international authorities for trial.

U.S. efforts—primarily through armed unmanned aerial vehicles—have killed numerous other senior Al Qaeda operatives in recent years. In August 2008, an airstrike was confirmed to have killed Al Qaeda chemical weapons expert Abu Khabab al-Masri, and two senior operatives allegedly involved in the 1998 embassy bombings in Africa reportedly were killed by an unmanned aerial vehicle strike in January 2009. Following the killing of Bin Laden, three top operational leaders, Ilyas Kashmiri, Attiyah Abd al-Rahman, and Abu Yahya al-Libi were killed in Pakistan by reported U.S. drone strikes in June and August 2011 and June 2012, respectively.

Hikmatyar Faction (HIG)

Another significant insurgent leader is former *mujahedin* party leader Gulbuddin Hikmatyar, who leads Hizb-e-Islami-Gulbuddin (HIG). The faction received extensive U.S. support against the Soviet Union, but turned against its *mujahedin* colleagues after the Communist government fell in 1992. The Taliban displaced HIG as the main opposition to the 1992-1996 Rabbani government. HIG's areas of activity include Kunar, Nuristan, Kapisa, and Nangarhar provinces, north and east of Kabul, but it is not a major factor on the Afghanistan battlefield. The group is ideologically and politically allied with Al Qaeda and Taliban insurgents, but its fighters have sometimes clash with the Taliban over control of territory. A suicide bombing on September 18, 2012, which killed 12 persons, including eight South African nationals working for a USAID-chartered air service, was allegedly carried out by a female HIG member. HIG claimed responsibility for a suicide bombing in Kabul on May 16, 2013, that killed six Americans, including two soldiers and four Dyncorps contractors. On February 19, 2003, the U.S. government formally designated Hikmatyar as a "specially designated global terrorist," under Executive Order 13224, subjecting it to a freeze of any U.S.-based assets. The group is *not* designated as a "Foreign Terrorist Organization" (FTO).

Although it continues to conduct attacks, HIG is widely considered amenable to a reconciliation deal with Kabul. In January 2010, Hikmatyar outlined conditions for reconciliation, including elections under a neutral caretaker government following a U.S. withdrawal. On March 22, 2010, both the Afghan government and HIG representatives confirmed talks in Kabul, including meetings with Karzai, and Karzai subsequently acknowledged additional meetings with group representatives. Some close to Hikmatyar attended the consultative peace *loya jirga* on June 2-4, 2010, which discussed the reconciliation issue. HIG figures met government representatives at a June 2012 academic conference in Paris and a follow up meeting in Chantilly, France, on December 20-21, 2012.

Haqqani Faction

Another militant faction, cited by U.S. officials as perhaps the most potent threat to Afghan security, is the "Haqqani Network," founded by Jalaludin Haqqani, a *mujahedin*commander and U.S. ally during the U.S.-backed war against the Soviet Union. He subsequently joined the Taliban regime (1996-2001), serving as its Minister of Tribal Affairs. Since 2001, the network has staunchly opposed the Karzai government, and his faction is believed closer to Al Qaeda than to the Taliban—in part because one of the elder Haqqani's wives is Arab. Over the past few years, he has delegated operation control to his sons Siraj (Sirajjudin), Badruddin, and Nasiruddin, although Badruddin was reportedly killed in a U.S. or Pakistani strike in late August 2012.

Suggesting it may sometimes act as a tool of Pakistani interests, the Haqqani network, which reputedly has 3,000 fighters and supporters, has primarily targeted Indian interests. It claimed responsibility for two attacks on India's embassy in Kabul (July 2008 and October 2009), and is considered likely responsible for the August 4, 2013 attack on India's consulate in Jalalabad. No Indian diplomats were injured in the Jalalabad attack, but nine Afghans were killed. U.S. officials attribute the June 28, 2011, attack on the Intercontinental Hotel in Kabul; a September 10, 2011, truck bombing in Wardak Province (which injured 77 U.S. soldiers); and attacks on the U.S. Embassy and ISAF headquarters in Kabul on September 13, 2011 to the Haqqani group as well.

That the faction is tolerated or protected in the North Waziristan area of Pakistan and also its purported ties to Pakistan's Inter-Services Intelligence Directorate (ISI) has caused U.S. criticism of Pakistan. The ISI is believed to see the Haqqanis as a potential ally in any Afghan political structure that might be produced by a political settlement in Afghanistan. The most widely cited criticism was by then Joint Chiefs of Staff Chairman Mullen, following September 2011 attacks on U.S. Embassy Kabul, who testified (Senate Armed Services Committee) on September 22, 2011, that the Haqqani network acts "as a veritable arm" of the ISI. Other senior officials issued more nuanced versions of that assertion.

Many consider the faction less ideological than the Taliban—interested primarily in earning funds through licit and illicit businesses in Pakistan and the Persian Gulf and in controlling parts of Khost Province. Such interests could make the faction amenable to a political settlement. On November 13, 2012, a top Haqqani commander said that the Haqqani Network would participate in political settlement talks with the United States if Taliban leader Mullah Umar decided to undertake such talks, and a Haqqani representative reportedly was stationed at the Taliban office in Doha, Qatar that was opened on June 18, 2013 but later closed. It has also been reported that U.S. officials met with Haqqani representatives in 2011 in UAE.

The faction's calculations might be affected by how the United States characterizes the group. In July 2010, then-top U.S. commander in Afghanistan General David Petraeus advocated that the Haqqani network be named as an FTO under the Immigration and Naturalization Act. Some in the State Department reportedly opposed an FTO designation because that could complicate efforts to conduct reconciliation talks with the faction or create pressure for Pakistan to be named a state sponsor of terrorism. A number of Haqqani leaders had already been sanctioned as Specially Designated Global Terrorists (SDGT) under Executive Order 13224. In the 112th Congress, S. 1959 (Haqqani Network Terrorist Designation Act of 2012), enacted on August 10, 2012 (P.L. 112-168). It required, within 30 days of enactment, an Administration report on whether the group meets the criteria for FTO designation and an explanation of a negative decision. On September 9, 2012, the Administration reported to Congress that the Haqqani Network meets the criteria for FTO designation.

Pakistani Groups

A major Pakistani group, the Pakistani Taliban (Tehrik-e-Taliban Pakistan, TTP), primarily challenges the government of Pakistan, but it supports the Afghan Taliban and some of its fighters reportedly are operating from safehavens in Taliban-controlled areas on the Afghan side of the border. Based in part on a failed bombing in New York City in May 2010 allegedly by the TTP, the State Department designated the TTP as an FTO on September 2, 2010. Its current leader, Hakimullah Mehsud, was named as terrorism supporting entities that day. He succeeded Baitullah Mehsud, who was killed in a U.S. drone strike in August 2009.

Another Pakistani group said to be increasingly active inside Afghanistan is Laskhar-e-Tayyiba (LET, or Army of the Righteous). LET is an Islamist militant group that has previously been focused on operations against Indian control of Kashmir.

Some assess the group as increasingly active in South Asia and elsewhere, and could rival Al Qaeda or Al Qaeda affiliates as potential threat to U.S. interests. Another Pakistan-based group that is said to be somewhat active in Afghanistan is Lashkar-i-Janghvi—it was accused of several attacks on Afghanistan's Hazara Shiite community during 2011-2012.

Insurgent Tactics

As far as tactics, prior to 2011, U.S. commanders worried most about insurgent use of improvised explosive devices (IEDs), including roadside bombs. In January 2010, President Karzai issued a decree banning importation of fertilizer chemicals (ammonium nitrate) commonly used for the roadside bombs, but there reportedly is informal circumvention of the ban for certain civilian uses, and the material reportedly still comes into Afghanistan from at least two major production plants in Pakistan.

U.S. commanders have said they have verified some use of surface-to-air missiles. It does not appear that sophisticated missiles were involved in the shootdown of a U.S. Chinook helicopter that killed 30 U.S. soldiers on August 6, 2011.

Some insurgents have used bombs hidden in turbans, which had, until October 2011, generally not been searched out of respect for Afghan religious traditions. Such a bomb killed former President Rabbani on September 20, 2011, as noted above. A suicide bomber who wounded intelligence chief Asadullah Khalid in December 2012 might have had explosives surgically sewn into his body. A major concern, particularly during 2012, has been "insider attacks"

(attacks on ISAF forces by Afghan security personnel, also known as "green on blue" attacks). These attacks, some of which apparently were carried out by Taliban infiltrators into the Afghan forces, declined by late 2012 but have continued occasionally in 2013.

INSURGENT FINANCING: NARCOTICS TRAFFICKING AND OTHER METHODS

All of the insurgent groups in Afghanistan benefit, at least in part, from narcotics trafficking. However, the adverse effects are not limited to funding insurgents; the trafficking also undermines rule of law within government ranks. At the same time, narcotics trafficking is an area on which there has been progress in recent years, although some question whether progress is sustainable. The trafficking generates an estimated $70 million-$100 million per year for insurgents. A UNODC report released on November 20, 2012, assessed the number of poppy free provinces remained at the previous year's level of 17 (but down from 20 in the 2010 report), but said that area under cultivation increased 18% from the previous year (154,000 hectares compared to 131,000 hectares under cultivation in 2011). The agency attributed the increase to high opium prices.

The Obama Administration approach focuses on promoting legitimate agricultural alternatives to poppy growing in line with Afghan government preferences. In July 2009, the United States ended its prior focus on eradication of poppy fields on the grounds that this practice was driving Afghans to support the Taliban as protectors of their livelihood. This put aside the long-standing differences with Karzai over whether to conduct aerial spraying of fields. Congress sided with Karzai's view; successive annual appropriations laws since FY2008 have prohibited U.S. counter-narcotics funding from being used for aerial spraying on Afghanistan poppy fields without Afghan concurrence. The Afghan government does conduct eradication, and it announced in March 2013 that it plans to destroy 37,000 acres of poppy fields in 2013. Some U.S. programs, such as "Good Performance Initiative" (GPI) funds, give an incentive to provinces to actively work against cultivation.

The U.S. military flies Afghan and U.S. counter-narcotics agents (Drug Enforcement Agency, DEA) on missions and identifying targets; it also evacuates casualties from counter-drug operations and assists an Afghan helicopter squadron to move Afghan counter-narcotics forces around the country. To help break up narcotics trafficking networks, the DEA presence in Afghanistan is expanded from 13 agents in 2008 to over 80 by 2013.

The Bush and Obama Administrations have exercised waiver provisions to required certifications of full Afghan cooperation needed to provide more than congressionally stipulated amounts of U.S. economic assistance to Afghanistan. Although successive appropriations have required certification of Afghan cooperation on counter-narcotics, no funds for Afghanistan have been held up on these grounds. Narcotics trafficking control was perhaps the one issue on which the Taliban regime satisfied much of the international community. However, cultivation flourished in provinces under Northern Alliance control, such as Badakhshan.

Donations from Gulf State individuals

The Obama Administration has placed additional focus on the other sources of Taliban funding, including continued donations from wealthy residents of the Persian Gulf. It established a multinational task force to combat Taliban financing generally, not limited to narcotics, and U.S. officials are emphasizing with Persian Gulf counterparts the need for cooperation. On June 29, 2012, the Administration sanctioned (by designating them as terrorism supporting entities under Executive Order 13224) two money exchange networks (*hawalas*) in Afghanistan and Pakistan allegedly used by the Taliban to move its funds earned from narcotics and other sources. However, the sanctions prevent U.S. persons from dealing with those money exchanges, and will likely have limited effect on the networks' operations in the South Asia region.

THE U.S.-LED MILITARY EFFORT: 2001-2008

During 2002-2009, most U.S. forces were in eastern Afghanistan, leading Regional Command East (RC-E) of the NATO/ISAF operation. The most restive provinces in RC-E have been Paktia, Paktika, Khost, Kunar, and Nuristan. Helmand, Qandahar,

Uruzgan, Zabol, Nimruz, and Dai Kundi provinces constituted a "Regional Command South (RC-S)," a command formally transferred to NATO/ISAF responsibility on July 31, 2006. The increased U.S. troop strength in RC-S in 2009 and 2010—a product of the fact that most of the 2009-2010 U.S. "surge" was focused on the south—prompted a May 2010 NATO decision to bifurcate RC-S, with the United States leading a "southwest" subdivision (RC-SW) for Helmand and Nimruz, and later leading both RC-S and RC-SW. About 4,000 U.S. forces have been under German command in RC-North, headquartered in Konduz, and Italy has led RC-West. Turkey commands ISAF forces in the capital, Kabul, and on October 7, 2011, Turkey agreed to continue in that role for another year. Afghan forces are in overall lead in the capital, however.

During 2001 to mid-2006, U.S. forces and Afghan troops fought relatively low levels of insurgent violence with focused combat operations mainly in the south and east where ethnic Pashtuns predominate. These included "Operation Mountain Viper" (August 2003); "Operation Avalanche" (December 2003); "Operation Mountain Storm" (March-July 2004); "Operation Lightning Freedom" (December 2004-February 2005); and "Operation Pil" (Elephant, October 2005). By late 2005, U.S. and partner commanders considered the insurgency mostly defeated and NATO/ISAF assumed lead responsibility for security in all of Afghanistan during 2005-2006. The optimistic assessments proved misplaced when violence increased significantly in mid-2006.

NATO operations during 2006-2008 cleared key districts but did not prevent subsequent re-infiltration. NATO/ISAF also tried preemptive combat and increased development work, without durable success. As a result, growing U.S. concern took hold, reflected in such statements as a September 2008 comment by then Joint Chiefs of Staff chairman Admiral Mike Mullen that "I'm not sure we're winning" in Afghanistan. Major incidents supporting that assessment included: (1) expanding Taliban operations in provinces where it had been inactive; (2) the January 14, 2008, attack on the Serena Hotel in Kabul; and (3) the June 12, 2008, Sarposa prison break in Qandahar that freed several hundred

Taliban captives. Reasons for the deterioration included popular unrest over corruption in the Afghan government; the absence of governance or security forces in many rural areas; the safe haven enjoyed by militants in Pakistan; the reticence of some NATO contributors to actively combat insurgents; a popular backlash against civilian casualties caused by military operations; and unrealized expectations of economic development.

While not neglecting these many factors, the United States and its partners decided to respond to the deterioration primarily by increasing force levels. The Bush Administration moved to partly fulfill a mid-2008 request by then top U.S. and NATO commander General David McKiernan for 30,000 additional U.S. troops. The decision whether to fulfill the entire request was deferred to the next Administration. U.S. troop levels started 2006 at 30,000; climbed slightly to 32,000 by December 2008; and reached 39,000 by April 2009. Partner forces increased by about 6,000 during this time, to a total of 39,000 at the end of 2009— achieving rough parity between U.S. and non-U.S. forces.

In September 2008, the U.S. military and NATO each began strategy reviews. The primary U.S. review was headed by Lieutenant General Douglas Lute, the Bush Administration's senior adviser on Iraq and Afghanistan (who is in the Obama NSC with responsibility for Afghanistan). These reviews were briefed to the incoming Obama Administration.

OBAMA ADMINISTRATION SURGE

The Obama Administration maintained that Afghanistan needed to be given a higher priority than it was during the Bush Administration, but that the U.S. mission in Afghanistan not be indefinite. The Administration integrated the reviews underway at the end of the Bush Administration's into an overarching 60-day inter-agency "strategy review," chaired by South Asia expert Bruce Riedel and co-chaired by then SRAP Holbrooke and then-Under Secretary of Defense for Policy Michele Flournoy. President Obama announced a "comprehensive" strategy on March 27, 2009, including deployment of an additional 21,000 U.S. forces—most of General McKiernan's request for 30,000 additional forces.

McChrystal Assessment and December 1, 2009, Surge Announcement

On May 11, 2009, then-Secretary of Defense Gates announced the replacement of General McKiernan with General Stanley McChrystal, who headed U.S. Special Operations forces from 2003 to 2008. He assumed the command on June 15, 2009, and, on August 30, 2009, delivered a strategy assessment that recommended that:

- the goal of the U.S. military should be to protect the population rather than to focus on searching out and combating Taliban concentrations. Indicators of success such as ease of road travel, participation in local *shuras*, and normal life for families are more significant than counts of enemy fighters killed.
- there is potential for "mission failure" unless a fully resourced, comprehensive counter-insurgency strategy is pursued and reverses Taliban momentum within 12-18 months. About 44,000 additional U.S. combat troops (beyond those approved in March 2009) would be needed to provide the greatest chance for his strategy's success.

The assessment set off debate within the Administration and another policy review.

Some senior U.S. officials, such as then-Secretary of Defense Gates, were concerned that adding many more U.S. forces could create among the Afghan people a sense of "occupation" that could prove counter-productive. The high-level review included at least nine high-level meetings, chaired by President Obama, who announced the following at West Point academy on December 1, 2009:

- That 30,000 additional U.S. forces (a "surge") would be sent—bringing U.S. levels close to 100,000—to "reverse the Taliban's momentum" and strengthen the capacity of Afghanistan's security forces and government.
- There would be a transition, beginning in July 2011, to Afghan leadership of the stabilization effort and a corresponding drawdown of U.S. force levels.

NATO Decision on Transition by the End of 2014/Petraeus Takes Command

The Obama Administration argued that a transition to Afghan security leadership beginning in July 2011 would compel the Afghan government to place greater effort on training its own forces. However, Afghan and regional officials viewed the deadline as signaling a rapid decrease in U.S. involvement.

To address that perception, on August 31, 2010, the President asserted that the pace and scope of any drawdown would be subject to conditions on the ground. The debate over the July 2011 deadline abated substantially following the November 19-20, 2010, NATO summit in Lisbon, which decided that the transition to Afghan leadership would begin in 2011 and would be completed by the end of 2014.

As this debate over transition timeframes was taking place, on June 23, 2010, President Obama accepted the resignation of General McChrystal after comments by him and his staff to *Rolling Stone* magazine that disparaged several U.S. civilian policymakers on Afghanistan. General Petraeus was named General McChrystal's successor; he was confirmed on June 30, 2010, and assumed command on July 4, 2010.

U.S. Strategy Definition: to build capable and transparent Afghan security and governing institutions and move to a support role (formally accomplished on June 18, 2013), and then transfer full responsibility to the Afghans by the end of 2014. A residual force - likely consisting of about 10,000 U.S. troops and 5,000 allied forces - will conduct training and some combat against high value targets after 2014. Residual U.S. force depends on finalization of a Bilateral Security Agreement that grants U.S. troops immunity from Afghan law.

Surge and then Drawdown: Following the 2009 "surge," U.S. force levels reached a high of 100,000 in mid-2011, then fell to 90,000 by the end of 2011 and to 68,000 ("surge recovery) by September 20, 2012. U.S. troop levels are to fall to 34,000 by February 2014. Current U.S. troop levels are about 52,000, almost all under NATO/ISAF command.

Long-Term Involvement. A strategic partnership agreement, signed in Kabul on May 1, 2012, pledges U.S. security and economic assistance to Afghanistan until 2024.

Reintegration and Reconciliation: to support Afghan efforts to reach a settlement with insurgent leaders.

Pakistan/Regional: to enlist Pakistan's cooperation against militant groups, such as the Haqqani network, that have a measure of safe haven in Pakistan.

Economic Development: To build an economy that can be self-sufficient by 2024 by further developing agriculture, collecting corporate taxes and customs duties, exploiting vast mineral deposits, expanding small industries, and integrating Afghanistan into regional diplomatic and trading and investment structures..

TRANSITION AND DRAWDOWN: AFGHANS IN THE LEAD

Despite doubts about the durability of progress, the results of the surge were considered sufficient to permit the transition to Afghan security leadership to begin on schedule in July 2011. The transition was divided into five "tranches"—the first was announced by Karzai in March 2011, the second in November 2011, the third in May 2012, the fourth (52 districts) on December 31, 2012, and the fifth and final tranche (91 districts along the Pakistan border) on June 18, 2013. The process of completing the transition to Afghan responsibility takes 12-18 months; the process in the first four tranches were either completed or fully underway by mid-2013, and the transition in the fifth tranche began in June 2013.

Afghan Forces Assume Leadership Role/ISAF Moves to Support Role

The announcement of the final tranche coincided with the announcement by President Karzai and visiting NATO Secretary General Anders Fogh Rasmussen that day (June 18, 2013) that Afghan forces were now in the lead role throughout Afghanistan and NATO/ISAF had moved to a supporting role. That shift in roles occurred in line with plans discussed by President Obama on March 15, 2012, and then announced formally in a joint statement following a meeting between President Karzai and President Obama on January 11, 2013. According to that joint statement, the move to a support role implies that U.S. forces have ceased patrolling Afghan villages.

In concert with the transition to Afghan security lead, there has been a gradual drawdown of U.S. forces. President Obama took into account the assessment that the killing of Osama Bin Laden represented a key accomplishment of the core U.S. mission, and financial needs to reduce the size of the U.S. budget deficit. On June 22, 2011, he announced that

- 10,000 U.S. forces would be withdrawn by the end of 2011. That drawdown was accomplished, then bringing U.S. force levels to 90,000.
- 23,000 forces (the remainder of the surge forces) would be withdrawn by September 2012. This draw-down, completed as of September 20, 2012, brought U.S. force levels to 68,000.
- In the February 12, 2013, State of the Union message, President Obama announced that U.S. force level would drop to about 34,000 by February 2014. This reduction is underway, and current U.S. force levels there are about 52,000. The remainder of the U.S. contingent that will exit by the 2014 transition deadline are likely to be withdrawn after the April 5, 2014, Afghan presidential elections.

In concert with the U.S. drawdown, some U.S. airpower in country has left, reducing the capability to conduct strike missions against insurgent positions. Many of the approximately 150 U.S.-run bases are being closed down or turned over to Afghan forces, and will consolidate to about 50 by the end of 2014. The provincial reconstruction teams (PRTs), are being turned over to Afghan institutions. DOD is planning how to move the approximately $36 billion worth of U.S. military equipment out of Afghanistan, including 28,000 vehicles and trailers.

Security Assessments

The NATO/ISAF move to a support role went forward based on assessments of the security situation and the performance of the ANSF. Prior to the implementation of the surge, the Afghan Interior Ministry estimated (August 2009) that the Karzai government controlled about 30% of the country, while insurgents controlled 4% (13 out of 364 districts) and influenced or operated in another 30%. Tribes and local groups with varying degrees of loyalty to the central government controlled the remainder. Some outside groups report higher percentages of insurgent control or influence. The Taliban had named "shadow governors" in 33 out of 34 of Afghanistan's provinces, although many provinces in northern Afghanistan were assessed as having minimal Taliban presence.

Assessments of the prospects for long-term stability, as presented in the DOD report on security and stability in Afghanistan released in July 2013 (covering October 2012 through March 2013), are relatively positive. According to the report: (1) Taliban territorial influence is decreasing; (2) the ANSF has lost no major bases or district centers; (3) the Afghan government is executing on its budget and is delivering basic goods and services; and (4) the transfer of responsibilities to the ANSF has undercut the Taliban effort to portray itself as resistant to foreign occupation. Other officials and sources note that 80% of the violence occurs in areas with only 25% of the Afghan population, and that U.S. casualties in Afghanistan in mid-2013 have been at a five-year low as the ANSF bears the brunt of the fighting. Others cite revolts against Taliban infiltration of parts of Ghazni and Qandahar provinces during 2012-2013 as a sign that the Taliban is rejected by the population. In a May 2013 press interview, prior to the NATO/ISAF announcement of its move to a supporting role, General Dunford said that he is optimistic that Afghan forces will be able to take the lead security role in 2013, protect the 2014 elections, and assume full security responsibility by the end of 2014.

Less optimistic assessments are based on observations that the insurgents continue to be able to penetrate into normally quiet provinces and cities, and to conduct high profile attacks in many places, including Kabul. Others note that ANSF casualties are high, potentially reducing recruitment and commitment to serving in the security forces. The DOD report released July 2013 said that there had been some "regression" (loss of security) in several provinces, including Wardak, Faryab, Farah, and Herat. A major blow to the coalition came on September 14, 2012, when 15 militants penetrated the perimeter of the British Camp Bastion airbase in Helmand and destroyed 8 Marine Harrier jets before being killed. On October 26, 2012, an insurgent bomb killed more than 40 worshippers at a mosque in previously quiescent Faryab Province. On November 23, 2012, a suicide truck bomb leveled several government buildings in the capital of Wardak Province. On April 3, 2013, 46 persons were killed in a Taliban attack on the governor's compound in Farah province, another infrequent target. The widely respected reformist provincial governor of Lowgar, Arsala Jamal, was killed by a Taliban bomb in a mosque on October 15, 2013. The DOD report also notes that Afghan insurgents use sanctionaries in Pakistan to attempt to regain lost ground and influence.

Legislatively Mandated Accelerated Drawdown?

In Congress, some have expressed support for winding down the U.S. involvement in Afghanistan more rapidly than the rate implemented by the Administration. H.Con.Res. 248, requiring a withdrawal, failed by a vote of 356 to 65 on March 10, 2011. In the 112th Congress, after the death of Osama Bin Laden on May 1, 2011, an amendment to the defense authorization bill (H.R. 1540) requiring a plan to accelerate the transition to Afghan-lead security failed by a vote of 204215 on May 26, 2011. On May 25, 2011, an amendment to that same bill that would require U.S. troops to withdraw most of its forces failed 123-294. A provision of the FY2013 defense authorization bill (Section 1226 of P.L. 112-239) expresses the Sense of Congress that the United States draw down troops at a steady pace through the end of 2014.

ASSISTANCE TO ETHNIC AND RELIGIOUS FACTIONS IN AFGHANISTAN

Others are puzzled by Iran's support of Taliban fighters who are Pashtun, because Iran has traditionally supported Persian-speaking or Shiite factions in Afghanistan, many of whom have been oppressed by the Pashtuns. Some of Iran's funding has been intended to support pro-Iranian groups in the west as well as

Hazara Shiites in Kabul and in the Hazara heartland of Bamiyan, Ghazni, and Dai Kundi, in part by providing scholarships and funding for technical institutes. Iran has used some of its funds to construct mosques in Herat, pro-Iranian theological seminaries in Shiite districts of Kabul, and Shiite institutions in Hazara-dominated areas. Iran also offers scholarships to Afghans to study in Iranian universities, and there are consistent allegations that Iran has funded Afghan provincial council and parliamentary candidates who are perceived as pro-Tehran. These efforts have helped Iran retain close ties with Afghanistan's leading Shiite cleric, Ayatollah Mohammad Mohseni, as well as a Hazara political leader Mohammad Mohaqiq.

Iran's Development Aid for Afghanistan

Iran's economic aid to Afghanistan does not conflict with U.S. efforts to develop Afghanistan. Iran has pledged about $1 billion in aid to Afghanistan, of which about $500 million has been provided to date. The funds have been used mostly to build roads and bridges in western Afghanistan. In cooperation with India, Iran has been building roads that would connect western Afghanistan to Iran's port of Chahbahar, and provide Afghan and other goods an easier outlet to the Persian Gulf. In late July 2013, Iran and Afghanistan signed a formal agreement allowing Afghanistan to use the port. Iran also has provided credits to the Afghan private sector and helped develop power transmission lines in the provinces bordering Iran, two of which were turned over to Afghan ownership in January 2013. Some of the funds reportedly are funneled through the Imam Khomeini Relief Committee, which provides charity in Iran and worldwide. Iran also provides gasoline and other fuels to Afghanistan, although a SIGAR report in January 2013 said that some U.S. funds might have been used to purchase fuels from Iran for Afghanistan. U.S. sanctions bar virtually all U.S. energy transactions with Iran.

India

The interests and activities of India in Afghanistan are the inverse of those of Pakistan: India's goals are to deny Pakistan "strategic depth" in Afghanistan, to deny Pakistan the ability to block India from trade and other connections to Central Asia and beyond, and to prevent militants in Afghanistan from attacking Indian targets in Afghanistan. India saw the Afghan Taliban's hosting of Al Qaeda during 1996-2001 as a major threat to India itself because of Al Qaeda's association with radical Islamic organizations in Pakistan, such as LET (Laskhar-e-Tayyiba, or Army of the Righteous), one of the groups that was formed in Pakistan to challenge India's control of part of the disputed territories of Jammu and Kashmir. Some of these groups have committed major acts of terrorism in India, including the terrorist attacks in Mumbai in November 2008 and in July 2011. Pakistan accuses India of using nine consulates in Afghanistan to spread Indian influence in Afghanistan. According to Afghan officials, India has four consulates (in the major cities of Qandahar, Jalalabad, Mazar-e-Sharif, and Herat) and no security presence in Afghanistan.

Afghanistan has sought close ties to India—in large part to access India's large and rapidly growing economy—but without alarming Pakistan. In May 2011, India and Afghanistan announced a "Strategic Partnership" agreement that demonstrated India's support for U.S. efforts to better integrate Afghanistan into regional political, economic, and security structures. On October 5, 2011, Karzai visited Delhi to sign the pact. The pact affirmed Pakistan's worst fears because it gave India, for the first time, a formal role as one of the guarantors of Afghan stability, and it provided for expanded India-Afghanistan political and cultural ties. Indian experts noted that no Indian troops or security forces would deploy to Afghanistan as a consequence of the pact, but it did produce a late 2011 agreement for India to train some ANSF personnel in India. As an outgrowth of a four-day Karzai follow-up visit to India in November 2012, India reportedly agreed to train up to 600 ANSF per year at the Indian Army's jungle warfare school. In the immediate aftermath of the Afghanistan-Pakistan border clashes in early May 2013, Karzai visited India later in May 2013, reportedly to seek sales of Indian artillery, aircraft, and other systems that would help it better defend its border with Pakistan.

The signing of a strategic partnership with Afghanistan could reflect India's concerns about potential preponderant Pakistani influence in post-2014 Afghanistan. India, which supported the Northern Alliance against the Taliban in the mid-1990s, has been stepping up its contacts with those factions to discuss possible contingencies in the event of an Afghan settlement deal. Many Northern Alliance figures have lived in India at one time or another, although Indian diplomats stress they have long also had close connections to Afghanistan's Pashtuns. As noted above, Karzai studied there. In addition, Tajikistan, which also supported the mostly Tajik Northern Alliance against the Taliban when it was in power, allows India to use one of its air bases. Still, India reportedly does not want to be saddled with the burden of helping secure Afghanistan as U.S.-led forces depart. India has stressed its economic aid activities there, showcased by its hosting of a June 28, 2012, meeting in Delhi to discuss investment and economic development in Afghanistan.

India's Development Activities in Afghanistan

India is the fifth-largest single country donor to Afghan reconstruction, funding projects worth over $1.5 billion, with an additional $500 million announced during the Singh visit to Kabul in May 2011. Indian officials assert that all their projects are focused on civilian, not military, development and are in line with the development priorities set by the Afghan government. India, along with the Asian Development Bank, financed a $300 million project, mentioned above, to bring electricity from Central Asia to Afghanistan. It has also renovated the well-known Habibia High School in Kabul and committed to a $67 million renovation of Darulaman Palace as the permanent house for Afghanistan's parliament. India and Afghanistan finalized the construction plans for that building in early 2012. At a cost of about $85 million, India financed the construction of a road to the Iranian border in remote Nimruz province, linking landlocked Afghanistan to Iran's Chahbahar port on the Arabian Sea. India is currently constructing the 42 megawatt hydroelectric Selwa Dam in Herat Province at a cost of about $77 million, expected to be completed in late 2012. This will increase electricity availability in the province. In December 2011, an Indian firm, the Steel Authority of India, Ltd. (SAIL) was declared winning bidder on three of four blocs of the

Hajji Gak iron ore project in Bamiyan Province. This led to assessments that India is also an economic beneficiary of international intervention in Afghanistan, without taking the risk of involving India militarily there.

India is also helping Afghanistan's Independent Directorate of Local Governance (IDLG) with its efforts to build local governance organizations, and it provides 1,000 scholarships per year for Afghans to undergo higher education in India. Some Afghans want to enlist even more Indian assistance in training Afghan bureaucrats in accounting, forensic accounting, oversight, and other disciplines that will promote transparency in Afghan governance.

Russia, Central Asian States, and China

Some neighboring and nearby states take an active interest not only in Afghan stability, but in the U.S. military posture that supports U.S. operations in Afghanistan. The region to the north of Afghanistan is a growing factor in U.S. efforts to rely less on routes through Pakistan to bring out the substantial amount of equipment that will be withdrawn as most U.S. forces depart.

Russia/Northern Distribution Network

Russia wants to reemerge as a great power and to contain U.S. power in Central Asia. At the same time, by supporting the "Northern Distribution Network" supply route for NATO forces in Afghanistan, Russia supports U.S. and NATO efforts against militants who have posed a threat to Russia itself. Fearing that Afghanistan could become unstable after international forces draw down in 2014, Russian officials said in mid-May 2013 that Russia might deploy border guards at the Afghanistan-Tajikistan border after the ISAF drawdown. Previously, Russia had kept a low profile in the country because it still feels humiliated by its withdrawal in 1989 and senses some Afghan resentment of the Soviet occupation. Since 2002, Russia has only been providing small amounts of humanitarian aid to Afghanistan.

In line with Russian official comments in June 2010 that more economic and social assistance is needed for Afghanistan, Russia is investing $1 billion in Afghanistan to develop its electricity capacity and build out other infrastructure. Included in those investments are implementation of an agreement, reached during a Karzai visit to Moscow on January 22, 2011, for Russia to resume long dormant Soviet occupation-era projects such as expanding the Salang Tunnel connecting the Panjshir Valley to Kabul, hydroelectric facilities in Kabul and Baghlan provinces, a customs terminal, and a university in Kabul.

During the 1990s, after its 1989 withdrawal and the breakup of the Soviet Union, Russia supported the Northern Alliance against the Taliban with some military equipment and technical assistance in order to blunt Islamic militancy emanating from Afghanistan. Although Russia supported the U.S. effort against the Taliban and Al Qaeda in Afghanistan out of fear of Islamic (mainly Chechen) radicals, Russia continues to seek to reduce the U.S. military presence in Central Asia. Russian fears of Islamic activism emanating from Afghanistan may have ebbed since 2002 when Russia killed a Chechen of Arab origin known as "Hattab" (full name is Ibn al-Khattab), who led a militant pro-Al Qaeda Chechen faction. The Taliban government was the only one in the world to recognize Chechnya's independence, and some Chechen fighters fighting alongside Taliban/Al Qaeda forces have been captured or killed.

Northern Distribution Network and Other Aid to Afghan Security

Russian cooperation is crucial to the U.S. effort in Afghanistan. In February 2009, Russia paved the way for the expansion of the Northern Distribution Network supply route into Afghanistan by allowing the resumption of shipment of non-lethal equipment into Afghanistan through Russia. Russia suspended the shipments in 2008 over differences over the Russia-Georgia conflict. About half of all ground cargo for U.S. forces in Afghanistan has flowed through the Northern Distribution Network as of 2011, and the United States has emphasized this network at time of strains in U.S. relations with Pakistan, even though the costs to ship goods through the route are far greater than the Pakistan route. The northern route could play a significant role in removing much U.S.

equipment as the U.S. drawdown proceeds. As noted above, Russia has also responded to NATO requests to provide helicopters and spare parts to the Afghan forces (which still make heavy use of Russian-made Hind helicopters) as well as fuel, and to provide new helicopters.

In November 2010, in its most significant intervention in Afghanistan since its occupation, Russian officers reportedly joined U.S. and Afghan forces attempting to interdict narcotics trafficking in Afghanistan. However, the move prompted a complaint by President Karzai because he was not consulted about the inclusion of the Russians.

CENTRAL ASIAN STATES

These states are crucial to the U.S. transition in Afghanistan, as discussed in a Senate Foreign Relations Committee staff report released December 19, 2011, entitled "Central Asia and the Transition in Afghanistan." As shown in Table 6, Uzbekistan, Turkmenistan, Tajikistan, and Kazakhstan are pivotal actors in U.S. efforts to expand the Northern Distribution Network supply route. Kyrgyzstan is key to the U.S. ability to fly troops and supplies in and out of Afghanistan. These states are also becoming crucial to the New Silk Road (NSR) strategy that seeks to help Afghanistan become a trade crossroads between South and Central Asia—a strategy that could net Kabul substantial customs duties and other economic benefits. An increasing amount of trade is flowing from Afghanistan to and through the Central Asian states. The railway lines are being built to Uzbekistan. The Panj bridge, built largely with U.S. funds, has become a major thoroughfare for goods to move between Afghanistan and Tajikistan. Kazakhstan is funding a $50 million program to develop Afghan professionals. The revival of a long-standing plan to establish Afghanistan as a transit hub for Central Asian natural gas (*TAPI* pipeline) is discussed later in this report under "Development in Key Sectors."

The Central Asian countries have long had an interest in seeing Afghanistan stabilized and moderate. In 1996, several of the Central Asian states banded together with Russia and China into the SCO because of the perceived Taliban threat.

Tajikistan

On security cooperation, Tajikistan allows access primarily to French combat aircraft, and Kazakhstan has allowed use of facilities in case of emergency. In May 2011, Kazakhstan became the first Central Asian state to pledge forces to Afghanistan (four non-combat troops). Earlier, in April 2010, Kazakhstan agreed to allow U.S. over flights of lethal military equipment to Afghanistan, allowing the United States to use polar routes to fly materiel directly from the United States to Bagram Airfield.

Uzbekistan

Uzbekistan, a sponsor of Afghan faction leader Abdul Rashid Dostam, an ethnic Uzbek, allowed use of Karshi-Khanabad air base by OEF forces from October 2001 until a rift emerged in May 2005 over Uzbekistan's crackdown against riots in Andijon. Uzbekistan's March 2008 agreement with Germany for it to use Karshi-Khanabad air base temporarily, for the first time since the rift with the United States, suggested potential for resumed U.S.-Uzbek cooperation on Afghanistan. Renewed U.S. discussions with Uzbekistan apparently bore some fruit with the Uzbek decision in February 2009 to allow the use of Navoi airfield for shipment of U.S./NATO goods into Afghanistan. As a rift with Pakistan widened in September 2011, the United States launched new overtures to Uzbekistan, including a call from President Obama to Uzbek President Islam Karimov congratulating him on 20 years of independence from Russia/Soviet Union. Subsequently, the Administration opened formal negotiations with Uzbekistan to enlist its cooperation with further expansion of the Northern Distribution Network. However, in late August 2012, Uzbekistan's parliament advanced legislation that would ban foreign military bases on Uzbekistan territory—a move widely interpreted as reluctance to resume permission for U.S. forces to expand operations in Uzbekistan.

During Taliban rule, Russian and Central Asian leaders were alarmed that radical Islamic movements were receiving safe haven in Afghanistan. Uzbekistan, in particular, has long asserted that the group Islamic Movement of Uzbekistan (IMU), allegedly responsible for four simultaneous February 1999 bombings in Tashkent that nearly killed President Islam Karimov, is linked to Al Qaeda. One of its leaders, Juma Namangani, reportedly was killed while commanding Taliban/Al Qaeda forces in Konduz in November 2001. Kazakhstan and Kyrgyzstan do not directly border Afghanistan, but IMU guerrillas transited Kyrgyzstan during incursions into Uzbekistan in the late 1990s.

Turkmenistan

Currently, perhaps to avoid offending Pakistan or other actors, Turkmenistan takes a position of "positive neutrality" on Afghanistan. It does not allow its territory to be part of the Northern Distribution Network. No U.S. forces have been based in Turkmenistan.

This neutrality essentially continues the policy Turkmenistan had when the Taliban was in power. Turkmenistan was the only Central Asian state to actively engage the Taliban government, possibly viewing engagement as a more effective means of preventing spillover of radical Islamic activity from Afghanistan. It saw Taliban control as facilitating construction of the TAPI natural gas pipeline, that was under consideration during Taliban rule and discussion of which has been revived in recent years. The September 11 events stoked Turkmenistan's fears of the Taliban and its Al Qaeda guests, and the country publicly supported the U.S.-led war.

China

China's involvement in Afghanistan policy appears to be growing, primarily to secure access to Afghan minerals and resources but perhaps also to help its ally, Pakistan, avoid encirclement by India. That was exemplified on September 23, 2012, when a senior Chinese official made a rare visit to Afghanistan to sign security and economic agreements with Afghanistan, including a pledge to help train, fund, and equip the ANP. Like Pakistan, China has been a rival of India. China also is concerned about the potential for Islamic militancy in Afghanistan to inflame Islamist sentiment among China's Uighur community in China. A major organizer of the Shanghai Cooperation Organization, China has a small border with a sparsely inhabited sliver of Afghanistan known as the "Wakhan Corridor," and it is building border access routes and supply depots to facilitate China's access to Afghanistan through the corridor.

Chinese delegations continue to assess the potential for new investments in such sectors as mining and energy, and the cornerstone is the development of the Aynak copper mine south of Kabul. In early 2012, China National Petroleum Co. was awarded the rights to develop oil deposits in the Amu Darya basin. Since 2002, China has pledged about $255 million in economic aid to Afghanistan, about 75% of which has been provided to date.

Prior to the September 2012 agreements China had taken only a small role in securing Afghanistan. No Chinese forces have deployed to Afghanistan, and it trained small numbers of ANP at a People's Armed Police facility in China since 2006, with a focus on counter-narcotics. It also has offered training for ANSF officers at People's Liberation Army training colleges and universities. On the sidelines of the SCO meeting during June 7-8, 2012, China agreed on a strategic partnership with Afghanistan that includes security cooperation.

During the Taliban era, in December 2000, sensing China's increasing concern about Taliban policies, a Chinese official delegation met with Mullah Umar. However, China did not enthusiastically support U.S. military action against the Taliban, possibly because China was wary of a U.S. military buildup nearby.

PERSIAN GULF STATES

The Gulf states are considered a key part of the effort to stabilize Afghanistan. As noted, the late Ambassador Holbrooke focused substantial U.S. attention—and formed a multilateral task force—to try to curb continuing Gulf resident donations to the Taliban in Afghanistan. He maintained that these donations are a larger source of Taliban funding than is the narcotics trade. The Gulf states have also been a source of development funds and for influence with some Afghan clerics and factions.

Two Gulf states, UAE and Bahrain, have contributed some of their small forces to Afghanistan security missions. The UAE has deployed about 250 troops to OEF and ISAF security missions in southern Afghanistan, including Helmand province. Some are military medical personnel who run small clinics and health programs for Afghans in the provinces where they operate. The UAE said in March 2013 it would keep at least some forces in Afghanistan after 2014. In January 2009, Bahrain sent 100 police officers to Afghanistan on a two-year tour to help U.S./NATO-led stabilization operations there. Their tour has been extended until the end of the NATO mission at the end of 2014.

Saudi Arabia

Saudi Arabia has a role to play in Afghanistan in part because, during the Soviet occupation, Saudi Arabia channeled hundreds of millions of dollars to the Afghan*mujahedin,* primarily the Islamist factions. In so doing, Saudi Arabia developed extensive intelligence ties to these factions as well as to the Taliban. A majority of Saudi citizens practice the strict Wahhabi brand of Islam similar to that of the Taliban, and Saudi Arabia was one of three countries to formally recognize the Taliban government. Some press reports indicate that, in late 1998, Saudi and Taliban leaders discussed, but did not agree on, a plan for a panel of Saudi and Afghan Islamic scholars to decide Bin Laden's fate.

Saudi Arabia has played a role as a go-between for negotiations between the Karzai government and "moderate" Taliban figures. This role was recognized at the London conference on January 28, 2010, in which President Karzai stated in his opening speech that he sees a role for Saudi Arabia in helping stabilize Afghanistan. Some observers say that a political settlement might involve Mullah Umar going into exile in Saudi Arabia.The Afghan government also sees Saudi Arabia as a potential new source of investment; in early November 2012 it was reported that the Saudis will fund a $100 million mosque and education center in Kabul. Some see the investment as a Saudi effort to enhance its influence in Afghanistan as international involvement there wanes.

According to U.S. officials, Saudi Arabia cooperated extensively, if not publicly, with OEF. It broke diplomatic relations with the Taliban in late September 2001 and quietly permitted the

United States to use a Saudi base for command of U.S. air operations over Afghanistan, but it did not permit U.S. airstrikes from it.

UAE

The United Arab Emirates, the third country that recognized the Taliban regime, is emerging as another major donor to Afghanistan. In addition to deploying about 250 troops to the U.S.-led effort (most of which are not under ISAF command), the UAE has donated at least $135 million to Afghanistan since 2002, according to the Afghan Finance Ministry. Projects funded include housing in Qandahar, roads in Kabul, a hospital in Zabol province, and a university in Khost. At the same time, the UAE property market has been an outlet for investment by Afghan leaders who may have acquired their funds through soft loans from the scandal-plagued Kabul Bank or through corruption connected to donor contracts or other businesses.

Qatar

Until 2011, Qatar was not regarded as a significant player on the Afghanistan issue. It had not recognized the Taliban regime when it was in power, and was said to have little influence with Taliban figures interested in reconciliation. Since late 2011, Qatar has increased its profile as host of some Taliban negotiators there and, more recently, the Taliban political office. The United States views Qatar as less influenced by Pakistan than is Saudi Arabia, and this might explain why the United States pushed for Qatar to be the host of Taliban political office outside Afghanistan. Karzai's two visits to Qatar in 2013, were related to the opening of the Taliban office in Doha.

AID AND ECONOMIC DEVELOPMENT

Experts have long believed that accelerating economic development is pivotal to Afghanistan's stability after 2014, at which time donors are likely to reduce their financial involvement in Afghanistan as their military involvement declines. In December 2011, the World Bank released a report warning that an abrupt aid cutoff could lead to fiscal implosion, loss of control over the security sector, the collapse of political authority, and possible civil war. The role of the economy in the success of post-2014 Afghanistan is discussed in an Administration report released in December 2011, called the "U.S. Economic Strategy for Afghanistan."

The Obama Administration maintains relative optimism about the Afghan economy's ability to withstand the military and donor drawdown. The DOD report issued July 2013 says the economy (Gross Domestic Product, GDP) grew 12% in 2012, and other sources say growth has averaged 9% per year since 2001, although much of that growth was fueled by donor aid that accounts for more than 95% of Afghanistan's GDP. Afghan officials stated in December 2011 that Afghanistan will need at least $10 billion in donated funds per year from 2014 until 2025, at which time Afghanistan expects to be financially self-sufficient.

The DOD report says the government is increasingly able to execute parts of its budget and deliver basic goods and services - even though the government is working with very small amounts of domestically-generated revenue. Government revenues have increased steadily, but still only totaled about $2 billion in revenue for all of 2012. The government had predicted $2.5 billion in revenue for 2013 out of the total $7 billion budget adopted, but revenue was reported in April 2013 to be running about 20% lower than projections. The Afghan government revenue comes mostly through taxation (68%), including through a flat 20% corporate tax rate, and most of the remainder from customs duties. Afghan officials say that uncertainty about stability after 2014 has caused some provincial governors to withhold customs revenue from the central government—one key cause of the reported revenue shortfall. The tax system has been computerized since 2001. Because the government takes in so little revenue relative to its needs, donors provided at least two-thirds of total Afghan government expenditures (operating budget and development budget) in 2012.

Since the international community intervened in Afghanistan in 2001, there have been debates over many aspects of aid to Afghanistan, including amounts, mechanisms for delivery, donor coordination, and distribution within Afghanistan. Some of the more stable provinces, such as Bamiyan and Balkh, complain that

80% of international aid has flowed to the restive provinces and ignoring the needs of poor Afghans in peaceful areas.

Adding to the complexity of strategy development is the analysis that some economic sectors in Afghanistan have been developed largely with private investment, including by wealthy or well-connected Afghans who have founded companies. Therefore, it is often difficult to determine the effects on Afghanistan's economy of aid, as compared to the effects of investment, trade, and other variables. As noted above, as part of the U.S. strategy, in July 2011 then Secretary of State Clinton and other U.S. officials articulated a post-transition vision of greater Afghan economic integration in the region and its role in a "New Silk Road" trading pattern that would presumably accelerate Afghan private sector growth and customs revenue receipts.

Further hindering Afghanistan is that its economy and society are still fragile after decades of warfare that left about 2 million dead, 700,000 widows and orphans, and about 1 million Afghan children raised in refugee camps outside Afghanistan. More than 3.5 million Afghan refugees have since returned, although a comparable number remain outside Afghanistan. The literacy rate is very low and Afghanistan has a small, although growing, pool of skilled labor, middle managers, accountants, and information professionals. And, the widespread government corruption in Afghanistan, which is analyzed in greater detail in CRS Report RS21922, *Afghanistan: Politics, Elections, and Government Performance*, by Kenneth Katzman, has caused some donors to withhold funds or to avoid giving aid directly to the Afghan government.

U.S. Assistance to Afghanistan

During the 1990s, the United States was the largest single provider of assistance to the Afghan people even though no U.S. aid went directly to the Taliban government when it was in power during 1996-2001; monies were provided through relief organizations. Between 1985 and 1994, the United States had a cross-border aid program for Afghanistan, implemented by USAID personnel based in Pakistan. Citing the difficulty of administering this program, there was no USAID mission for Afghanistan from the end of FY1994 until the reopening of the U.S. Embassy in Afghanistan in late 2001.

For all of FY2002-FY2012, the United States provided about $83 billion in assistance, including military "train and equip" for the ANA and ANP (which is about $51 billion of these funds). The figures in the tables, which include aid costs for FY2012 and the request for FY2013, do not include costs for U.S. combat operations. Those costs amount are/estimated to be about $90 billion in FY2010, $104 billion for FY2011, $93 billion for FY2012, and $82 billion for FY2013. When those costs are included, the United States has spent about $557 billion on the Afghanistan effort during FY2002-2012.

Aid Oversight and Conditionality

Some laws have required the withholding of U.S. aid subject to Administration certification of Afghan compliance on a variety of issues, including: counter-narcotics efforts, corruption, vetting of the Afghan security forces, Afghan human rights practices and protection of women's rights, and other issues. Prior to 2013, required certifications had been made and virtually no U.S. funds had been withheld. In mid-2013, following reports that the CIA has been giving cash payments to President's Karzai's office and National Security Council to be used at their discretion, the Ranking Senator of the Senate Foreign Relations Committee, Senator Bob Corker, placed a hold on about $75 million in U.S governance funds, subject to Administration explanations of the rationale for the payments. Legislation proposed in the 113th Congress would have reduced U.S. aid to Afghanistan by a multiple of the amount of funds Afghanistan sought to charge the U.S. military to ship equipment out of the country. The U.S. outcry against the fines apparently caused the Afghan government to drop the levy in early August 2013.

Some in Congress want to ensure independent oversight of U.S. aid to Afghanistan; the conference report on the FY2008 defense authorization bill (P.L. 110-181) established a "special inspector general" for Afghanistan reconstruction, (SIGAR) modeled on a similar outside auditor for Iraq. The SIGAR issues quarterly reports and specific audits of aspects of Afghan governance and security, with particular attention to how U.S.-provided funds have been used. The SIGAR, as of July 2012, is John Sopko. Some Executive branch agencies, including USAID, have criticized some SIGAR audits as inaccurate or as highlighting problems that the agencies are already correcting.

Aid Authorization: Afghanistan Freedom Support Act

A key post-Taliban aid authorization bill, S. 2712, the Afghanistan Freedom Support Act (AFSA) of 2002 (P.L. 107-327, December 4, 2002), as amended, authorized about $3.7 billion in U.S. civilian aid for FY2003-FY2006. The law, whose authority has now expired, was intended to create a central source for allocating funds; that aid strategy was not implemented. However, some of the humanitarian, counter-narcotics, and governance assistance targets authorized by the act were met or exceeded by appropriations. No Enterprise Funds authorized by the act have been appropriated. The act authorized the following:

- $15 million per year in counter-narcotics assistance FY2003-FY2006);
- $10 million per year for FY2003-FY2005 for political development, including national, regional, and local elections;
- $80 million total to benefit women and for Afghan human rights oversight ($15 million per year for FY2003-FY2006 for the Afghan Ministry of Women's Affairs, and $5 million per year for FY2003-FY2006 to the Human Rights Commission of Afghanistan);
- $425 million per year for FY2003-FY2006 in humanitarian and development aid;
- $300 million for an Enterprise Fund; and
- $550 million in drawdowns of defense articles and services for Afghanistan and regional militaries. (The original law provided for $300 million in drawdowns. That was increased by subsequent appropriations laws.)

A subsequent law (P.L. 108-458, December 17, 2004), implementing the recommendations of the 9/11 Commission, contained "The Afghanistan Freedom Support Act Amendments of 2004." The subtitle mandated the appointment of a U.S. coordinator of policy on Afghanistan and requires additional Administration reports to Congress.

A bill in the 110th Congress to reauthorize AFSA, H.R. 2446, passed by the House on June 6, 2007 (406-10). It would have authorized about $1.7 billion in U.S. economic aid and $320 in military aid (including drawdowns of equipment) per year for several years. A Senate version (S. 3531), with fewer provisions than the House bill, was not taken up by the full Senate.

Direct Support to the Afghan Government

Currently, the United States disburses more than 47% of its donated aid funds through the Afghan government. The Kabul Conference (July 20, 2010) communique endorsed a goal of increasing that to about 50% and for 80% of all funds to align with Afghan government priorities. USAID has approved 14 ministries to receive direct U.S. aid.

The United States channels much of its direct aid through the Afghanistan Reconstruction Trust Fund (ARTF), run by the World Bank. Donors have contributed about $6 billion to the ARTF, the funds of which are about equally split between funding Afghan salaries and priority development investments. Through FY2012, the USAID has provided about $2 billion to the ARTF.

National Solidarity Program

Through the ARTF, the United States supports an Afghan government program that promotes local decision making on development—the "National Solidarity Program" (NSP). Donors have provided the program with over $600 million, about 90% of which has been U.S. funding. The program provides block grants of up to $60,000 per project to local councils to implement their priority projects, most of which are water projects. The program has given at least 20,000 grants to a total of 21,600 villages that participate in the program—participation requires setting up a Community Development Council (CDC) to help decide on what projects should be funded. The Afghan implementer is the Ministry of Rural Rehabilitation and Development. It is widely hailed by many institutions as a highly successful, Afghan-run program, although its contributions to improving local governance are unclear. U.S. funds for the program are drawn from a broad category of ESF for "good governance." P.L. 111-32, a FY2009 supplemental, earmarked $70 million to defray a large part of a shortfall in that program. The FY2010 consolidated appropriation (P.L. 111-117) earmarked another $175 million in ESF for the NSP.

Afghanistan Infrastructure Trust Fund

A fund was set up in early 2013 to channel some U.S. aid directly to Afghanistan, other than the U.S. aid already going directly. The Afghanistan Infrastructure Trust Fund is managed by the Asian Development Bank. An initial U.S. contribution of $45 million was made in March 2013, but is expected to be followed by tens of millions more to support a power grid project running north-south.

OTHER DONOR AID

As shown in Table 9, non-U.S. donors, including such institutions as the EU and the Asian Development Bank, have provided over $29 billion in assistance to Afghanistan since the fall of the Taliban. When combined with U.S. aid, this by far exceeds the $27.5 billion for reconstruction identified by the IMF as required for 2002-2010. Major pledges have been made primarily at donor conferences such as Tokyo (2002), Berlin (April 2004), Kabul (April 2005), London (February 2006), Paris (June 2008), and London (January 2010).

Among multilateral lending institutions, the World Bank is expected to be key to sustaining Afghanistan long term. In May 2002, the World Bank reopened its office in Afghanistan after 20 years. Its projects have been concentrated in the telecommunications and road and sewage sectors. The Asian Development Bank (ADB) has also been playing a major role in Afghanistan, including in financing railway construction. Another of its projects in Afghanistan was funding the paving of a road from Qandahar to the border with Pakistan, and as noted above, it is contributing to a project to bring electricity from Central Asia to Afghanistan. On the eve of the London conference on January 28, 2010, the IMF and World Bank announced $1.6 billion in Afghanistan debt relief.

July 8,2012, Tokyo Conference

Identifying sources of post-2014 assistance (2012-2022 is termed the "transformation decade") was the focus of an international conference on Afghanistan in Tokyo on July 8, 2012. At the conference, the United States and its partners pledged a total of $16 billion in aid to Afghanistan through 2015 ($4 billion per year for 2012-2015) and agreed to sustain support through 2017 at levels at or near the past decade. As part of that overall pledge, at the conference, then Secretary Clinton said the Administration would ask Congress to sustain U.S. aid to Afghanistan at roughly the levels it has been through 2017. Among other major pledges, Japan pledged $5 billion over five years (2012-2017), and Germany pledged $550 million over four years (2014-2016).

The Tokyo Mutual Accountability Framework issued in concert with the final conference declaration lays out requirements of the Afghan government in good governance, anti-corruption, holding free and fair elections, and human rights. As an incentive, if Afghanistan meets the benchmarks, the Framework will increase (to 10% by 2014 and to 20% by 2024) the percentage of aid provided through the Afghanistan Reconstruction Trust Fund (ARTF) and other incentive mechanisms. The ARTF gives Kabul the maximum discretion in use of the donated funds. A senior officials meeting held in Kabul on July 3, 2013 to review the Afghan performance found that the Afghan government had met only a few of the stipulated benchmarks and was making slow progress on most of the others.

Development in Key Sectors

Efforts to build the legitimate economy are showing some results, by accounts of senior U.S. officials. Some sectors are being developed primarily (although not exclusively) with private investment funding. There has been substantial new construction, particularly in Kabul, including luxury hotels; a $25 million Coca Cola bottling factory (opened in September 2006); apartment and office buildings; and marriage halls and other structures. The bottling factory is located near the Bagrami office park (another private initiative), which includes several other factories. The Serena luxury hotel was built by the Agha Khan foundation, a major investor in Afghanistan. Phase one of a major, multi-billion dollar development near the Kabul airport, called "New Kabul City," is in the early stages of construction. An arm of DOD, called the Task Force for Business and Stability Operations facilitated some of the private investment that has occurred.

On the other hand, uncertainty about the post-2014 political and security situation is causing some Afghan businessmen to relocate outside the country, or to develop external components of their business in case the situation in Afghanistan deteriorates. Others say that private investment could have been healthier if not for the influence exercised over it by various faction leaders and Karzai relatives.

Education

Despite the success in enrolling Afghan children in school since the Taliban era (8 million in school, of which about 40% are girls), continuing Taliban attacks on schools have caused some to close. Afghanistan's university system is said to be highly underfunded, in part because Afghans are entitled to free higher education (to the B.A. level) by the Constitution, which means that demand for the higher education far outstrips Afghan resources. The shortfall is impeding the development of a large enough pool of skilled workers for the Afghan government. Afghanistan requires about $35 million to operate its universities and institutes for one year; USAID spent about $20 million to help fund those activities in FY2012. A substantial portion of USAID funds have gone directly to the Ministry of Education for the printing and distribution of textbooks.

Health

The health care sector, as noted by Afghan observers, has made considerable gains in reducing infant mortality and giving about 65% of the population at least some access to health professionals. Some USAID funds for health have gone directly to the Ministry of Health to contract with international NGOs to buy medical supplies for clinics. Egypt operates a 65-person field hospital at Bagram Air Base that instructs Afghan physicians, and Jordan operates a similar facility in Mazar-e-Sharif. A SIGAR report of early September 2013 said that no further U.S. funding should be provided to the Public Health Ministry "until program costs are validated as legitimate" - a recommendation focused on a $236 million USAID program called "Partnership Contracts for Health" that provides immunizations, prenatal exams, and equipment and salaries in 13 provinces. However, USAID said no U.S. funds are directly provided to the ministry and that USAID had set up a unit in the ministry to monitor grants and contracts.

Roads

Road building is considered a U.S. priority and has been USAID's largest project category there, taking up about 25% of USAID spending since the fall of the Taliban. Roads are considered key to enabling Afghan farmers to bring legitimate produce to market in a timely fashion, and former commander of U.S. forces in Afghanistan General Eikenberry (later Ambassador) said "where the roads end, the Taliban begin." About 3,000 miles of roads have been built since 2001, with another 1,500 miles under construction. The major road, the Ring Road, has been completely repaved using funds from various donors, including substantial funds from the Asian Development Bank. Among other major projects completed are a road from Qandahar to Tarin Kowt, (Uruzgan province) built by U.S. military personnel, inaugurated in 2005; a road linking the Panjshir Valley to Kabul; a Khost-Gardez road; and a Salang Bypass Road through Bamiyan province. In several of the most restive provinces, U.S. funds, including CERP, have been used to build small roads linking farming communities to the markets for their products.

The Afghan government has committed to developing an East-West road across Afghanistan, from Herat to Kabul. However, funding only for a few segments (Herat to Chest-e-Sharif, and Maidany Shar to Bamiyan, and Bamiyan City to Yakowlang in that same province) has been identified, from Italy and Japan.

Bridges

Afghan officials say that trade with Central Asia increased after a bridge over the Panj River, connecting Afghanistan and Tajikistan, opened in late 2007. The bridge was built with $33 million in (FY2005) U.S. assistance. The bridge is helping what press reports say is robust reconstruction and economic development in the relatively peaceful and ethnically homogenous province of Panjshir, the political base of the Northern Alliance.

Railways

Afghanistan is beginning to develop functioning railways—a sector it lacked as a legacy of security policy during the late 19th century that saw railroads as facilitating invasion of Afghanistan. Rail is considered increasing crucial to Afghanistan's ability to develop its mineral wealth because it is the means by which minerals can be exported to neighboring countries. Three railway projects are underway. One, a 75 mile line from Mazar-i-Sharif to Hairaton, on the border with Uzbekistan, was completed in March 2011 with $165 million from the Asian Development Bank. It began operations in early 2012 and shortly thereafter began carrying its peak capacity of 4,000 tons of cargo per month. In September 2012, the government established the Afghan Rail Authority to maintain and regulate this sector.

Some planned rail lines might not get built if foreign investors believe they will not yield a significant payoff for their projects in the mining sector. In particular, China has committed to building a rail line from its Mes Aynak copper mine project to the northern border. A spur to the Hajji Gak iron mine would be funded by India (about $1 billion) as part of its project there. However, there are indications India and China might opt instead truck their minerals out, a process that would slow full exploitation of these mines. There are also plans to build a line from Herat and Kabul to Qandahar, and then on to the border with Pakistan. The planned railways will link Afghanistan to the former Soviet railway system in Central Asia, and to Pakistan's railway system, increasing Afghanistan's economic integration in the region.

Electricity

This sector has been a major U.S. focus because the expansion of electricity proves popular with the Afghan public. USAID has spent $88 million to help the national power company, Da Afghanistan Breshna Sherkas (DABS), generate revenue from power provision and manage the nation's electricity grid. However, the SIGAR reported in an April 2013 audit that DABS will require Afghan government subsidies beyond March 2014, at which time it was supposed to become self-sufficient financially. Some additional U.S. funding for Afghanistan power projects come from an "Infrastructure Fund" funded by DOD. That authority was provided in the FY2011 DOD authorization bill (P.L. 111-383).

The Afghan government set a goal for electricity to reach 65% of households in urban areas and 25% in rural areas by 2010—a goal that was not met—but USAID says that as of April 2013, DABS serves about 28% of the population. Power shortages in Kabul, caused in part by the swelling of Kabul's population to about 4 million, have been alleviated as of 2009 by Afghan government agreements with several Central Asian neighbors to import electricity, as well as construction of new plants such as that at Tarakhil in north Kabul. Kabul is now generally lit up at night. There has been some criticism of the 105 Megawatt Tarakhil plant, built at a cost of about $300 million, because of the high costs of fuel, the questionable need for it, and the possible inability of the Afghan authorities to maintain it. USAID has spent a $35 million to help the national electric utility—operate and maintain the plant. In January 2013, Afghanistan gained formal title to the Tarakhil plant as well as two less efficient power plants built by Iran in western Afghanistan. Russia has refurbished some long dormant hydroelectric projects in Afghanistan that were suspended when Soviet troops withdrew in 1989.

Much of the U.S. electricity capacity effort has been focused on southern Afghanistan. The key long-term project is to expand the capacity of the Kajaki Dam, located in Helmand Province ("Kandahar-Helmand Power Project," KHPP). Currently, two turbines are operating—one was always working, and the second was repaired by USAID contractors. This has doubled electricity production in the south and caused small factories and other businesses to come to flourish. As of December 31, 2012, USAID has obligated $140 million to the project. USAID had planned to further expand capacity of the dam by installing a third turbine (which there is a berth for but which never had a turbine installed.) In September 2008, 4,000 NATO troops (Operation Ogap Tsuka) delivered components of the third turbine to the dam. The third turbine was expected to be operational by late 2009 but technical and security problems delayed the project. USAID funded a $266 million contract to Black and Veatch in December 2010 to complete the installation of the third turbine. However, in early 2013, USAID decided to instead provide these funds to DABS so that it could contract for completion of the work. Some critics say that decision might derail the third turbine project entirely. Another $205 million will be spent by the Army Corps of Engineers to improve power lines and substations fed by the dam.

In the interim, and to the consternation of some who want long-term, sustainable solutions for Afghanistan rather than short-term palliatives, since early 2011 the U.S. military and USAID have implemented a plan ("Kandahar Power Bridging Solution") to build smaller substations and generator projects that can bring more electricity to Qandahar and other places in the south quickly. The initiative was pursued in order to facilitate the U.S.-military led counter-insurgency strategy in Qandahar. Some of the power provided by additional diesel generators is being used to supply the Qandahar Industrial Park. However, the SIGAR reported in July 2012 that five of the seven projects of the Bridging Solution are at least six months behind schedule, and that many aspects of the project depend on progress on the Kajaki Dam and other projects that have completion dates beyond 2014. President Karzai has said in interviews, including on CNN on June 26, 2011, that he favors the longer-term Kajaki Dam project rather than the interim generator project. Other criticism centers on the cost of fuel for the diesel generators, for which the Afghans are dependent on continued U.S. funding.

The SIGAR also recommended that some attention be shifted to building up northern power distribution routes rather than focusing exclusively on the south and east. Some of the USAID funds provided to DABS, including through the Afghanistan Infrastructure Trust Fund above, are being used to build a north-south power grid.

There is also an apparent increasing emphasis on providing electricity to individual homes and villages through small solar power installations. A contractor to USAID, IRG, has provided small solar powered-electricity generators to homes in several districts of Afghanistan, alleviating the need to connect such homes to the national power grid. However, there are technical drawbacks, including weather-related inconsistency of power supply and the difficulty of powering appliances that require substantial power. The U.S. broadcasting service to Afghanistan, Radio Azadi, run by Radio Free Europe/Radio Liberty, has given out 20,000 solar-powered radios throughout Afghanistan.

Agriculture

Even though only about 12.5% of Afghanistan's land is arable, about 80% of Afghans live in rural areas and the agriculture sector has always been key to Afghanistan's economy and stability. The late Ambassador Holbrooke, including in his January 2010 strategy document, outlined U.S. policy to boost Afghanistan's agriculture sector not only to reduce drug production but also as an engine of economic growth. Prior to the turmoil that engulfed Afghanistan in the late 1970s, Afghanistan was a major exporter of agricultural products. From 2002 until the end of 2012, USAID has obligated $1.9 billion to build capacity at the Ministry of Agriculture, Irrigation, and Livestock (MAIL), increase access to markets, and provide alternatives to poppy cultivation, according to the January 30, 2013, SIGAR report.

USAID programs have helped Afghanistan double its legitimate agricultural output over the past five years. One emerging "success story" is growing Afghan exports of high-quality pomegranate juice called Anar. Other countries are promoting not only pomegranates but also saffron rice and other crops that draw buyers outside Afghanistan. Another emerging success story is Afghanistan's November 2010 start of exports of raisins to Britain. Wheat production was robust in 2009 because of healthy prices for that crop, and Afghanistan is again self-sufficient in wheat production. The U.S. Department of Agriculture has about 110 personnel in Afghanistan on long-term and priority projects; there are also at least 25 agriculture experts from USAID in Afghanistan. Their efforts include providing new funds to buy seeds and agricultural equipment, and to encourage agri-business. In addition, the National Guard from several states deployed nine "Agribusiness Development Teams" to help Afghan farmers with water management, soil enhancement, crop cultivation, and improving the development and marketing of their goods.

U.S. strategy has addressed not only crop choice but also trying to construct the entirety of the infrastructure needed for a healthy legitimate agriculture sector, including road building, security of the routes to agriculture markets, refrigeration, storage, transit through Pakistan and other transportation of produce, building legitimate sources of financing, and other aspects of the industry. U.S. officials in Kabul say that Pakistan's restrictions on trade between Afghanistan and India had prevented a rapid expansion of Afghan pomegranate exports to that market, but the transit trade agreement between Afghanistan and Pakistan is expected to alleviate some of these bottlenecks. Dubai is another customer for Afghan pomegranate exports.

There is a vibrant timber industry in the northeast provinces. However, the exports are illegal. Deforestation has been outlawed because of the potential for soil erosion and other economic and environmental effects.

In terms of specific programming, USAID has a $150 million program for the relatively safe areas of Afghanistan to continue to develop licit crops. The Incentives Driving Economic Alternatives for the North, East, and West (IDEA-NEW) program is planned to run through FY2014. In southern and eastern areas of the country where counterinsurgency operations are ongoing, USAID's $474 million Afghanistan Vouchers for Increased Production in Agriculture (AVIPA-Plus) program ran through FY2011 and includes initiatives coordinated with U.S. counterinsurgency operations in Helmand and Qandahar provinces. The program provides vouchers for wheat seed, fertilizer, and tools, in addition to supporting cash for work programs and small grants to local cooperatives.

Telecommunications

Several Afghan telecommunications firms have been formed and over $1.2 billion in private investment has flowed into this sector, according to the DOD Task Force for Business and Stability Operations. With startup funds from the Agha Khan Foundation (the Agha Khan is leader of the Isma'ili community, which is prevalent in northern Afghanistan), the highly successful Roshan cellphone company was founded. Another Afghan cellphone firm is Afghan Wireless. The most significant post-Taliban media network is Tolo Television, owned by Moby Media. U.S. funds are being used to supplement the private investment; a $4 million U.S. grant, in partnership with the Asia Consultancy Group, is being used to construct communication towers in Bamiyan and Ghor provinces. The Afghan government is attempting to link all major cities by fiber optic cable.

Airlines

The 52-year-old national airline, Ariana, is said to be in significant financial trouble due to corruption that has affected its safety ratings and left it unable to service a heavy debt load. However, there are new privately run airlines, such as Safi Air (run by the Safi Group, which has built a modern mall in Kabul), and Kam Air. Another, Pamir, was ordered closed in 2010 due to safety concerns. In January 2013, the U.S. military ceased contracting with an Afghan airline, Kam Air, on the grounds that it was helping traffic opium; the U.S. military rescinded the ruling after Afghan complaints that questioned the allegation. The Afghan government agreed to investigate the allegations.

Mining and Gems

Afghanistan's mining sector has been largely dormant since the Soviet invasion. Some Afghan leaders complain that not enough has been done to revive such potentially lucrative industries as minerals mining, such as of copper and lapis lazuli (a stone used in jewelry). The issue became more urgent in June 2010 when the DOD Task Force for Business and Stability Operations announced, based on surveys, that Afghanistan may have untapped minerals worth over $1 trillion. Although copper and iron are the largest categories by value, there are believed to also be significant reserves of such minerals as lithium in western Afghanistan—lithium is crucial to the new batteries being used to power electric automobiles. However, as noted above, some of the expected revenue from this sector might not materialize if investors decide not to build rail lines needed to export the minerals from Afghanistan in large volumes. An additional brake on investment is the lack of legislative action on a new Law on Mines. The Afghan cabinet approved a draft in February 2013 and sent it to the National Assembly in July 2013, but the Assembly has not acted on it to date.

Mes Aynak Copper Field. A major project, signed in November 2007, is with China Metallurgical Group for the company to invest $3.0 billion to develop Afghanistan's Mes Aynak copper field in Lowgar Province. The agreement, viewed as generous to the point where it might not be commercially profitable for China Metallurgical Group, includes construction of two coal-fired electric power plants (one of which will supply more electricity to Kabul city); a segment of railway; and a road from the project to Kabul. Work on the mine reportedly has been slowed by various factors, including the need to clear mines in the area and to excavate ancient Buddhist artifacts that local activists insist be preserved. Actual extraction was expected to begin in mid-2012, but has not begun as of April 2013. U.S. forces do not directly protect the project, but U.S. forces have set up small bases on some of the roads leading to the mine project to provide general stability there.

Hajji Gak Iron Ore Project. In September 2011 seven bids were submitted for another large mining project, the Hajji Gak iron ore mine (which may contain 60 billion tons of iron ore) in Bamiyan Province. The bids—from Chinese, Indian, and other firms—were evaluated and, in late 2011, the Steel Authority for India Ltd. (SAIL) was awarded the largest share of the project. One of the four blocs of the project was awarded to Kilo Gold of Canada. As of the end of 2012, the contract had not been finalized. The project is expected to generate $200 million in annual government revenues when fully operational—expected by 2017—although this level might not be reached unless the associated rail lines are built to allow export in high volumes.

Other mining projects have been awarded (subject to finalized contract negotiations):

- The Balkhab coooper mine in Sar-i-Pol Province, awarded to Afghan Gold and Minerals Co.
- The Shaida copper mine in Herat Province, awarded to Afghan Minerals Group
- The Badakshan gold project, in that province, awarded to Turkish-Afghan Mining Co.
- Zarkashan copper and gold project (Ghazni Province), awarded to Sterling Mining/Belhasa International LLC.

Oil, Gas, and Related Pipelines

Years of war have stunted developed of a hydrocarbons energy sector in Afghanistan. The country has no hydrocarbons export industry and a small refining sector that provides some of Afghanistan's needs for gasoline or other fuels. Most of Afghanistan's fuel comes from neighboring states. However, Afghanistan's prospects in this sector appeared to brighten by the announcement in March 2006 of an estimated 3.6 billion barrels of oil and 36.5 trillion cubic feet of gas reserves, amounts that could make Afghanistan self-sufficient in energy or even able to export. In a major development, on December 15, 2010, the Afghan government let a six-month contract to a local firm, Ghazanfar Neft Gas (Ghazanfar Group), to collect and market crude oil from the Angot field in northern Afghanistan (part of a field that may contain 80 million barrels of oil), initially producing at the low rate of 800 barrels per day.

The energy sector took a major step forward with the awarding in early 2012 of development rights to the Amu Darya basin (northern Afghanistan) oil fields to China National Petroleum Co. The field began producing at about 5,000 barrels per day in early

2013, with a longer-term potential of 145,000 barrels per day. However, the production did not increase in 2012 because the companies involved did not reach agreement to sell or process the crude oil from the field. The $3 billion development has a local partner, the Watan Group, owned by Karzai relatives Rashid and Rateb Popal.

Among pending development, in November 2012 a consortium consisting of Kuwait Energy, Dragon Oil of UAE, Turkey's state-owned TPAO, and the Ghazanfar Group had bid to develop part of the "Afghan-Tajik Basin," estimated to hold 950 million barrels of oil, 7 trillion cubic feet of gas, and other gas liquids. A solicitation is to be offered later in 2013 to develop a large oil field in Balkh Province (Kasha Kari bloc), estimated to hold 1.8 billion barrels of oil. Exxon-Mobil is reportedly weighting a bid on the project—an action that Afghan officials say would instill substantial confidence in the investment climate in Afghanistan.

USAID has funded test projects to develop gas resources in northern Afghanistan. A key project is to build a 200 megawatt gas-fired thermal plant and associated transmission lines in northern Afghanistan ("Shehbergan Program"). The plant would be part of a plan to link Afghanistan's natural gas field in Shehbergan to the population center in Mazar-e-Sharif. The total cost of the project, targeted for 2016 completion, is estimated at $580 million, provided by USAID, the Overseas Private Investment Corp. (OPIC), the Asian Development Bank, and the Afghan government.

Another pilot project, funded by the Task Force for Business and Stability Operations, is to develop filling stations and convert cars to use compressed natural gas (CNG), which is produced in the gas field in Shehbergan and could provide an inexpensive source of fuel in the future.

TAPI (Turkmenistan-Afghanistan-Pakistan-India) Gas Pipeline Project.

Another long-stalled major energy project appears to be gaining momentum. During 1996-1998, the Clinton Administration supported proposed natural gas and oil pipelines through western Afghanistan as an incentive for the warring factions to cooperate. A consortium led by Los Angeles-based Unocal Corporation proposed a $7.5 billion Central Asia Gas Pipeline that would originate in southern Turkmenistan and pass through Afghanistan to Pakistan, with possible extensions into India. The deterioration in U.S.-Taliban relations after 1998 suspended hopes for the pipeline projects. At a summit meeting in late May 2002, the leaders of Turkmenistan, Afghanistan, and Pakistan agreed to revive the project. Sponsors held an inaugural meeting on July 9, 2002, in Turkmenistan, signing a series of preliminary agreements. On December 12, 2010, in the Turkmenistan capital Ashkabad, the relevant leaders reaffirmed their intent to complete the project. In late 2011, the Asian Development Bank has agreed to finance the project, removing what had been a major hurdle. U.S. officials view this project as a superior alternative to a proposed gas pipeline from Iran to India, transiting Pakistan.

TRADE PROMOTION/RECONSTRUCTION OPPORTUNITY ZONES

The key to U.S. economic strategy, as exemplified by the New Silk Road strategy, is to encourage Afghanistan's trade relationships. The United States is doing so by promoting regional economic integration as well as through bilateral economic agreements with Afghanistan. A key to the strategy was accomplished in 2011 when Afghanistan and Pakistan finalized provisions to implement their 2010 transit trade agreement. To facilitate Afghanistan's ability to increase trade, USAID is funding a five year project ($63 million total during 2010-2014) to simplify the customs clearance process. This includes new import procedures that have reduced the time needed for imports to clear customs by 45%. On December 13, 2004, the 148 countries of the World Trade Organization voted to start membership talks with Afghanistan.

Earlier, in September 2004, the United States and Afghanistan signed a bilateral trade and investment framework agreement (TIFA), and most of Afghanistan's exports are eligible for duty free treatment under the enhanced Generalized System of Preferences (GSP) program. The Administration economic strategy report of December 2011 says the Administration is reaching out to Afghan exporters and U.S. importers of Afghan products to make increased use of the GSP program. The TIFA is seen as a prelude to a broader and more complex bilateral free trade agreement, but negotiations on an FTA have not yet begun.

Another initiative supported by the United States is the establishment of joint Afghan-Pakistani "Reconstruction Opportunity Zones" (ROZs) which would be modeled after "Qualified Industrial Zones" run by Israel and Jordan in which goods produced in the zones receive duty free treatment for import into the United States. Bills in the 110th Congress, S. 2776 and H.R. 6387, would have authorized the President to proclaim duty-free treatment for imports from ROZs to be designated by the President. In the 111th Congress, a version of these bills was introduced (S. 496 and H.R. 1318). President Obama specifically endorsed passage of these bills in his March 2009 strategy announcement. H.R. 1318 was incorporated into H.R. 1886, a major Pakistan aid appropriation that passed by the House on June 11, 2009, and was then appended to H.R. 2410. However, the version of the major Pakistan aid bill that became law (S. 1707, P.L. 111-73) did not authorize ROZs.

7

Status of Women in Post Taliban Afghanistan

This chapter attempts to study, investigate and analyse the condition and status of womenfolk in Afghanistan after the United States-led invasion of the country in November-December 2001. It includes information and findings to clearly illustrate the actual state of affairs relating to women in the war-ravaged country. On the basis of data collection and findings, the paper aims at drawing conclusions and making recommendations for the improvement of the situation and status of the women in present-day Afghanistan.

Although it looks at the condition of women in Afghanistan after the fall of the Taliban regime, makes the Taliban era a point of reference against which to measure up the efforts made by the current U.S-installed regime with regard to women's rights. This, however, does not imply a comparative approach with the women's rights situation under the Taliban. What it does imply, however, is an assessment of the stated objectives regarding the liberation of women, laid out by the NATO and the Allied occupation forces in Afghanistan.

After the Allied victory in Afghanistan in 2001, hopes regarding a new Afghanistan ushering in a liberation and deliverance for womenfolk who had been suffering in the war-torn country were high. After the intense international criticism of the Taliban's treatment of women in the country, it was expected that the international community would help bring about a radical positive change in the lives of women, as per their commitments. A number of reforms were in fact initiated and development projects launched. Ambitious targets regarding women's liberation were set. Nine years since then, an objective assessment of the fulfilment of the original commitment to the cause can be made only through a thorough explanation and understanding of the actual condition of women in Afghanistan. To assess the real situation and status of the Afghan woman today, one needs to study the extent of freedom they have for making their own choices in important matters of their lives_ education, career, marriage etc. It also involves an assessment of the security of environment for women to conduct their affairs, the efficiency of education and health facilities for them as well as their access to a fair justice system. A significant improvement in these at par with the original goals and targets set out can help lead towards a genuine conclusive appraisal of the women's rights situation in present-day post-Taliban Afghanistan.

BACKGROUND

When the Taliban took over Afghanistan, an ever-increasing stream of criticism of their orthodox ideology and policies directed itself at the new regime. Among numerous criticisms levelled at the regime was the allegation that the Taliban oppressed and victimized women through their orthodox interpretation of religious law and its ruthless imposition. The traditional Afghan 'burqa' became a symbol of oppression and pictures of women being beaten by the Taliban in public for offences were telecast all across the globe. On September 22 2001, CNN aired the documentary 'Beneath the Veil', which claimed an audience of five million Americans, building revulsion in their minds against burqa-clad women being beaten up. The documentary was aired several times on numerous channels in various talk shows and was perhaps the most watched documentary in CNN's history.[i]In fact, one of the primary factors leading to the rise of censure and disapproval of the Taliban was their treatment of women. The level of attention this issue managed to get was 'unparalleled.' International feminist NGOs were at the forefront of this campaign highlighting the abuse of women's rights under the Taliban and pressed hard the case against the US's recognition of the Taliban regime_ successfully. In 1997, the US State Department criticized the Taliban on the grounds of gender discrimination 'officially' in the annual report. Two years later, the US Senate passed a unanimous resolution condemning the treatment of women by the Taliban. A 1998 Security Council Resolution no. 1214 demanded the Afghans to stop discriminating against women and girls.

The media gave great attention to the issue as the number of articles on the theme rose dramatically by more than 30 times from August to November 2001. This, therefore, became one of the primary reasons for the US invasion of the country, other than, of course, the foremost 'harbouring terrorists' factor. In fact, Afghanistan became a country where *'for the first time women's rights were used as a justification for international intervention.'* First lady Laura Bush claimed in a radio address on November 17, 2001, *"The fight against terrorism is also a fight for the rights and dignity of women."*

Following the US-aided fall of the Taliban, international organizations, Human Rights NGOs rallied to the assistance of women, *'bolstered up by media images of women in burqas, the full-body veil.'*

According to the Communique of the Revolutionary Association for Women in Afghanistan on December 10, 2007, *"The United States and its allies tried to legitimize their military occupation of Afghanistan under the banner of 'bringing freedom and democracy to the Afghan people."* The same organization, in its March 2008 Communique states, *"After the United States and its allies invaded Afghanistan seven years ago, they misleadingly claimed to bring peace and democracy and to liberate Afghan women from the bleeding fetters of the Taliban..."*

THE CHANGE SETTING IN

Women's rights groups working in Afghanistan both government sponsored and independent do agree that women in Afghanistan today have acquired a variety of rights, at least on paper. Mechanisms employed to empower Afghan women by the new regime after the Taliban's ouster include:

- financial assistance and aid channelized for women's uplift projects and schemes;
- new laws and amendments to previous laws in order to do away with gender bias in the letter of the law;
- fixing quotas for women in government/decision-making institutions;
- the establishment of the Ministry of Women's Affairs which supervises multifarious women's rehabilitation and uplift projects; efforts to politically empower women.

Shortly after the fall of the Taliban to the NATO-Northern Alliance forces, the victors began to manifest their commitment to the objectives originally laid out as a rationale for the invasion. This materialized during the United Nations peace negotiations held in Germany in November and December 2001. According to the settlement, the 1964 constitution of Afghanistan was revived, and was to be reviewed by the elected parliament for amendments. It gave the women of Afghanistan the rights to:

*vote in elections

*serve in the government

*be elected to the parliament

Soon after this, the interim president Hamid Karzai, in a ground-breaking move, appointed two women ministers out of a total of 29 cabinet positions. The Emergency Loya Jirga of June 2002 gave women a 12% representation. President Karzai followed this by appointing four women to key positions in the government, namely: the head of the Afghanistan Independent Human Rights Commission, Health, Women's Affairs and a senior advisory position in the cabinet.

Non Governmental Organizations and Human Rights Groups:

From 2003-2005, the international community has channellized financing worth $72.5 million to Afghanistan through NGOs working for women's rights. The Afghan Human Rights Commission began operation by setting up a special women's rights unit. Under the gender unit of the United Nations Assistance Mission in Afghanistan (UNAMA), international donor agencies committed themselves to women's rights projects. These agencies brought together *'excellent expertise on gender and peace building and women's human rights.'* After the Taliban, a number of NGOs who had quit the country, returned to Pakistan and began to work actively in order to raise awareness about the situation of Afghan women and refugees. These NGOs helped fill the gap in public services whose capacity had been destroyed after prolonged war. Most of the NGOs in Afghanistan work in the areas of women's education, health and income generation. In comparison with the number of such NGOs, there is a relatively fewer number of NGOs working for the advocacy of human rights on the legal front and capacity building within the present infrastructure.

Some of the NGOs currently working in Afghanistan for women's rights include :

i) Afghan Women's Mission
ii) Revolutionary Association of Women of Afghanistan (RAWA)
iii) Afghan Women's Network
iv) Afghanistan Women's Council
v) Afghanistan Women's Education Centre
vi) Canadian Women for Women in Afghanistan
vii) Feminist Majority Foundation
viii) Global Fund for Women
ix) Medica Morale
x) Refugee Women in Development
xi) Womankind Worldwide
xii) FemAid
xiii) PARWAZ
xiv) NEGAR
xv) Voice of Women
xvi) Women for Women International
xvii) Humanitarian Assistance for Women and Children of Afghanistan
xviii) Women's Alliance for Peace and Human Rights in Afghanistan (WAPHA)

Over the years, NGOs for women in Afghanistan have worked consistently for the improvement of women's lives, and have acquired successes on various fronts. So far, almost a 100,000 women have benefited from micro financing loans through international NGOs in the country. Research has been conducted on various sensitive issues regarding women, and the plight of women has been brought into the limelight, and built a strong case for women's rights advocacy and reviewing of government policy and legal stance on specific women-related issues.

These organizations have also sought a return of women into public life. Today several job openings for women in fields such as education, medicine, the media and journalism exist. Radio and television broadcasts in Kabul have once again featured women commentators. Units have been established by these for providing emergency obstetric care and family planning services. Women have been trained as midwives to provide domestic reproductive health services. Roughly 10,000 women have received training for several skills helping them set up small scale cottage industrial units. The training has been provided by the All Afghan Women's Union as well as Women for Women International and the Self Employed Women's Association (SEWA).

The plight of widows in Afghanistan has always been an area of concern. Under the World Food Programme, flour is supplied to women in refugee camps, in particular to destitute war widows or independent mothers, which allows them to bake the traditional bread and sell it for small profit. This has helped generate nominal income for families.

GREATER PARTICIPATION IN POLITICAL ACTIVITY AND ROLE OF THE MEDIA

Important measures by the government include the allotment of 25% seats for women in the lower house of the parliament (Wolesi Jirga), and 17% women's seats in the upper house (Meshrano Jirga). Furthermore, the October 2004 elections showed a massive turnout of women voters. Interestingly, although women comprise 40% of the electorate, the number of women voters outnumbered that of men.

An important step forward has been the establishment of the Ministry of Women's Affairs by the government in early 2002. The Ministry comprises of several resource Centres for women spread over many provinces. These centres are actively imparting vocational training to a number of women. The MOWA has a staff numbering 1,200 working in Kabul and it runs Departments of Women's Affairs in 28 provinces of the country. It has an annual fiscal budget of $ 1.25 million. The mandate of the MOWA as stated in their official documents is *"to support the government in its response to the needs and issues affecting women in all sectors of life in order to attain gender equality and full enjoyment of women's human rights; to ensure Afghan women's legal, economic, social, political and civic rights_ including their rights to be free from all forms of violence and discrimination_ are respected, promoted and fulfilled."* The MOWA aims to work in the following priority areas: health, education, legal protection and economic empowerment. It monitors women's development programmes throughout the country and helps create employment and business opportunities for women. Due to lack of state funds, the MOWA is being financed by the United Nations Development Programme. According to the U S State Department, the United States is spending $2.5 million for the functioning of Women's Resource Centres in 14 provinces. Other international organizations and agencies like the Japanese International Co operation Agency and the German Technical Co operation have also funded some centres. The Microsoft company, Gateway and America On Line Time Warner donate computer equipment and impart technical assistance and training to the Ministry. Hence the MOWA is less of a state institution and is described as 'a large NGO.'

Afghan women have benefited from a variety of training sessions, including United Nations Assistance Mission in Afghanistan (UNAMA)'s induction course for the female delegates of the Loya Jirga and other women in public offices.

The Afghan media has developed considerably, and has helped highlight women's rights issues. Radio transmission reaches 65% of an overwhelmingly illiterate populace. Radio programmes help educate women, and a number of NGOs use radio to get their message across and educate women on important gender issues. The US based NGO Internews is funding 18 radio stations in Afghanistan. Most radio stations broadcast women's programmes on a daily basis. With funds from the United Nations Educational, Scientific and Cultural Organisation (UNESCO), the country's first women-operated FM station 'Voice of Afghan Women' is currently operating. According to Jane Mc Elhone, project director of an NGO IMPACS states *"For many Afghan women who still live very isolated lives, radio can serve as a bridge to the outside world. It can help them develop skills to survive in their daily lives. It can make them feel less alone."*

Role of the International Community

In early 2006, leaders of the Afghan government and the international community met in London to decide goals to be achieved by the country by 2010. One of the goals was to increase the enrolment of women in universities from the current 10,000 to 40,000. The Ministry of Education also decided to make more girls' schools and high schools. In March 2005, the UNICEF and the Ministry of Education began a national campaign to boost girls' education. It has been decided that 75,000 religious workers will be recruited in the campaign to inform the people that educating sons and daughters alike was a duty laid down by Islam.

The Bonn Agreement of 2001 proved to be instrumental in setting the agenda for women's rights in Afghanistan under the interim government. Agence France Press reports a UN representative in the conference states: *"Afghan women have been silenced more than any other group, and the United Nations believes it is important to give them a chance to express their views about what they want the future of Afghanistan to be."*

Reform through State and International Law

On January 12 2002 Afghanistan signed the Declaration of the Essential Rights of the Afghan Women in Dushanbe, Tajikistan, which had been prepared by 300 Afghan women under the auspices of the NEGAR-Support of Women of Afghanistan, a French NGO. The document calls for*'equality between men and women, equal* *protection under the law, institutional education in all disciplines, freedom of movement, freedom of speech and political participation, and the right to wear or no to wear the burqa or the scarf.'* In 2003, Afghanistan signed and ratified the Convention on the Elimination of All Forms of Discrimination Against Women (CEDAW).

The Afghanistan government has entered into numerous treaties and ratified various conventions internationally which pertain to women's human rights. Afghanistan is a member of:

- International Covenant on Economic, Social and Cultural Rights
- International Covenant on Civil and Political Rights
- Convention on the Elimination of all forms of Discrimination Against Women
- Universal Declaration of Human Right

From these it follows that the Afghanistan government has an international obligation to protect the women of Afghanistan. This commitment is reiterated clearly in the Afghan Constitution which was revised and brought into effect by the interim government. The Afghan Constitution mentions the government's duty to observe and respect the rights of women:

Article 7 of the Constitution states, *"The State must abide by the United Nations Charter, international treaties and international conventions that Afghanistan has signed, and the Universal Declaration of Human Rights."*

Article 22 of the Constitution further elaborates: *"Any kind of discrimination and privilege between the citizens of Afghanistan is prohibited. The citizens of Afghanistan, whether men or women, have equal rights and equal duties before the law."*

According to articles 43 and 44 of the Constitution the government is tasked with taking necessary measures to eliminate illiteracy and develop women's education. Article 52 lays down that the state must provide free health care and medical assistance to women.

In March 2005, the Afghan Supreme Court approved a new marriage contract (nikah nama) in order to check forced marriages and child marriages, and to empower women's legal status after marriage. This new marriage document stipulates that if a man wants to marry, he must first make sure that the prospective wife is at least sixteen years of age. This is a legal requirement now. No marriage certificates can be issued for underage brides. This step has been termed as 'courageous reform' by international observers.

According to the Afghan National Development Strategy of 2007 that the government laid out, the government has committed itself to eliminate poverty among women by at least 20%, and ensure that women make up 20% of all public bodies by the year 2010. The Ministry of Women's Affairs has declared the year 2020 as the 'target year' to eliminate gender discrimination in the society at all levels.

The Convention on the Elimination of all forms of Discrimination Against Women (CEDAW) that Afghanistan is signatory to, states in its article 10 that the government is obligated to make efforts in providing for equal rights of men and women in terms of education. In its article 12 the Convention goes on to say that signatory states must take necessary steps for the complete eradication of discrimination in all its forms and manifestations against women, and to prepare grounds for women's access to health services as well as suitable food during pregnancy and lactation. The Convention in its article 14 makes clear that all citizens of a state will be equal before courts and tribunals, and that everyone will have the same rights to a fair and public hearing by an independent and impartial tribunal in accordance with the law. Article 16 of the same reads: *"States shall take all appropriate measures to eliminate discrimination against all matters related to marriage and family relations, and in particular, shall ensure, on the basis of the equality of men and women, the same right to freely choose a spouse."*

According to the International Covenant on Civil and Political Rights that Afghanistan has ratified, no marriage can be entered into without the free and full consent of the intending spouses (article 23, part 3).

The Judicial Reform Commission (JRC) was established in November 2002 and has been mandated, as set out in the Bonn

Agreement, to rebuild the domestic legal *system "in accordance with Islamic principles, international standards, the rule of law and Afghan legal traditions"*. The JRC is responsible for preparing drafts of new Criminal, Criminal Procedure and Family Codes, and for surveying the existing judicial system in Afghanistan. It has also been involved in the training for judges.

Other than that, the Afghan government, recognizing the important role that religious leaders and tribal elders can play in bringing about a positive improvement in the lives of Afghan women, has tried and continues to use religious experts to change attitudes and legitimize rights that the government is under obligation to grant to the women. Fatwas (religious rulings) have been issued in favour of girls' education, as well as for the political participation of women through voting in elections and being part of the democratic process.

It is important to note that Afghanistan's international commitments with regard to improving the status of women at home entail an important responsibility and in fact a legal obligation on the part of the interim government. According to Amnesty International, *"the international standards provide the essential framework for developing national legislation and measures to uphold women's human rights. The government of Afghanistan has the responsibility under international human rights law, and must take every possible step to ensure that women's human rights are protected throughout all stages of the reconstruction process."*

While the government and the international partners of the new regime have made considerable effort in this regard, a true assessment of the sincerity, efficiency and success of these efforts and measures can only be made by looking at the current state of affairs with regard to Afghan women. The 'other side' of the picture, the effects and results of the new policies and efforts, and the lives of women in Afghanistan today.

Women's rights groups claim that women in Afghanistan at present have a variety of rights they did not enjoy earlier. In practice, however, one finds that the changes initiated by the topmost echelons of the administration have not quite filtered through to the grassroots as of yet. For one, the work of NGOs in Afghanistan is severely hampered by the atmosphere of insecurity. The government is as yet unable to restore an atmosphere of security and stability. In fact, human rights activists complain of being subjected to intimidation and threat. The former head of the Ministry of Women's Affairs Safia Amajan was shot dead, and security threats keep numerous others indoors. A worker at the MOWA Headquarters says, *"Women in Afghanistan today no more want to step out of their homes due to the atmosphere of insecurity."* Though women in Afghanistan have managed to hold 25% of seats in the parliament, female politicians and activists face intimidation and violence. Brita Fernandes Schmidt of Womankind Worldwide says, *"My message to the international community is that you need to address specific security issues for women. Activists are being killed and it is not going to be changed unless drastic action is taken."*

Independent organizations and activists working in Afghanistan criticize the government for failing to provide security and materializing commitments made, by not seeing them through to implementation.

The gaping loophole is that the current interim setup includes numerous elements of the anti-Taliban and pro-US/NATO Northern Alliance with a criminal past record. Warlords of yore rule the roost and enjoy power which is used to maintain the status quo for women. Besides, the unlimited powers these warlords enjoy at the behest of their foreign backers give them a free hand in managing international funds and aid, most of which is embezzled and is hence not spent on development and humanitarian assistance work. Corruption is a major impediment in the task of raising the status of women in Afghanistan. Mariam Rawi of the Revolutionary Association of the Women of Afghanistan believes the government has fallen into the hands of criminals and looting and destruction is being carried out without check. The Northern Alliance warlords who spread chaos from 1992-1996 before the Taliban takeover left behind a legacy of tens of thousands of deaths and destruction as well as homelessness. They are ruling again with guns and money and the real power behind them, the United States of America, is letting it be. She said: *"You might expect me to talk about Afghanistan as a free, peaceful and liberated country, but painfully and unfortunately the reality is not what you might be aware of through the media. After 9/11, subsequent military intervention in Afghanistan in the name of the War on Terror and liberating Afghan women_ despite the tall claims of the United States and its allies_ Afghanistan is still burning in a two-fold fire. On one hand the Northern Alliance warlords supported by the US and on the other hand the Taliban and Al Qaeda terrorists supported by clandestine groups internationally; and moreover, an administration, legislature and judiciary under the domination of criminals and traitors will never do any good for our bereaved people. Treacherousness and corruption has meshed around the roots of the government very deeply."*

The Revolutionary Association of the Women of Afghanistan (RAWA) also reports that of the $10 to 12 billion received in aid from its international donors, not even a billion has been spent on the people of Afghanistan. Dr. Ramzan Bashar Dost, Afghan Member of Parliament says, *"Even if just one billion of aid money had been spent honestly, Afghanistan would have changed."* The Washington Post acknowledges that there exist *'serious flaws in American efforts to rebuild Afghanistan.'* Corruption and inefficiency are rife and millions of dollars have been wasted on 'useless projects.'

In a still more scathing critique in its 2007 Communique, the RAWA reports that *"after seven years there is no peace in Afghanistan. Destitution and suffering has doubled. Our people, especially women and children fall victim to fighting, non-stop US-NATO bombardments and terror attacks. The Northern Alliance bloodsuckers (sic) who are part of Karzai's team with key government posts continue to be the most serious obstacle towards the establishment of peace and democracy in Afghanistan. Human rights violations, crime and corruption have reached their peak, so much so that the president is now forced to request his MPs to 'keep some limits.'"*

In its report on human rights situation in Afghanistan pertaining to women, the Human Rights Watch maintains that women in the country today are still extremely vulnerable to reprisal at the behest of the different factions in the ongoing infighting. The prevalent insecurity restricts severely the activity and opportunities for women.

The worst hit among Afghanistan's suffering womankind are the women in the refugee camps who live in miserable conditions, as well as the numerous war widows struggling to survive. Kabul alone has around 40-50,000 war widows in dire need of rehabilitation.

Extreme poverty, lack of means of earning or a male relative to depend on alongwith children and dependents to support compels these despondent women to take to begging, petty crime or prostitution. As a result, the number of criminal women is increasing and this naturally has a disastrous effect on families. This devastation is the consequence of the decades of war and oppression in the country. Besides, interviews conducted by the Human Rights Watch with refugees along the Pakistan-Afghanistan border reveal that women in the refugee camps are invariably victims of widespread abuse.

Violence Against Women

Women and girls in Afghanistan are threatened with violence in every aspect of their lives, both in public and private, in the community and the family. Violence against women in the family including physical abuse and underage marriage is widely reported. Forced and underage marriage also occurs when women and girls are given in marriage as a means of dispute resolution by informal justice mechanisms. Rape of women and girls by armed groups continues to occur. The prevalence of violence against women and girls constitutes a grave threat to their right to physical and mental integrity.

Abuse and violence suffered by Afghan women takes various forms. Some of them are discussed below:

- Domestic (family) violence
- Underage marriages
- Forced marriages
- Temporary marriages
- Exchange marriages and trading and exchange of women as chattels
- Sexual abuse
- Rape
- Honour killings

Domestic (family) violence

Violence against women in the home by husbands, male family members and, on rarer occasions, female family members is widely reported. Majority of women in both rural and urban areas are faced with family violence. The Afghan Independent Human Rights Commission's report shows 50% of women undergo daily beatings at home. Few cases of abuse, however, are reported either to the authorities or NGOs. Severely injured women seek treatment at hospitals all over the country. According to one woman doctor interviewed by Amnesty International, *"domestic and physical violence are normal practice – we have a lot of cases of broken arms, broken legs and other injuries. It is common practice in Afghanistan – it is not something we should say is not in our region because most Afghan men are using violence."* A foreign doctor working in a hospital spoke of women victims of severe domestic violence undergoing hospital treatment at a rate of about one each week. No monitoring of domestic violence issues is undertaken and the doctor stated that she believed domestic violence often went unrecognized.

Physical violence against women in the family is an abuse of their human rights. The Committee on the Elimination of Violence against Women has stated, *"Family violence is one of the most insidious forms of violence against women. It is prevalent in all societies. Within family relationships women of all ages are subjected to violence of all kinds, including battering, rape, other forms of sexual assault, mental and other forms of violence, which are perpetuated by traditional attitudes. Lack of economic independence forces many women to stay in violent relationships. The abrogation of their family responsibilities by men can be a form of violence, and coercion. These forms of violence put women's health at risk and impair their ability to participate in family life and public life on a basis of equality."*

The BBC reports a young mother of three who suffered systematic daily violence at home. She narrated, *"My man beats me whenever he feels like. He broke my arms, then legs, and now again he has broken my arm. I try not to make a fuss about it for the sake of my children."* Such women, according to the local police, keep turning up in ever-increasing numbers. The police themselves are helpless against this. Another beaten woman says, *"The police have been to see my husband several times, and they made him sign a written undertaking not to beat me any more. But it just does not make any difference. I've asked my brother and my parents to help, but they say we are a very poor family and cannot afford to take you back."*

Subjection to continual physical violence is extremely traumatizing and results in chronic depression which at times is so severe that it can drive the victim to suicide and violent death through self-immolation. Suicide and self-immolation rates in Afghanistan remain high and the single most important reason for this is domestic violence and abuse which goes on unabated. It also leads to drug abuse by women seeking escape, rising prostitution and escape from home due to violence and severe restrictions. AIHRC reports that in Kandahar alone, there are over 300 women seeking shelter at rehabilitation centres who have escaped domestic violence at home. Tragically, however, on discovery of having 'run away' by the family, the victimizers get the woman back and subject her to even more violent punishment than she had sought escape from.

Underage marriages

The legal age for marriage in Afghanistan for men is 18 and for women is 16 years of age. However, a clear pattern of widespread underage marriage of girls emerges, particularly in rural areas. It appears relatively rare for girls to remain unmarried by the age of 16. Amnesty International asked focus groups of women about the typical age of marriage in their communities. All groups gave the age at which girls married as typically between 12 to 16 years. A women's *shura* (traditional Afghan decision making body) in Nangarhar Province in eastern Afghanistan reported marriage age for girls to be between 10 and 12 years in the region. On occasion, girls are forced into marriage below the age of puberty, sometimes at extremely young ages.

Such cases include that of Fariba, aged eight, who was given in marriage to a 48-year-old man. The father of the girl reportedly received 600,000 Afghani for his daughter. Fariba was reported to have suffered sexual abuse by the husband. There exist countless such stories, and few girls have the opportunity to express their distress.

Underage marriage is a breach of Afghan law and Afghanistan's international obligations. In Afghan civil law, the legal age of marriage is given in the article 71 of the constitution: *"Marriage or the consummation of marriage is not allowed before the age of 16."* However, early marriages are part of Afghanistan's traditions and continue to take place despite the law. There exists no punishment for violators and the percentage of child brides remains shockingly high. The UNICEF reports that over 57% of girls in Afghanistan get married before the age of 16. Humaira Daqiq, a policewoman in Kabul is reported by the BBC saying *"Due to poverty many parents marry their daughters off to wealthy old men when the girls are still very young and often when they are underage."*

Humaira, an 18 year old student at Mazar e Sharif was promised in marriage to a much older man when she was just a few months old. He has now returned to claim her and she is distraught. *"I went to the police but they could not help me. His family says if I do not go through with the marriage then my father should kill me."* The trend of underage marriages has dampened down the chances of women acquiring education or pursuing careers.

Forced Marriages

Forced marriages are those that do not include the consent of the intending spouses, and are contracted under pressure or through the use of force by a third party within or without the family. According to law and international conventions Afghanistan is signatory to, clear and explicit consent by both partners is required before a marriage can be contracted. However, the law is routinely violated in Afghanistan and is almost never punished by authorities. The roots of this practice again reach deep into the traditions of Afghan society.

Women in focus groups in a survey conducted by Amnesty International described marriage practices that denied them the right to choose a spouse. A husband would be chosen by the father or another close male relative, and the marriage imposed upon girls and women, if necessary in the face of protest and against their will. This oppressive process reflects in part the fact that girls and women are treated as an economic asset, with families receiving a price from the family of the groom on marriage in all communities where Amnesty International conducted research. They are also reflective of the pervasive control exerted by husbands and male relatives on women's lives.

The prime reason for forced marriages is the use of women to settle family or tribal feuds. In such cases huge dowries are demanded and women are subjected to entering into engagement without their consent. In Afghanistan today, 50% of women get married not merely without their consent, but positively against their will and are hence not happy with their spouses, leading to disturbed family life and worse still, domestic violence. The Minister of Women's Affairs stated that at present two in every five marriages that take place in Afghanistan are forced. Another survey conducted by Womankind Worldwide shows that 60-80% of marriages in Afghanistan are forced. According to a survey conducted by the United Nations News Centre, most people in Afghanistan believe the primary reason for violence against women was forced and child marriages. Forced marriages can lead to drastic consequences, and often the husbands who are generally much older to their young wives, subject them to sexual abuse and violence. An even more heinous practice is marrying daughters by force to families who later use them as prostitutes to bring income for the family. The law seems to be helpless against this as *'in only a very small fraction of cases will any sanction be imposed on perpetrators of domestic violence.'*

Temporary Marriages

There is another terrible aspect of Afghanistan's women's life, and that is temporary marriage. Temporary marriages have made some women fate-less. According to this practice which is common among the Afghan Shiite community, the wife and the husband can be separated after the fixed period or change the temporary marriage to a permanent one. The husband and wife can marry and live together for a day or till whenever they want, but after the end of the fixed period the legal relationship ends and the wife is illegal to the husband. This leaves women hanging in the balance, shelterless and undecided about the future. The stigma of having been in a marital relationship makes seeking a new relationship almost impossible for the woman. She has no legal rights to demand anything from the husband in case of a temporary marriage.

Exchange marriages or trading of women as chattel

In Afghanistan, marriages take place with intimidation by powerful people in order to repay debts. Poor families who cannot afford to pay off debts in cash, sell off their daughters as chattel under pressure from creditors. Other than that, families also resolve disputes with other families or tribes by handing over daughters in marriage, or exchanging girls through marriage. Blood feuds are settled through the same practice. Women are exchanged instead of blood money to avenge murders. Naturally, the woman is later subjected to extreme violence, abuse and punishment as the second family 'sees the killer in her.'

Forced marriage of girls and women also occurs as a result of decisions of *jirgas*. People report the giving of girls, usually below the legal age of marriage, as the preferred means of resolving cases of unintentional killing. Typically, the family of the perpetrator will be ordered to provide a girl, or girls, to the family of the deceased, in order to compensate for the alleged crime. Girls "exchanged" are then forcibly married to male members of the victim's family.

Girls exchanged in marriage or given as chattel are treated very badly after marriage. Amnesty International reports, *"Women speak of the particularly harsh treatment of girls given in dispute resolution and subsequently married. Their own families might sever contact with them, and the family of the groom regards them as tainted by the circumstances of the marriage."*

Girls are used as currency in Afghanistan and this trend has intensified due to poverty and infighting in which blood feuds and disputes are settled through this practice. Many Afghan poor families sell their daughters as brides. Nazir Ahmad who lived in Jalalabad was forced to pay a debt of less than $200 by selling his 16 years old daughter to marry the lender's son. RAWA investigated about 500 cases of girls given in marriage to settle blood feuds and found only four or five that ended happily. Such girls are often beaten and sometimes killed because when the family looks at her, they see the killer.

Sexual Abuse and Rape

Girls and women married by force below the legal age or used as chattel are the worst victims of sexual abuse by the male members of the family. Other than that, sexual harassment of women, sexual sadism and marital rape are also common all over the country. Due to the notion of 'honour' involved, such cases are almost never reported. Amnesty International reports, *"The exact extent and prevalence of such abuses remains unclear owing to the reluctance of most victims to speak out and the limited capacity for monitoring."*

Abuses perpetrated by armed groups against women and girls since the fall of the Taleban government in November 2001 include rape, abduction, and forced and underage marriage. The failure to establish security and legitimate government in many parts of Afghanistan has left women and girls at continuing risk of rape, sexual violence and intimidation. They are extremely vulnerable today to rampant sexual abuse and assault by the different factions in the ongoing infighting, in the face of which the interim government seems to be utterly powerless to exert control. In its October 2008 official statement, the Revolutionary Association of the Women of Afghanistan (RAWA) states:*"The country has been turned into a mafia state and rape and abduction of women and children has no parallel in the history of Afghanistan. Rapists are not only protected from prosecution due to their influence, but have even been forgiven as Karzai announced a general amnesty."*

RAWA reports that eleven year old Rahima, 14 year old Fatima and her mother were raped by warlords and gunmen. In another case 9 year old Saima was tortured and raped by warlords as punishment for her father's crime. Human rights are in crises as criminal warlords hold high office and child abuse and gang rapes are on the increase.

Amnesty International's research indicates a systematic pattern of abuse against women and girls in Mazar-e Sharif, and incidence of abuse in both Nangarhar and Bamiyan provinces. Human Rights

Watch has reported on the occurrence of rape of women, girls and boys in southeast Afghanistan, including in Laghman, Ghazni, Gardez and Nangarhar provinces, and in Paghman district of Kabul province. Incidents reported to Amnesty International included the rape of four girls by members of an armed group. The youngest, aged 12, was unconscious as a result of her injuries when brought to hospital by her parents. UNAMA has investigated a number of incidents of abuse of women and girls by members of armed groups, including incidence of forced marriage of girls as young as 12.

In its report on human rights violation in Afghanistan Amnesty International states: *"Amnesty International is deeply concerned by reports that in certain cases, members of the police or the Afghan National Army (ANA) may be involved or colluding in such abuses. In one incident, said to be indicative of a pattern of abuse, a woman was reported to have been detained at an ANA checkpoint and handed over to the commander of an armed group. Her fate remained unknown, but it was understood that she would be transferred as a "gift" to different commanders. Amnesty International was informed of incidents of police colluding in such abuses. There are also reports of women's reluctance to report such abuse because they fear government involvement. One individual told Amnesty International, "These cases remain secret because if a government official becomes aware they will start abusing the woman".*

Due to the weakness of the criminal justice system, and the fact that it is dominated by the influence of misogynistic and criminal elements, seeking justice for victimized women is almost impossible. Women reporting rape run the risk of being imprisoned for having committed adultery outside marriage, especially if the rapist happens to be a person of influence. There also is evidence that cases relating to women have been judged unfairly. Investigation of crimes against women is poorly carried out both due to lack of will and lack of resources. Warlords continue to intimidate women's rights activists. Courts pay little attention to such issues and decisions are often made in the absence of the woman involved, because the family's sense of honour does not allow the woman to be presented in public. There is increased vulnerability of women to abuse owing to the involvement in some cases of commanders or members of armed factions in the criminal justice system.

Testimony on such abuses is extremely difficult to collect owing to the shame and secrecy surrounding rape and the fear inspired by perpetrators. In Afghanistan, where the criminal justice system is perceived as ineffective and prosecution for rape is extremely rare, few incidents of rape and sexual violence are reported to the authorities. The possibility of any investigation by the criminal justice system may be entirely ruled out when powerful members of armed factions exert control over the police and the judiciary. Amnesty International reports, *"In parts of Afghanistan, women have stated that the insecurity and the risk of sexual violence they face make their lives worse than during the Taleban era. Women expressed a greater sense of fear and intimidation arising from the behaviour of illegally and heavily armed groups in parts of Mazar-e Sharif and Jalalabad."*

An increasing incidence of sexual abuse has been reported among women in prisons. No safeguards are in place to protect women from sexual abuse while in police custody. Amnesty International has received reports of sexual abuse of women prisoners in official detention centres in Herat, Mazar-e Sharif and Kabul. In Herat in early 2003, a riot by women prisoners was alleged to have been a response to sexual abuse by staff. Assaults by staff and incidents of members of armed factions being allowed to abuse women prisoners were reported in Mazar-e Sharif. When women are arrested for adultery, they face the risk of sexual abuse and transfer to different police stations where they are repeatedly abused. One woman told Amnesty International: *"If the commanders arrest a girl in a case of adultery when her case is going to the first district police station, they are sexually abusing her saying you had relations with a man so you should with us also. Then they transfer the woman from station to station."*

Honour Killings

Ms. Hannah Irfan, a Human Rights lawyer defines 'honour killing' as an act of murder of a person assumed or alleged to be guilty of what is seen as sexual transgression by the victim's family tarnishing the family's sense of honour. The 'sense of honour', the violation of which leads to violence on the victim leading to death, is a part of Afghan tribal tradition. The incidence of honour killings in the country is on the rise and often involves influential families. Women are judged to have committed sexual transgression through primitive tribal jirgas, which decree punishment on the woman by the family which considers itself to have been shamed by the act. The punishment almost invariably, is death. No due legal process is required in such cases.

Due to this strong notion of 'honour', no woman is to be seen in public unaccompanied by a man. Women seen 'unaccompanied' are usually suspected of sexual offences. Moreover, women who seek escape from domestic violence or forced marriage are also alleged with illicit sexual activity. The United Nations News Centre reports, *"Once a woman has spent even a single night away from family control, it becomes a dead end in her life. The stigma attached with this makes her be refused by her family, or accepted only to face punishment, often death."*

Amnesty International received reports of women and girls killed by family members. These included the shooting of a woman by her father for refusing his choice of husband. The district governor of the woman's village attempted to bring the alleged killer to justice, but was frustrated in his efforts when the alleged killer was given sanctuary by members of an armed group to whom he is reportedly affiliated.

Amnesty International also received reports of two 12-year-old girls killed by their husbands. Amnesty International's research indicated that in some parts of the country custom or tradition is used to legitimize the violent deaths of women.

In eastern Afghanistan, wherever women and girls are alleged to have committed adultery or eloped, the family deals with the situation by killing the woman involved. In some parts of Afghanistan, adultery, "running away from home" and unlawful sexual activity are invariably, and with or without circumstantial evidence and due legal procedure, punishable by death. Some women in such circumstances are also at risk of being killed if released.

The Afghan state has a duty under international treaties to which it is a party to exercise due diligence to ensure that all cases of rape or other serious sexual assault are effectively investigated and the perpetrators brought to justice.

The effects of systematic abuse and violence which women in Afghanistan routinely suffer are devastating on the victims. Due to lack of security and fear of violence, many Afghan women and girls no more want to travel alone or even get out of the house. They do not want to work outside their homes and women alone in public are often threatened and harassed. The psychological impact of it can be assessed by the rising incidence of suicide attempts and self-immolation by victimized women. Afghan women are resorting to desperate means to try to escape violence and victimization. A woman seeking refuge at a women's shelter says,"*I want to die. I come here to the shelter to ease my pain. When I am at home I feel as though someone is choking me.*" Doctors, NGOs and focus group participants in certain regions reported to Amnesty International a pattern of suicide by women made desperate by sustained violence in the family. A common form of suicide is self-immolation.

Several individual cases of suicide arising from violence against women have been reported. An international organization working with community groups in Afghanistan reported the case of a young girl whose father beat her so much that she killed herself by self-immolation. In another case a woman fell in love with someone that her family did not approve of. Her brother became aware of this, and was reported to have beaten her so severely that she committed suicide by taking an overdose of tablets. Amnesty International states, "*Although the exact rate of such suicides remains unknown, their apparent frequency reflects the very few options and forms of assistance available to women experiencing physical violence in the home.*" Shaimi Amini who works at Heart Hospital tells of at least 53 cases of self-immolation the hospital received in merely six months. She says, "*If someone sees what is happening and acts fast enough then there is a chance to save such women, but in most cases they die. The girls who survive such an attempt are disfigured for the rest of their lives. This brings them even more suffering.*"

The Afghanistan Independent Human Rights Commission is worried by the rising numbers of forced marriages and self-immolation cases involving women. 154 cases of self-immolation have been reported from Western Afghanistan alone, 144 reports of forced marriages, 25 marriages of exchange in Helmand alone and 230 attempted suicides. Afghanistan Online reports Soraya Subhrang of AIHRC on the rising rates of women committing suicde through self-immolation, slashing of veins and taking lethal drug doses. Rape and violence are dramatically increasing with 1545 reported cases in 2006 and 2374 cases in 2008. While the Taliban were condemned for their treatment of women, the AIHRC has reported more cases of violence against women since then, and in Kabul and Herat where there is almost no Taliban influence. "There are so many more unregistered cases," adds Dr. Sobhrang. Afghanistan Online reports 1000 cases of violence against women in Kunduz and 77 cases of rape in the same district in 2007. The same source also reports an increase by 40% in registered cases of rape and violence since March 2007.

According to Yakin Erturk, the Special Rapporteur of the United Nations Human Rights Violations against Women, forced and child marriages, physical and sexual abuse and honour killings on the orders of local warlords alongwith rising self-immolation cases have become a 'dramatic problem' in Afghanistan. He further states, *"The violence has to come to an end. There is no reason under the sun that can legitimize any of these acts, and if the government is going to gain legitimacy and credibility, it has to find ways of dealing with these issues… Girls burn themselves to death because they have no other way to escape violence, not only from husbands, fathers and fathers-in-law, but even mothers-in-law."*

The international NGO Womankind Worldwide reports, *"Seven years after the US invasion, gender violence has reached shocking and worrying levels in Afghanistan and efforts must be redoubled to tackle it. Our findings clearly indicate that that despite over 6 years of international rhetoric about Afghan women's emancipation and development, a real tangible change has not touched the lives of millions of women in the country. Guarantees given to Afghan women after the Taliban have not translated into real change."*

According to Amnesty International, women in Afghanistan continue to suffer widespread abuse that goes unpunished. Few Afghan women are safe from violence and there is a daily risk of abduction, rape, forced marriage and trading as chattel to settle disputes and debts: *"such violence is widely accepted by local communities and inadequately addressed at the highest levels of government and judiciary."*

In its official Communique in 2008, the Revolutionary Association of the Women of Afghanistan (RAWA) states: *"After the United States and its allies invaded Afghanistan seven years ago, they misleadingly claimed to bring peace and democracy to liberate Afghan women from the bleeding fetters of the Taliban. However, in reality Afghan women are still burning in the inferno of violence. Women are exchanged with dogs, girls are gang-raped, men kill their wives viciously and violently..."*

INSTITUTIONALIZED DISCRIMINATION

Other than the spate of violence victimizing women, there are also numerous other forms of injustice and discrimination that the women of Afghanistan routinely suffer, and most of these relate to the weaknesses and flaws in the legal system of Afghanistan and its feeble implementation. In its report 'Justice Denied', Amnesty International identifies these problems faced by women as :

a) Restrictions on mobility and public life due to insecurity
b) Lack of access to the right of divorce
c) Lack of information and awareness of women's rights
d) Inefficiency of the Criminal Justice System
e) Lack of adequate provisions for women in the legal system
f) Failure of police and courts to investigate crimes against women
g) Failure to investigate rape and forced marriage
h) Pressure by influential people on the Judiciary
i) Women's inability to reach courts of law
j) Confusion and lack of clarity about laws
k) Lack of adequate training and capacity in state institutions

l) Under-representation of women in the criminal justice system

m) Inadequate provision for shelter and legal aid for women

The Effects of Poverty

Widespread poverty in Afghanistan has had a debilitating effect on the lives of women. The 2005 report of the Millennium Development Goals reports that the average per capita income in Afghanistan is less than 200$. Only 13% of Afghan families have access to a sustainable source of income. The worst hit, of course, are the women in refugee camps and the war widows who often have no means of sustained income at all. Women are considered dependents in Afghan society, hence the idea of a woman earning for the family is not accepted at large. This makes the dilemma worse for widows, most of whom have to raise an average of four children without any male relative to support them. As a result, these women take up begging or petty crimes. The number of female beggars and criminals in Kabul alone has reached record high levels. Zuleika is such a woman in Kabul who has three children to support. The family begs in Kabul from 7 a.m in the morning to 6 p.m in the evening and collects up to 100 Afghanis a day (U.S $ 2) which is barely enough for bread and tea. Zuleika's husband was killed in the factional infighting in 1999, and now she has nobody to help her. Hers is just one of numberless stories of shelterless widows and orphans. Afghanistan today has the highest number of widows in the world due to armed conflicts that have bedeviled the country for over 20 years. There exist almost 2 million widows in the country today, 50,000 of whom are in Kabul alone. The average age of these war widows is 35, yet remarriage is not an option for them any more. It is like being 'second hand property.' Seeking employment is impossible too as 94% of these women are illiterate, with an average of four children. They battle for survival begging on roadsides, taking to prostitution or weaving carpets as under-paid daily wage workers in small industrial units. Widows are socially excluded, have no educational or employment opportunities and as a result have severe psychological and emotional problems. In a survey it was revealed that 65% of Kabul's widows 'want to commit suicide.'

Soraya Subhrang of the AIHRC criticizes the government for not doing enough to alleviate the plight of Afghanistan's widows. They have no voice to represent their problems and no representation in public institutions. They live in indescribably wretched conditions.

Another trend that has directly resulted from the extreme poverty in the country is prostitution which is dramatically on the rise since the US invasion. Roughly 25,000 women in the country work as prostitutes. Out of these, 5,000 are in Kabul alone. Due to extreme poverty and no means of earning, women are forced to sell themselves into the trade. In some cases, families force women to indulge in the practice to bring income for the family. Widows looking after large families having no opportunities amidst high inflation in the country to deal with are the prime recruits for the expanding illicit trade.

One of the many effects of rising poverty is an increasing trend of exchange marriages and women as chattel. This is because due to crushing poverty families often run into huge debts impossible to pay off. This leads to exploitation by the lenders and creditors, forcing families to bring into use the ancient custom of paying debts through women and girls. Poverty also forces extremely poor families to sell their children due to destitution and starvation. Opium farmers in the country often sell off their daughters to cover debts to drug traffickers. The Independent reports, *"Afghanistan is becoming a narco-state right under the nose of the NATO authorities. 60% of the country's income today is through drug trade. When the government tries to intervene or restrict poppy growth, the loss of the crop leaves farmers unable to pay off piling debt to drug traffickers who lent money to buy the seeds. In desperation, they turn to the traditional practice of paying off debts by handing over a daughter to the creditor. Usually there is a marriage ceremony for the sake of propriety, but the woman will always be treated as property."*

Health Conditions

Health facilities for women are abysmal, and, as reported by AIHRC, most women have no access to basic health services due to long distance to the nearest health centre. This makes it harder for women to seek medical help, and only 5 to 7% of women in the country can get that access. In many districts throughout the country, there is no female doctor or even health worker available. As custom and tradition does not allow women to be checked up by male physicians, absence of female health personnel means women cannot get medical services at all.

Afghanistan today faces a health disaster 'worse than the Tsunami.' 700 children and around 70 women perish every single day due to lack of health services, from illnesses 87% of which are preventable. Even the healthcare facilities that are present are inadequate for the rapidly growing population. The few hospitals in the bigger cities are overwhelmed with patients and have very little medical staff available to tackle with them. Due to lack of communication facilities, often patients cannot reach medical aid and die before the nearest hospital arrives. Although some health centres and maternity clinics have opened up lately, yet still a lot more needs to be done. Every 30 minutes a woman in Afghanistan dies in childbirth because of lack of proper medical facilities. Afghanistan Online reports 3,900 die while delivering a child annually in Kabul alone, and these rates become higher in rural areas of Urozgan and Zabul provinces in the south. The annual maternity death rate in the country is 15,000 to 24,000, which is the second highest in the world. The Ministry of Women's Affairs (MOWA) reports that 2,000 out of every 10,000 women die in childbirth. 50% of all pregnant women are iron deficient. Importantly, the number of women dying in Afghanistan due to lack of health facilities is 25 times higher than the number of people dying due to security-related problems.

Poverty and economic hardship directly affects women's access to health facilities, as do chauvinistic and conservative attitudes. Malnutrition among women, low age of marriage, high fertility rates and lack of family planning leading to no spacing out of childbirth put women and children's health at high risk. Malnutrition among women and expectant mothers is caused not only by food shortage due to drought and prolonged conflict in the country, but also due to the traditional preference of the male in Afghan households. Women's fertility rates at an average of 6.6

are the highest in the world. Frequent pregnancies put the health of women in danger and prevent them from gainful economic opportunities. Small numbers of women doctors, nurses and health staff prevent women from seeking medical aid. Living standards are extremely low and potable water is not available. Only 23% of the population has access to safe water and at least 15,000 Afghans die of tuberculosis yearly, 64% of whom are women. Only 15% of births are attended by trained health workers, while more than 90% of births take place at home. Due to all of these causes, the average woman in Afghanistan has a lifespan of 42-45 years, around 20 years short of the global average.

Education

Education for women is another area directly influenced by poverty and chauvinistic attitudes among families. The statistics as they stand are depressing indeed and show clear discrimination between boys and girls in Afghanistan. The number of girls going to schools is less than half the number of boys. In the Zabul province the ratio is 3:97. The number of girls schools in the country has dramatically declined over the years, especially high school due to few enrollments.

UNICEF reports that 60% of girls under the age of 11 are not going to school. In Urozgan and Zabul provinces of the south, 90% of girls do not go to schools. UNIFEM reports more than 90% of women in the country are illiterate.

The reasons for girls not going to schools are both the unwillingness and inability of girls to continue their education owing to a variety of factors some of which are:

* widespread gender discrimination
* poverty
* security challenges
* shortage of female schools
* early marriages

Insecurity which keeps most girls home results from a number of reasons, and is not quite without basis. According to a UN survey, 300 schools in south Afghanistan were set on fire and a number of teachers were killed. In Zowjan province, owing to these conditions, presently not a single school for girls exists. Radio Liberty reports 600 more schools in the country have closed down due to insecurity. Afghan authorities say they are facing a tough task forcing parents to send their daughters to school because attacks on female students have increased throughout the country. Three girls sustained severe burns in Kandahar as unknown men sprayed acid on a group of 15 school-going girls. One of them permanently lost her eyesight as a result of this. After this incident, only 35 out of the total 1300 students of the school turned up the next day. Numerous such incidents have occurred and although no one has claimed responsibility for such attacks, Taliban are usually blamed. Anonymous leaflets have been distributed in some villages warning parents against sending their daughters to school. According to the Ministry of Education, 120 schools have been burnt down. In 2007, two girl students were shot dead by unknown armed men as they were walking to school. A resident of Kandahar whose two daughters have been victims of acid-throwing says, *"I always wanted my daughters to get an education and not to be left illiterate like their parents. But now I am having second thoughts. I will not send my girls to school again. Would you?"* The government has utterly failed to provide security and reassure parents to continue their children's education.

This, however, is of course not the only reason. OXFAM reports that out of 110,000 girls who began school in 2006, only one third are still continuing their education. According to a local school principal, most girls drop out of school in grades 7 to 9 (ages13 to 15). The reason is that people stop sending their daughters to school because 'they become adults during this age.' Girls' education is generally undervalued. Nader, father of a girl student in Kabul informs, *"Girls are only allowed to go to mosques between 5 to 8 years, to learn to read the Quran. After age 9 they stop going as they are not allowed to go out or be seen by other men, meaning they cannot go to school either."* 18 year old Diba's father from Kunduz forced her to discontinue her education. She says, *"I love the white scarf and the black uniform of school, but my father hates it. Now I wash the dishes at home. And when I hear the sound of the school bell going,*

I become very sad." Her father tells his side of the story: *"I do not let my daughter go to school because we have a conservative society. Nobody allows their daughters to continue going to school after class 4 or 5. If I let her go to school my relatives will say bad things about me. Girls should work inside the home, not study or work outside the home."*

ATTITUDES AND MINDSETS

Afghanistan has a traditionally patriarchal tribal society that dates back to thousands of years of its history, most of which has been overshadowed by conflict. The society is introverted and conservative, and is based on the patriarchal values of male dominance. Other than that, a strong sense of 'honour' which strictly defines 'modesty' of women is integral to the Afghan mindset.

It is important to realize here that this mindset pre-dates the Taliban regime, and that women of Afghanistan have been subjected to male dominance_ and still are_ with or without the Taliban, contrary to what has been portrayed in the media. In as early as 1978, the Communist Party of Afghanistan attempted to introduce radical reforms for gender equality by prohibiting and banning ancient traditions and customs. The reaction to this from the population was strong and family after family began to leave Afghanistan as a form of resistance to this attempt. During the jihad against the Soviets, the Islamic fighters revived the traditional role of the Afghan woman in the family as the daughter, sister, mother or wife.

The chaotic years of infighting after that offset widespread poverty and destruction which revived the cycle of victimization of women amidst rising insecurity. Women began to be treated as spoils of war and the traditional notions of honour and shame in Afghan culture re-emerged in a perverted form, often brutally subjecting women to patriarchal authority and leading to crimes against women. Armed warlords today use these cultural norms as weapons of war, engaging in rape and assault against women as the ultimate means of dishonouring families, tribes or entire communities. Due to rising insecurity in the country, restrictions on women's freedom have become severe, on the excuse of 'protecting the security of women.' This automatically implies enforcement of policies regarding women, and severer punishments for violations. This was just what the Taliban regime had come under fire for, but the trend continues today all the same, minus the scrupulous criminal justice system of the Taliban. Maryam Aslan, the Program Director of UNIFEM says *"With or without the Taliban, Afghanistan was and still is in a miserable situation."*

Religion forms an important part of life and society in Afghanistan. However, due to the country's preoccupation with war and conflict, and no opportunities to develop intellectually both in religious and secular studies, custom and tradition is mixed with religion, and sometimes seeks justification through it. Religious values and laws are interpreted narrowly and even incorrectly. The justice system is still primitive, giving the final word to traditional tribal jirgas headed by tribal elders. These jirgas have outdated means of investigation and prosecution which do not require circumstantial evidence and do not give the right of appeal. Jirgas are headed by patriarchal heads believing in the inferiority and subjection of women to masculine authority. Hence the sentences handed down by jirgas are often unfair to women, even brutal.

Widows are viewed as social outcasts owing to the attitude of considering the woman as a dependant. Hussain Ali Moin of the Ministry of Women's Affairs states, *"In Afghanistan, the death of a husband diminishes a woman's economic independence and damages her sense of social protection."*

The same attitude creates immense difficulties for women victimized by sexual violence and rape:*"In highly conservative Afghanistan, only a fraction of women dare to breach social taboos and publicly speak out against the violence they suffer. They face a social stigma if they appear at police stations and courts to reclaim their rights."* Rape crimes are not discussed and court proceedings are carried out entirely by males in the absence of the even the female victim herself. Moreover, the notions of 'honour' stigmatize women who attempt to escape domestic violence or forced marriage. 'Running away' is seen as evidence of illicit sexual relations, and there is no sympathy for such women. 17 year old Fatima who refused to be forced into marriage narrates her story: *"I was put into chains for a whole month by my father. I ran away twice but was returned home by the police. Everyone says I am guilty and that my father has the right to beat me."*

Discriminatory attitudes towards women run deep and have affected all sections of the society, even the topmost state institutions, in spite of the fact that women are now part of the political administration. Hawa Alam, an Afghan MP says, *"Women in the parliament get very few opportunities to express themselves as the speaker and administrative staff of the house think women do not have the capacity to engage in high politics."* Owing to this, the Bill of Rights of the Afghan women tabled by women parliamentarians calling for mandatory female education, equal representation in the assembly, criminalization of sexual harassment and domestic violence and the right to marry and divorce has still not been made part of the constitution. The Chairman of the Afghan Loya Jirga is reported to have said, *"God has not given you equal rights because under His decision, two women are equal to one man."*

A similar situation exists even in the judiciary where women are under-represented and some of the highest judges have prejudices against women. In two divorce proceedings observed by Amnesty International delegates, women claimed that they had been physically abused by their husbands. However, in both of the cases, the judges failed to view the physical abuse allegations as giving rise to any form of criminal liability on the part of the husband. In one divorce case, it was reported that a woman was beaten in the street by her husband, and that witnesses supporting her claim appeared in court. However, the judges reportedly stated that as her arm was only lightly injured and not broken, there were no proper grounds for a divorce. Some of the statements below give a fuller picture of discriminatory attitudes against women:

"A man killed his wife when he found her with a cousin. No one did anything about the case because he had strong reasons."

"When a woman is killed [in a case of alleged adultery] *it is the family of the woman who carries out the killing...These things are secret, they are happening inside homes."*

"*They* [family members] *will kill man and woman* [in certain cases of rape]. *If married she should go back to her father, because her husband will not keep her... If unmarried she will be killed.*"

"*Where a father kills his daughter, he will never go to court, no one will be aware because it is a big shame and no one can bear it.*"

"*If a woman or girl doesn't want to respect what her family is saying, of course she will commit suicide or her family will do this to her* [kill her and make it appear as suicide]."

Both women's education and health have remained resistant to positive change for the same reasons. Despite efforts at making laws, establishing rehabilitation centres and financing NGOs, real change will not materialize except with a gradual change of attitudes in the society. This, of course, requires an insightful approach which the actors involved have not demonstrated so far.

On the other extreme of the spectrum is the mindset and attitude of some of the women's human rights NGOs and the international community that has shown a rather condescending and condemnatory approach towards indigenous Afghan customs, traditions, values and religious beliefs. This mindset has led to an approach that calls for an eradication of these from the body-politic of Afghanistan, and their replacement with modern Western secular values. Well-intentioned as it may be, it quite misses the point. A noteworthy instance is when a representative from an international NGO approached an Afghan judge requesting him to legalize consensual sexual relations. The elderly judge responded, "*We welcome your programme of reform, but let me tell you, you can never change our values. If you attempt to change our values, the whole nation will rise up against you.*" According to 'Women Waging Peace, "*Attempts by aid workers to assist women in conservative areas may backfire if Afghans feel they are trying to change hundreds of years of culture rather than simply fulfilling basic human needs.*"

Another related matter is that of the attitude towards the Muslim 'veil' and its traditional Afghan form, the full body covering called 'burqa.' It is a fact that Western organizations rushed for aid to Afghanistan bolstered up by the media images of women in 'burqas.' The 'burqa' became a symbol of oppression and subjugation, a sort of punishment on the suffering women of Afghanistan. Hence it became an obsession with the Western NGOs, who equated liberation of the Afghan woman with the taking off of the oppressive veil. What came as a surprise, however, was that long after the departure of the Taliban, the women of the country still invariably carry on with it, and in fact, *'do not want to stop wearing the burqa.'* The implication is clear: the veil in fact is a deep-rooted Afghan tradition and cannot be shed off. In fact, most women find it secure and comfortable to be seen with the 'burqa' in public. The Policy Paper of 'Women Waging Peace' includes an interesting article titled 'Why the Burqa Misses the Point': *"For men and women around the world, the 'burqa' is the simplest and the most profound symbol of Afghan women's repression. The media, and women's organizations in the West, have used it to successfully attract the attention of mainstream Western audiences. Therefore, it may seem paradoxical that Afghan women are appealing to the public to end their fixation with the 'burqa.' In an interview with female teachers in Kandahar in December 2001, a respondent said, "The burqa is not out problem. We need education, we need to be able to see a doctor, we need to feed our families. We don't mind the burqa at all." She urged Western women to go beyond the 'burqa.' Afghan women worry that the international community's obsession with the burqa distracts attention from their more pressing issues."*

The international community needs to disassociate religion and traditional values from oppressive cultural practices and to not make the mistake of painting all with the same brush. A common perception is that discrimination and oppression is rooted in religion, and that to do away with this, religion must be abandoned altogether. Honour killings, for instance, are considered to be a result of religious condemnation of sexual liberty. According to Human Rights lawyer Hannah Irfan, *"Honour killings have nothing to do with religion, and it is important to see that. Islam clearly forbids such a practice and in fact, has liberated women from the fetters of this and such oppression thousands of years before any other system or law could. The Quran itself mentions the enormity of the sin of burying girls alive or alleging them with sexual misconduct without a stringent legal procedure and absolutely foolproof evidence."*

Similarly, the potential to liberate women in Afghan religion and values must be recognized and utilized, as some NGOs are beginning to do so by seeking help from traditional tribal elders and religious elders to push forth the agenda for progress and development. The UNICEF representative in Afghanistan said, *"We must tell the people how Islam makes education compulsory for both girls and boys, so that they start going to school."* Instead of condemning traditional laws and values, some of the international workers and government officials acknowledge that *"No law (neither civil nor the Shariah) accepts child marriages, that a 6 year old, for example, is marriageable. The awareness of such law must be made available, as it belongs to Afghan traditional values and is not a foreign imposition."*

Years ago after the fall of the Taliban, Afghanistan's new government pledged swift action to improve the lives of women. According to Womankind Worldwide, *"Millions of Afghan women and girls continue to face criminal violence everyday."* Despite the drafting of new laws and granting of rights, women do not enjoy these rights. Some independent analysts are bitterly critical of the failure to achieve the promised objectives: *"Seven years back the United States government and its allies were successfully able to legitimize their military invasion of Afghanistan and deceive the people of the US and the world under the banner of 'liberating Afghan women', 'democracy' and the 'War on Terror'. Our people were filled with hope, but soon their dream of the establishment of security, democracy and freedom was shattered in the most painful manner."* According to the Human Rights Watch report of 2005, *"Women face more peril with the intensification of the conflict after 9/11. Today there is impunity characterizing Afghanistan's civil war."*

The reason for this has been attributed to several factors. According to RAWA spokeswoman Mariam Rawi, *"The compromising government of Karzai has proven itself to be unable to solve the smallest of issues. The US has never truly been concerned about the roots of terrorism in our country, and has made a grave mistake by replacing the Taliban with the Northern Alliance criminal warlords, bringing them back in power. It is clear to us that the international community does not desire peace and democracy here at all."* Moreover, *"The mafia government of Karzai is tirelessly trying to conciliate with the criminals and award medals to those who should be prosecuted for their crimes and looting. Unaware of the realities, some people considered the presence of women in the parliament as a symbol of democracy, development, freedom and women's rights. But it is clear now that these women are related to intelligence agencies or fundamentalist bands and are like dolls in the hands of the warlords who are calmly watching the adversity of our unfortunate women and instead of revealing and protesting against the horrible condition of women, are busy in corruption and collaboration with the sworn enemies of women's rights and keeping their positions in the parliament. If these women were truly the representatives of the Afghan women, they should have stood firmly beside victimized women to fulfill their obligation towards our people and country with honesty and sincerity."*

Corruption in the ranks of the government is also a major reason for this general disappointment with the regime and its failure to fulfill commitments: *"The reality is that till now a big part of international aid has fattened the wallets and waists of the Northern Alliance mafia, national and international NGOs and the corrupt government authorities... the U.S disguised the dead rats of yesterday in suits and ties and released them like wild wolves on our people, and are doing nothing about the current crimes, violation of human rights, looting of millions of dollars of aid by warlords and corrupt NGOs. If the billions of dollars of aid had been directed in the name of reconstruction were not poured in the pockets of criminals in the parliament and the cabinet, so many lives would not have been taken. Even if a small portion of that wealth was used for the relief of people, the living conditions of our people, especially women, would not have been so tragic."*

Independent analysts heavily criticize the lack of sincerity and in fact expediency and hypocrisy of the United States and its allies towards Afghanistan. Mariam Rawi continues: *"The U.S remained silent from 1992 to 1996 when Northern Alliance warlords were getting power and were committing shocking crimes against our people, especially women. The Northern Alliance, in fact, was made an ally to oust the Taliban and was never made accountable. These criminals were imposed on us with US support, left free to make the lives of our women more miserable. If the US believed in freedom, it would have condemned and punished the Northern Alliance military groups who are the main violators of values."* In its December 2007 Communique, the Revolutionary Association of the Women of Afghanistan states: *"The United States and its allies tried to legitimize their military occupation of Afghanistan under the banner of 'bringing peace and democracy for afghan people.' But as we have experienced in the past from the fate of our own people, the US considers her own political and economic interests and has empowered and equipped the most traitorous, anti-democratic, misogynistic and corrupt gangs in Afghanistan. The US created a government out of those responsible for massacres. For the US, defeating Terrorism so that our people can be happy has no significance, because they will have no excuse to stay in Afghanistan and realize its economic, political and strategic interests in the region."* Furthermore, *"The War on Terror is merely a showcase to justify the long military presence of the US in Afghanistan and in the region. Troops of the US and its allies bomb wedding parties and shower bullets on oppressed people, especially women and children."* This, in fact, has reached such high levels that *'it is believed that the Taliban are in fact the rescuing forces.' "During the Taleban era if a woman went to market and showed her flesh she would have been punished; now, she's raped."*

Since the number of women dying of violence is several times greater than those dying of terror attacks, it becomes clear that improving the lives of the oppressed needs to be the topmost government priority, hence the fixation with 'terrorism' is uncalled for.

Adrian Edwards of UNAMA says *"Women's development should not be compromised by security imperatives."* RAWA reports, *"Women's rights have fallen down the agenda behind countering a growing insurgency, tackling opium production and confronting endemic corruption."* Hangama Anwari of AIHRC notices the lowering of the priority of dealing with women's issues. She opines, *"Day by day the government's support for women's development fades."* The Human Rights Watch brings to attention the fact that *'discussion on the protection of women's rights during the US led attack on Afghanistan has been absent.'*

State institutions have systematically failed to protect women from abuse and violence within and outside families. A spokeswoman from the Afghan Women Affairs Ministry, Nooria

Haqnagar acknowledged the abuse, and that the number of such cases is rising. Brita Fernandes Schmidt of Womankind Worldwide says, "*The international community must fulfill the promises made after the Taliban to protect the women. Give women a greater voice in setting the agenda. Until basic rights are granted to Afghan women in practice as well as on paper, it cannot be said that the status of women in Afghanistan has changed significantly in the past few years.*"

CONCLUSION

Findings:

i) The liberation of women in Afghanistan from oppression by the Taliban was one of the primary reasons for the Allied invasion of Afghanistan in November 2001, and the allies declared their commitment to improving the lives of women.

ii) Efforts have been made to improve the situation of women in Afghanistan through ratification of international conventions, revival of and amendments to the Constitution, establishment and work of international human rights NGOs, international assistance, establishment of the Ministry of Women's Affairs, inclusion of women at all levels of public administration and increased role of the free media.

iii) Despite efforts, women's empowerment at the grassroots level has not yet materialized.

iv) Lack of security severely hampers women's return to active social and political life.

v) Poverty continues to make the lives of women refugees and war widows miserable.

vi) Violence and crimes against women remain high.

vii) Seeking justice is still tedious for a number of women due to weaknesses in the criminal justice system.

viii) Biases and prejudices still exist against women even within the judiciary and the parliament.

ix) Health and education of women remains abysmally low both due to lack of will and lack of ability to seek both.

x) Warlords and misogynistic criminals enjoy vast powers threatening the security situation and interfering in the fair execution of the justice system.

xi) The government has failed to provide even minimal security to the Afghan woman. Crime often goes unpunished.

xii) The lack of commitment to improve women's lives on the part of the government and the international community is clear, and proves that the invasion seven years ago was more about strategic interests than about liberating the oppressed women of Afghanistan. Hence the massive propaganda campaign against the Taliban too was politically motivated.

xiii) Patriarchal attitudes against women lie at the root of the discrimination faced by women.

xiv) Understanding of and respect for Afghan religion and culture is required in order to initiate enduring, meaningful reform within the system. Reform cannot be imposed from without.

xv) The government and its international partners put dealing with terrorism and security issues as their prime priority and preoccupation, which has eclipsed the pertinence of women's issues and has led to slackening of effort on this front.

xvi) The lives of Afghan women today are no better than under the Taliban after over seven years since the occupation. The plight of the woman in Afghanistan today, in fact, is perhaps worse than it has ever been before. Only, this time the international attention to her plight is not there, because it is not politically useful.

Recommendations:

i) Policy needs to be matched with implementation. Constitutional reform will only be effective if the criminal justice system and state institutions to administer it are reformed.

ii) Corruption of funds for women's development programmes by state officials and NGOs must be checked and effectively stemmed.

iii) Criminal elements in the administration must be flushed out. An independent inquiry of criminal past record of influential warlords and functionaries must be carried out and legal punishments accorded. Crime against women will not stop unless its influential sponsors are taken to task.

iv) All parties to the conflict in Afghanistan must abide by the commitment to observe international human rights and humanitarian law guaranteeing the protection of civilians, and to investigate and hold accountable military personnel responsible for violations. In particular, the U.S.-led alliance must ensure that human rights and humanitarian law is not violated in any circumstances.

v) It must be ensured that development and reconstruction programs are structured to ensure that girls and women have full access to programs for education, health care, job training and housing.

vi) The international community must ensure that any government established in Afghanistan is committed to fully respect the human rights of all the people of Afghanistan and to repealing laws and ending practices that discriminate against women.

vii) Police reforms and training must be carried out. More women need to be recruited in the police service.

viii) Women's access to justice through smaller courts in rural areas must be facilitiated. More women must be recruited into the judiciary.

ix) Registration of marriage and divorce, as well as accurate entry of birth records must be made compulsory and any breach should be punishable.

x) Laws regarding the legal age of marriage must be strictly implemented.

xi) Awareness of family laws, marriage and divorce laws must be created among women through education and the media.

xii) Rehabilitation centres for women must be increased and made approachable.

xiii) Widows and orphans as well as despondent women must receive monthly stipends in aid from international donors and NGOs through the Ministry of Women's Affairs.

xiv) More health centres providing reproductive health services for women should be established, especially in far-flung rural areas.

xv) Female staff must be recruited into the health system.

xvi) Training must be imparted to women for basic and emergency health services.

xvii) Training to develop skills must be given to women to encourage them to work from home.

xviii) Entrepreneurial skills should be taught to women to help them acquire independent means of earning.

xix) Domestic violence must be made legally punishable.

xx) More girls schools need to be established, especially in rural areas.

xxi) Security must be provided in schools and strict action taken against those who threaten girl students.

xxii) Religious leaders should be recruited to promote women's education and rights in the light of religion. Arrangements should be made to impart such education through religion to the public_ men and women alike.

xxiii) International NGOs must not advocate imposition of secular Western law, but help reform the system from within. They must build trust among the people through respect of ancient values and traditions.

xxiv) Misunderstanding regarding religious law should be dispelled, and awareness of its correct and progressive interpretation must be spread through the media. Religion must be delinked from false notions of 'honour and shame' and gender apartheid.

xxv) The media must not present the liberation of women cosmetically through the ornamentalization and exposure of women, but should play a proactive role in public education about women's rights.

xxvi) Edicts handed down by local jirgas must be licensed and approved by the Afghanistan Supreme Court.

xxvii) Discriminatory laws must be amended or repealed altogether.

xxviii) Gender issues must be accorded priority by the government and the international community.

xxix) Psychotherapy and counseling must be provided to women subjected to violence and abuse.

xxx) Active NGOs must be provided with an atmosphere of security to conduct their work.

xxxi) The international community and international media must bring attention to the current situation of women in Afghanistan and shed off the fixation with human rights violations committed in the Taliban era. Celebrating a cosmetic liberation of women in comparison with their status under the Taliban is misleading and deceptive. A forward-looking approach and a true commitment to improve the lives of Afghan women is the need of the day.

WOMEN'S RIGHTS IN THE TALIBAN AND POST-TALIBAN ERAS

The strict edicts issued by the Taliban during their five-year rule marginalized women and girls severely in all aspects of Afghan society. After the Taliban's ouster in November 2001, Afghan women became hopeful about regaining their rights. The first signs of progress appeared as early as December of the same year, when a peace conference in Bonn, Germany, re-introduced the concept of gender equality, and ensured women's participation in both an interim government and the drafting of a new constitution. In 2005, further advancement came as Afghan women achieved unprecedented levels of political representation through parliamentary elections. Despite these positive strides in legislation, indicators on the ground belie continuing vulnerability to discrimination and the denial of basic rights. This features explores the extent to which Afghan policies towards women have translated into actual change on the ground.

EDUCATION

Taliban Era

Before the Taliban came to power, women were active members of the educational system as students and teachers, representing 70 percent of teachers in the capital of Kabul in 1996. It was during the Taliban's five year rule that women's rights to education were revoked. The Taliban dismantled Afghanistan's co-educational system, transforming many of its former state-run girls' schools into all-male institutions.

One of the Taliban's edicts in 1997 called for a nationwide ban on public education for all women and girls. Adhering to the letter of the law, but still determined to educate their children, Afghan women set up hundreds of schools in private homes. On June 16, 1998, however, the Taliban responded by issuing an edict stipulating that privately funded education must be limited to girls under eight and restricted to the teachings of the Koran. Making an example of Kabul, members of the Taliban shut down 100 private schools there. Women's literacy rates across the country fell to some of the lowest in the world — 13 percent in urban areas and three to four percent in rural districts.

This increasingly oppressive environment necessitated secretively conducted classes, often putting the lives of female students and teachers at grave risk. One UN report stated that underground schools in private homes were reaching 300,000 Afghan children by 2001. The same report highlighted BBC educational radio broadcasts as one of few alternate resources available to women.

Post-Taliban Era

Since the fall of the Taliban in 2001, educational resources for women have become more readily available. The right to education for both girls and women is anchored in articles forty-three and forty-four of the 2003 constitution:

Education is the right of all citizens of Afghanistan, which shall be provided up to the level of the B.A. (license), free of charge by the state. The state is obliged to devise and implement effective programs for a balanced expansion of education all over Afghanistan, and to provide compulsory intermediate level education. The state is also required to provide the opportunity to teach native languages in the areas where they are spoken.

The state shall devise and implement effective programs for balancing and promoting of education for women, improving of education of nomads and elimination of illiteracy in the country.

In addition, Afghanistan also signed the Millennium Development Goals program in 2004, of which two of the eight goals are specific to female literacy:

In March 2002, 1.5 million children who had been barred from education returned to school. By December 2005, the number had grown to 5.2 million, of which almost two million were girls. Women's literacy levels are estimated to be up by seven percent overall.

Women are teaching and attending universities, and receiving degrees in disciplines ranging from medicine to police work. Although this progress is seen as a step in the right direction by women's rights groups and international bodies alike, many believe female enrollment and literacy rates should be drastically higher given post-Taliban political reforms.

While Afghanistan's new constitution recognizes the equality of men and women, many of its male population still do not. This conservative outlook is mirrored in the situation on the ground, with women seeking education continuing to be under threat. In February and March 2004, a UN envoy condemned the burning of approximately 30 girls' schools in Afghanistan. Human Rights Watch estimated that in 2005 and the first half of 2006, there were more than 204 attacks on teachers, students, and schools in the southern and northern provinces.

The Afghan Ministry of Education estimates that girl's schools make up 30 percent of the 9,000 schools in the country, most of which are primary level. But with the threat of a Taliban resurgence and enduring conservatism amongst the male population, it is difficult to determine how many girls will continue on to a secondary education.

EMPLOYMENT

Taliban Era

Afghan women's right to work and freely choose their profession was written into the constitution in 1980, when Afghanistan signed the Convention on the Elimination of Discrimination Against Women an international bill of rights for women issued by the UN in 1979. This convention states that the right to work is an 'inalienable right of all human beings.' After Afghanistan became a signatory nation, women became key participants in the economy, holding positions as teachers, farmers, doctors, engineers, and equal partners in civil service. In 1996 however, the Taliban immediately revoked this right to work and introduced other oppressive edicts specific to women. As a result, a majority of educated female professionals went abroad, creating a considerable brain drain in the country. Women who were left behind faced deteriorating economic and social conditions, especially in the case of Afghanistan's two million widows.

The Taliban's first edict on women's right to employment came in 1997, banning all women from working in public places. The health sector, where the Taliban had already imposed gender segregation, suffered most. After months of negotiations with the United Nations, the Taliban issued a revised policy on the employment of women. This new edict stated that employment in the health sector was limited to needy widows with no other means of support. Most widows were generally unskilled with no education and did not qualify for positions in this sector, forcing some into begging or prostitution. The ban on women's employment was also a detriment to boys' education, as the majority of teachers had been women.

Some women found alternate sources of income through international non-governmental organizations (NGOs). But in 2000, the Taliban's Council of Ministers banned Afghan women from working with both foreign and domestic NGOs. With few options available in the formal employment sector, some women set up home-based businesses in agriculture, animal husbandry, carpet weaving, tailoring, embroidery, soap making, candle making, honey production and baking. These forms of employment had very little impact on the status of women, requiring skills many did not have and offering poor pay. Also, the Taliban's restrictions on women's freedom of movement limited their access to the market place. In many cases, women had to rely upon potentially exploitative male middlemen in order to sell their products.

Post-Taliban Era

The new constitution of Afghanistan states that men and women are equal, officially encouraging gender equality and job and educational opportunities for women. In 2002, the transition administration allocated some $10 million to the Women's Affairs Ministry to help strengthen women's status in society. The Ministry has offices throughout the country and 75 percent of its employees are women. One of its main objectives is to help Afghan women find employment. Early signs of hope came in 2001 when the World Food Program conducted a major survey on food needs in Kabul. Of 3,612 surveyors employed, some 2,400 were women, the first significant boost to women's employment since the fall of the Taliban.

In 2005, the Grameen Foundation USA estimated that 11 percent of entrepreneurs in Afghanistan are women. The southern and eastern provinces have seen less progress; whereas areas in the west like the Balkh province – and especially its capital city of Mazar-i-Sharif – have seen unprecedented levels of success. The Women's Affairs department has started a program for women who want to open their own shops. Balkh's provincial governor also approved the construction of a complex called Bagh-e-Zanana, or Women's Garden, which will have 200 shops owned by women.

Still, female labor force participation in Afghanistan is among the lowest in South Asia at 35.8 percent. Afghan women remain restricted to employment in informal sectors like agriculture, where they comprise 65 percent of the workforce. In the case of the formal economy – e.g. education, health care, and service industries – women continue to be a minority. In contrast to the pre-Taliban era, when women made up 70 percent of the teachers in Afghanistan, the education sector today is largely dominated by men at all levels. Low participation in the formal economy is attributed to low skills sets and low female literacy rates of 18 percent, compared to 50 percent for men. Also, selling products in the market continues to be a major obstacle for women due to limited mobility caused by a lack of security.

HEALTH

Taliban Era

By the end of the Taliban's five-year rule in 2001, the condition of Afghanistan's health care system was near-total despair. Women and children were the main victims, with standard health indices being among the worst in the world – one quarter of children died before the age of five, with a mortality rate of 165 deaths for every 1000 live births per year.

The chance of a mother dying in child-birth was also the second highest in the world with 17 deaths for every 1000 live births per year. Life expectancy for women was 46 years. Although the shaky foundation of the health care system was attributed to socio-economic factors such as drought, earthquakes and war-driven displacement, it was undoubtedly exacerbated by Taliban policies.

Under the Taliban, health care providers were predominantly located in urban areas, as most hospitals and health care centers in the countryside were destroyed during the civil war. The Taliban perpetuated the uneven distribution of medical care by issuing an edict in 1998 that introduced gender segregation in the health sector. Men and women could no longer inhabit the same building, let alone room. To make matters worse, the Taliban's ban on female employment further restricted women's access to health care and contributed to the low doctor-patient ratio of one physician for every 50,000 people in the country. As a result, the percentage of women with access to even the most basic health services plummeted to a mere 12 percent.

In 1999, foreign intervention by international bodies like the Red Cross and the United Nations led the Taliban to relax the ban on female employment in the health sector. Approximately 40 female medical students, who had been forced to leave Kabul University before receiving medical degrees, were allowed to continue their education. And in 2000, the authorities in Kandahar permitted the World Health Organization and the Office of the Resident Coordinator of the UN to start a nursing school for 40 female and 50 male nurses. Still, according to the WHO, by 2001 only 12 percent of deliveries in Afghanistan were attended by trained health workers.

Fatal illnesses included easily curable diseases like diarrhea and easily preventable diseases like tuberculosis. Due to a lack of even basic health care, diarrhea was estimated to kill 85,000 children a year. Immunization levels were extremely low due to the high costs of injections, and a lack of health care professionals to perform innoculations.

Tuberculosis rates were among the highest in world – approximately 133,000 cases by 2001, of which 70 percent were females aged 15 to 45. Lack of immunization spurred a measles epidemic during the spring of 2000, killing one thousand children. Undernourishment and inadequate health care also resulted in a high rate of birth complications and giving rise to disabilities such as cerebral palsy.

Post-Taliban Era

In 2001, health care became a priority for the new interim government. Article fifty-two of the 2003 Afghanistan constitution stipulates that:

The state is obliged to provide free means of preventive health care and medical treatment, and proper health facilities to all citizens of Afghanistan in accordance with the law. The state encourages and protects the establishment and expansion of private medical services and health centers in accordance with law.

In March of 2003, the interim government also produced The Basic Package of Health Services for Afghanistan — a policy paper outlining both challenges and tangible goals for the Ministry of Health. Some of the most glaring problems identified in the package were a grossly deficient, and even absent, infrastructure; a health system that is top-heavy with doctors who are not trained to deal with priority, community-level problems, and who lack public health expertise; poorly distributed resources; health care delivered on a project basis by many distinct, relatively uncoordinated service providers, as opposed to health care delivered in accordance with a clear and coherent national health policy; and lack of practical, useful and coordinated information systems for management decision-making.

The package highlights seven major target areas: maternal and newborn health, child health and immunization, public nutrition, control of communicable diseases, mental health, disabilities, and essential drugs.

In 2006 an assessment of the Afghan public health sector was conducted by researchers from the Johns Hopkins Bloomberg School of Public Health and the Indian Institute of Health Management, surveying more than 8,200 households in rural areas in 29 of Afghanistan's 34 provinces. The study found that public health care in Afghanistan is improving steadily and the Ministry of Public Health is slowly getting closer to meeting its goals. Key indicators of improvement since the fall of the Taliban:

- In line with the Ministry of Public Health's goal of equitable health care, more female patients than male patients used outpatient services, and the poor were more likely to use public sector services than the non-poor.

-Infant mortality rates have dropped in 2000-2006 from 165 deaths per 1000 live births to 129 deaths per 1000 live births. In the same period, the under 5 mortality rate has dropped from 257 deaths per 1000 live births to 191 deaths per 1000 live births.

-The percentage of women in rural Afghanistan receiving prenatal care from a skilled provider increased from an estimated 4.6 in 2003 to 32.2 in 2006. Although there have been great strides, a March 2005 World Bank report noted that an estimated 40 percent of all basic health facilities still lack female staff, maintaining constraints on women's access to good health care. The level of female involvement in the health sector, however, appears to be gradually increasing as in May 2006, women made up nearly a quarter of medical school graduates from Kabul Medical University.

HUMAN RIGHTS

Taliban Era

Afghanistan possesses a cultural legacy of conservatism characterized by a strong division of gender roles. Political, economic, and social decision-making has been traditionally male-dominated. In the latter part of the 20th century, women were making steps forward, being granted the right to both employment and education. The Taliban's rise to power in 1996, however, reversed much of this progress and exacerbated the plight of Afghan women.

The Taliban's strict social code marginalized the role of women in the public sphere by confining them to their private homes and enforcing the wearing of the burkha's heavy garment covering the entire body with only a mesh window to see through. Some Afghan women have traditionally worn the head scarf; however it was not until the Taliban's regime that a dress code or punishment for its violation was imposed by the state.

The Taliban's policies also extended to matrimony, permitting and in some cases encouraging the marriages of girls under the age of 16. Amnesty International reported that 80 percent of Afghan marriages were considered to be by force.

Most Afghan women quietly submitted to the Taliban's strictures in fear of the consequences often brutally enforced by the Department for the Propagation of Virtue and the Suppression of Vice. These religious police regularly beat women as punishment for a broad spectrum of violations: exposing ankles, being outside without a male relative, laughing loudly, wearing shoes that made noise when walking, and/or wearing the wrong type of burkha. These penalties were often meted out on the spot without a right to be heard or any due process. A United Nations Economic and Social Council report from 2000 stated that there were several prisons where hundreds of women were arbitrarily detained in very poor conditions. In Kandahar province, a women's prison in Karez Bazaar was said to hold more than 400 women. In Nezarat Khan Prison, one woman was allegedly arrested for simply speaking to a man in the street.

The religious police also punished women who committed adultery and fornication. The justification for these punishments was anchored in the Taliban's interpretation of Sharia Law (Islamic Law). When alleging rape, women had to present the testimony of four male witnesses. If they failed to provide this testimony, they faced flogging or even stoning in the case of adultery. One of the two was the outcome in most cases.

The Taliban's policies towards women and the high number of domestic abuse cases resulted in various consequences for Afghan women, from depression to self-immolation.

Post-Taliban Era

In 2004, Afghans adopted a new constitution that recognizes the United Nations Charter, the UN Declaration on Human Rights, and itself devotes two articles to human rights:

The state is obliged to create a prosperous and progressive society based on social justice, protection of human dignity, protection of human rights, realization of democracy, and to ensure national unity and equality among all ethnic groups and tribes and to provide for balanced development in all areas of the country.

The State, for the purpose of monitoring the observation of human rights in Afghanistan, to promote their advancement and protection, shall establish the Independent Human Rights Commission of Afghanistan.

Any person, whose fundamental rights have been violated, can file complaint to the Commission. The Commission can refer cases of violation of human rights to the legal authorities, and assist in defending the rights of the complainant.

Still, Afghanistan remains plagued by the legacy of Taliban rule as human rights violations continue. The Council on Foreign Relations reported that an Afghan rights watchdog registered 704 cases of violence against women this year, but noted that cultural taboos discourage accurate reporting of such incidents. Amnesty International relates that women continue to be subject to attacks upon their persons and harsh punishments proscribed by local religious councils.

In a 2007 article published by the UN Commission on Human Rights, Dr. Sima Samar, the head of the Independent Human Rights Commission of Afghanistan, said, "Some past violations still continue: arbitrary detentions, private jails, the torture of prisoners and detainees police still think it is their right to torture a suspect or culprit.

Forced marriages and land grabbing are among the top violations that take place a lot. Lack of awareness [of human rights] is very widespread. Meanwhile there is no access to justice, there are no proper courts and some [in which] cultural practices have influenced local courts. If a woman goes to court she is seen as bad and of ill repute."

Despite the recognition of human rights in Afghanistan's constitution, the number of reported female suicides has increased. According to the Afghanistan Independent Human Rights Commission and Ministry of Women's Affairs, 250 cases of suicides, including self-immolation victims, were registered in the first six months of 2007. In contrast, only five cases were recorded in 2006. The increase in reports suggests that officials are no longer hiding suicide cases. But the fact that female suicides are occurring at an increasing rate indicates there are still problems to be addressed.

Herat doctor Nesar Ahmad Ferehmand, who regularly treats self-immolation victims, attributes the problem to women's fight to assert their rights: "In Kabul, women probably don't have as many problems because they have more rights – they are accepted in society and they are free to work and study. In Kandahar, women have no rights and they have accepted that they should not go outside the house or work. But in Herat women are struggling to get their rights, they are trying to go out and work and study but the men in their family are sometimes opposed to this and that's what creates this problem."

POLITICS

Taliban Era

The 1964 constitution of Afghanistan introduced universal suffrage and equal rights for women. It is estimated, that 10 to 15 percent of Afghan women, pre-Taliban, were engaged in leadership positions. During the Taliban regime, however, women were completely excluded from the political arena.

Post-Taliban Era

In December 2001, less than a month after a U.S. led coalition ousted the Taliban regime, the United Nations sponsored an Afghan peace conference in Bonn, Germany. The resulting agreement established the mechanisms that would govern the creation of Afghanistan's new government. One such mandate was to foster the political participation of women in constitutional deliberations and the interim administration.

The Interim Authority and the Special Independent Commission for the Convening of the Emergency Loya Jirga will ensure the participation of women as well as the equitable representation of all ethnic and religious communities in the Interim Administration and the Emergency Loya Jirga.

On January 4, 2004, the Constitutional Loya Jirga approved a new constitution and government structure. All citizens were granted equal rights and in the subsequent presidential election, Hamid Karzai's landslide victory made him Afghanistan's official president. Massouda Jalal, a female physician and U.N. staff member from Kabul, was the only woman who stood for the presidency, going on to win 1.1 percent of votes — the sixth highest number of votes out of 19 candidates.

Afghanistan held its landmark legislative elections in September 2005. The constitution reserved 25 percent of the lower house and 17 percent of the upper house of parliament for women. While overall voter participation was down from the 2004 presidential election, turn out by the female population was exponentially higher.

Despite the parliamentary election's relative success, women only accounted for 12 percent (328 out of 2707) of candidates for the lower house and 8 percent (247 out of 3025) of candidates for the upper house. Human Rights Watch interviewed several female delegates and found that the low number in female candidates could be attributed to the continuing intimidation of women in the political arena. The same report also found that women's voter registration and turnout rates fell far behind men's in the regions with the worst security. Afghanistan's southern provinces are among its most conservative and had appallingly low female registration rates – 9 percent in the Uruzgan province, 10 percent in Zabul, and 16 percent in Helmand.

Most female candidates in the parliamentary elections also chose to run without a party affiliation. This is partly attributed to their fear of being used to fulfill a quota. Human Rights Watch interviewed one woman who was providing candidate training and awareness programs that said, "We are telling women to be decision-makers, don't be used. The political parties are including them as members, but not in decision-making. They are using women only as a symbol." Many of the Afghan political parties are also composed of ex-warlords and Malalai Joya, an MP from the Farah province, is a staunch opponent of their inclusion in the government. Another open critic of their participation is female MP Shukria Barakzai who, six years after the removal of the Taliban, still receives death threats.

THE SITUATION OF WOMEN IN AFGHANISTAN

"Your country is now embarking on a process to create credible and accountable institutions in which all Afghans are represented. These are decisions for Afghan men and women to make. The role of the United Nations is to assist and encourage this process. But, I would like to take this opportunity to say to all Afghans: there cannot be true peace and recovery in Afghanistan without a restoration of the rights of women." UN Secretary-General Kofi Annan in his statement to the Afghan Women's Summit for Democracy (Brussels, 4 to 5 December 2001)

Afghanistan is a country of approximately 23 million which, after three years of severe drought, 23 years of war and devastation and five years under the Taliban authorities, has been left as one of the poorest countries in the world. Afghanistan has the second highest maternal mortality rate in the world. Even before the Taliban came to power, Afghanistan had high maternal and child mortality rates and a very low literacy rate for women. But women participated economically, socially and politically in the life of their societies. Women helped to draft the 1964 Constitution. In the 1970s, there were at least three women legislators in the Parliament. Up to the early 1990s, women were teachers, government workers and medical doctors. They worked as professors, lawyers, judges, journalists, writers and poets.

After the Taliban's rise to power, women and girls were systematically discriminated against and marginalized, and their human rights were violated. This resulted in the deteriorating economic and social conditions of women and girls in all areas of the country, in particular in areas under Taliban control. Women and girls continued to be severely restricted in their access to education, health care facilities and employment. During the Taliban's rule, only about 3 per cent of girls received some form of primary education. The ban on women's employment also affected boys' education, as the majority of teachers had been women. Poor health conditions and malnutrition made pregnancy and childbirth exceptionally dangerous for Afghan women.

The Taliban's policies also severely limited women's freedom of movement. Women could travel only when accompanied by a male relative, which put a particular strain on female-headed households and widows. In May 2001, a decree was issued by the Taliban, banning women from driving cars, which further limited their activities. The resulting seclusion of women to the home constituted a form of solitary confinement and also created obstacles to women meeting with each other. Women were harassed and beaten by the Taliban if their public appearance was perceived to be in contradiction with Taliban edicts. Women's removal from the public space also meant that women could not play any role in the political process and were excluded from all forms of formal or informal governance. Afghan women suffered domestic and other types of violence for the past 25 years, not just under the Taliban regime.

Prior to September 2001, the United Nations Resident/ Humanitarian Coordinator, with the UN agencies on the ground and UN senior staff within the UN Special Mission to Afghanistan (UNSMA) continued to address issues related to the discrimination against women and girls. They made numerous efforts to negotiate the withdrawal of various discriminatory decrees, including those banning women's employment, which nevertheless remained in effect. The Afghanistan 2001 consolidated inter-agency appeal emphasized that the assistance community would collectively aim to expand access for Afghan women to education, health services and employment and income-generating activities.

Despite many years of concern about the situation of Afghan women, it is only now, under conditions of extreme tragedy, political violence and destruction, that the situation has propelled Afghanistan and the plight of its women and girls firmly back into the global spotlight. For the first time outside of the setting of the United Nations and of the international community, there is a groundswell of concern, from Parliaments to First Ladies, from entertainers and media stars to non-governmental organizations, all calling for the full recognition of the rights of women and girls in Afghanistan.

ACTIONS BY THE INTERNATIONAL COMMUNITY

The United Nations Charter proclaims the equal rights of men and women. Two years ago, the groundbreaking United Nations Security Council resolution 1325 (2000) called for an end to impunity for war crimes committed against women and girls, but also recognized the need to increase women's role in peace negotiations and in peace-building. The United Nations has urged the Afghan parties to bring women into every stage of the political process; and the UN is recruiting Afghan women as quickly as it can to help to provide humanitarian assistance.

The United Nations and its family of organizations have had a long interest in Afghanistan. UNICEF set up its first office there 52 years ago. The situation of Afghanistan, in general, and the situation of women and girls in particular, have remained under intense scrutiny by several United Nations bodies, including the Security Council, the General Assembly, and several of the Economic and Social Council's functional commissions and expert bodies, in particular the Commission on Human Rights, the Sub-Commission on the Promotion and Protection of Human Rights, and the Commission on the Status of Women.

In November 1997, Angela E.V. King, the Special Adviser to the Secretary-General on Gender Issues and Advancement of Women, led an inter-agency gender mission in Afghanistan, to specifically address issues related to discrimination against women and girls under the Taliban. The mission made a set of recommendations aiming to improve the gender situation within Afghanistan and in the United Nations system, so as to better serve the needs of Afghan women. One such recommendation was the appointment of a senior UN adviser on gender in Afghanistan.

After September 2001, the Special Adviser on Gender Issues and Advancement of Women continued to address the situation of women's rights in Afghanistan in meetings with the Special Representative of the Secretary-General and other senior officials within the United Nations system, in inter-agency consultations and in meetings with representatives of non-governmental organizations. She also facilitated contacts between Afghan women and women's organizations and the UN system and supported the organization of the Afghan Women's Summit in Brussels, and follow-up meetings with the Secretary-General and members of the Security Council in an Arria Formula meeting. She also called on Afghan women to return to their country and former jobs, including in the civil service and elsewhere.

The first Integrated Mission Task Force, which was established at UN Headquarters to advise the Special Representative of the Secretary-General for Afghanistan, Lakhdar Brahimi, included a gender specialist from the Division for the Advancement of Women. Three Executive Committees, reporting to the Secretary-General, on Peace and Security, Humanitarian Affairs and the United Nations Development Group (UNDG), have been meeting regularly and have drawn up strategic recovery plans on the political process, humanitarian assistance and reconstruction of Afghanistan, including gender perspectives. In addition, the UNDG and Executive Committee on Humanitarian Affairs formed a Sub-Group on Gender in Afghanistan, to monitor developments on the ground in order to devise strategies to ensure that a gender perspective was mainstreamed in the peace negotiations and the reconstruction process.

On 14 November 2001, in its resolution 1378, the Security Council expressed its strong support for the efforts of the Afghan people to establish a new and transitional administration leading to the formation of a government, which would be broad-based, multi-ethnic and fully representative of all the Afghan people, and should respect human rights regardless of gender, ethnicity or religion.

Most recently, on 30 January 2002, the 26th session of the Committee on the Elimination of Discrimination against Women issued a statement of solidarity and support for Afghan women, which stated, among other things, that "The participation of Afghan women as full and equal partners with men is essential for the reconstruction and development of their country." The Committee also called upon all parties concerned to respect internationally recognized principles, norms and standards of human rights, particularly the human rights of women, in all their actions and activities, which the Committee considered essential to achieve peace and stability in Afghanistan.

Today, as the reconstruction and rehabilitation of Afghanistan continues, a number of United Nations entities continue to be actively involved in improving the situation of women and girls in Afghanistan. Some examples of this work includes:

- During the Taliban's rule of Afghanistan, bakeries sponsored by the World Food Programme (WFP) represented one of the few job opportunities open to women; WFP bakery projects employed 300 women in Kabul and 100 women in Mazar-I-Sharif before September 2001. Today, WFP is currently assisting about six million people in Afghanistan. Beginning in April 2002, the focus will shift from relief to recovery, with particular emphasis on school feeding for education.
- The United Nations Children's Fund (UNICEF) managed to implement a massive polio eradication campaign, which reached over 10 million children under five years of age, and delivered life-saving humanitarian assistance, including nutrition, water and environmental sanitation, emergency obstetric care and provision of non-food items.

- The UN has launched a large-scale drive to immunize Afghan children against measles - a major, yet preventable, killer disease among the young. Measles is responsible for an estimated 40 per cent of all vaccine-preventable childhood deaths in Afghanistan, killing about 35,000 Afghan children each year. The $8 million effort, which is being organized by WHO and UNICEF, aims to vaccinate up to 9 million Afghan children.
- In mid-November 2001, women national staff members of the Office of Humanitarian Affairs, UNICEF, WFP and other agencies returned to work in Kabul and were expected to resume their posts in other urban areas as well.
- In December 2001, WFP conducted a major survey on food needs in Kabul. Of 3,612 surveyors employed, some 2,400 were women, the first boost to women's employment since the fall of the Taliban.
- The World Health Organization (WHO) and UNICEF shipped emergency health kits into Afghanistan in October 2001 to serve more than a million people for three months.
- In late September 2001, responding to the grave health emergency facing Afghan women, the United Nations Population Fund (UNFPA) mounted its largest-ever humanitarian operation. Thousands of pregnant women were among the Afghan civilians who fled their homes and massed along the country's borders. The lack of shelter, food and medical care, and unsanitary conditions posed a serious risk to these women and their infant children. To provide displaced Afghan women with lifesaving reproductive health care services, UNFPA prepared to pre-position emergency relief supplies in the countries bordering Afghanistan. UNFPA, supported by non-governmental organizations, continues to provide its essential obstetric care services through a network of about 130 clinics.
- The Office of the UN High Commissioner for Refugees (UNHCR) focused on assistance to internally displaced persons inside Afghanistan and on the needs of refugees

in neighbouring countries, including the voluntary return of refugees.

- The Mine Action Programme initiated the clearing of an estimated 25,000 unexploded cluster bomblet units.
- In December 2001, the Office of the UN High Commissioner for Human Rights (UNHCHR) deployed a needs-assessment mission in Pakistan and Afghanistan to assess the human rights situation, which paid particular attention to the systematic discrimination against women and girls.
- Under the leadership of the World Bank, the Asian Development Bank (ADB) and the United Nations Development Programme (UNDP), a number of meetings were held to prepare and coordinate the efforts of the assistance community and donors in the reconstruction and rehabilitation process in Afghanistan.
- The World Bank, ADB and UNDP submitted a joint assessment, entitled "Afghanistan: preliminary needs assessment for recovery and reconstruction", to the International Conference on Reconstruction Assistance to Afghanistan (Tokyo, 21 and 22 January 2002). The assessment addressed gender equality as an important element for the overall reconstruction and development agenda.
- The United Nations system, in consultation with the Interim Authority and international and national organizations and non-governmental organizations, prepared a transitional assistance programme, which was presented to the donor community following the Tokyo Ministerial Meeting.

WOMEN'S ROLE IN THE REHABILITATION AND RECONSTRUCTION OF AFGHANISTAN

Since September 2001, Afghan women have begun to increase their activities. Numerous events were organized during the last few months by and with Afghan women's organizations inside and outside Afghanistan, such as panel discussions, conferences and international meetings, in order to ensure that the experiences and needs of Afghan women would receive the needed attention in all efforts directed at the post-Taliban Afghanistan.

For the first time in many years, new opportunities have been presented for women to reclaim their rights as active participants in the governance, as well as in the rehabilitation and reconstruction of Afghanistan. Schools for girls are being reopened, and young women are enrolling in universities. Women are seeking to return to their former jobs as teachers, doctors and civil servants. Radio and television broadcasts in Kabul once again feature woman commentators.

The United Nations Talks on a transitional government for Afghanistan began in Bonn on 27 November under the leadership of the Special Representative of the Secretary-General Lakhdar Brahimi. Representatives of four Afghan groups participated, representing the Rome process, linked to the former King; the United Front (also known as the Northern Alliance); the Cyprus Group and the Peshawar Group. All political groups had been encouraged by the UN to include women in their delegations and Afghan women's organizations were asked to contact the four groups for participation in the Talks. Two women, Sima Wali and Rona Mansuri, participated as full delegates of the Rome process; Amena Afzali participated as a full delegate of the United Front; Seddiqa Balkhi participated as adviser to the Cyprus Group; and Fatana Gilani participated as adviser to the Peshawar Group. The Agreement on Provisional Arrangements in Afghanistan pending the re-establishment of permanent government institutions was signed in Bonn on 5 December 2001.

In response to requests from Afghan women, a number of non-governmental organizations convened the Afghan Women's Summit for Democracy in Brussels, from 4 to 5 December 2001, in collaboration with the Office of the Special Adviser on Gender Issues and Advancement of Women and the United Nations Development Fund for Women (UNIFEM). About 40 Afghan women leaders from different ethnic, linguistic and religious backgrounds participated, including three who had also attended the UN negotiations in Bonn. The Summit concluded with the adoption of the Brussels Proclamation, which included concrete demands for the recovery of Afghan society in the areas of education, media and culture; health; human rights and the constitution; and refugees and internally displaced women. Participants of the Summit met with members of the European Parliament, members of the U.S. Congress, members of the Security Council in the Arria Formula meeting, and women ambassadors to the United Nations. In their talks, the Afghan women called for measures to increase security in Afghanistan and facilitate the disarmament of all warring factions.

UNIFEM organized a roundtable in Brussels from 10 to 11 December 2001 in cooperation with the Government of Belgium on "Building Women's Leadership in Afghanistan". The roundtable brought together Afghan women and UN agencies, the World Bank and donors, and issued an Action Plan calling for mechanisms to support the role and leadership of women in shaping the future of their country.

On 19 December 2001, the Special Adviser on Gender Issues and Advancement of Women organized a breakfast meeting between Afghan women non-governmental organizations and women ambassadors from the permanent missions to the UN, allowing Afghan women to share their vision and priorities for Afghan women. In addition, these Afghan women met with the Secretary-General to share such vision and their views about their role in the reconstruction of Afghanistan.

In January 2002, Hamid Karzai, the head of the Interim Administration, demonstrated his support for women's rights by signing the "Declaration of the Essential Rights of Afghan Women", which affirmed the right to equality between men and women. The Declaration had been adopted by a meeting of Afghans in Dushanbe, Tajikistan, in 2000.

When the Secretary-General visited Kabul on 25 January 2002, he made a symbolic visit to a girls school, which is assisted by UNICEF. Girls from six through 16 were preparing to resume their education after a Taliban-imposed break of five years.

Women are at the helm of two Ministries which are part of the new Interim Administration headed by Hamid Karzai. The Ministry of Women's Affairs, which had never existed before, is headed by Sima Samar, a physician and founder of the Shuhada Organization network of clinics, hospitals and schools in Pakistan and central Afghanistan. Ms. Samar is also one of the five Vice-Presidents of the Interim Administration. Suhaila Siddiq, a surgeon who continued to practice in Kabul throughout the Taliban regime, heads the Ministry of Public Health.

AFGHAN WOMEN, CULTURE, AND DEVELOPMENT

The situation of Afghan women who are jailed for committing "moral crimes." These women are accused of running away from abusive husbands or of committing adultery, while others were raped or were forced into prostitution. Within the next several days, more stories concerning the problems of Afghan women came to my attention, one on opium addicts and another on self-immolation. The plight of these women raises several questions: What will happen to them when U.S. and NATO forces withdraw? Will the Taliban gain control of the country again, restricting women to their houses and denying them the chance for education or employment? Will projects designed to protect women's rights fall by the wayside? And, how much progress has been made with respect to improving the lives of Afghan women?

As an anthropologist conducting research in Afghanistan, I find that whenever the gaze of the international media falls on Afghan women I feel uncomfortable. Implied in many reports is the suggestion that Afghan women need to be saved from their own culture. (an insightful piece on this is "Do Muslim Women Really Need Saving?" by Lila Abu-Lughod). The idea that the United States needed to help the women of Afghanistan was stronglypromoted in the early years of the conflict. For many, after reading about Afghan women certain questions arise: "What can we do? But, is anything we do hopeless, as these problems are deeply ingrained into the culture?" I also want to help Afghan women, especially those I know personally, but there is little I can, or should, do as a researcher. While voicing support for continued international military involvement against the Taliban might be one answer, the battles between insurgents and international forces in Afghanistan have increased instability, putting women in danger and possibly continuing a trend that has been going on for many years, whereby women's lives are more restricted as their families and communities try to protect them from both the gaze of outsiders and increased violence.

Is culture the problem?

The Taliban, and Islam, are often blamed for the oppression of Afghan women, yet another oft-named culprit is Afghan culture, due to practices, such as stoning and baad, that deny women basic rights. This point in itself is somewhat problematic, as Afghanistan is an incredibly ethnically and culturally diverse country. During the past two summers I conducted fieldwork with Afghan women working on international development projects in Jalalabad and Bamyan, Afghanistan. The lives of women in these two areas, the first populated by ethnic Pashtuns and the second by Hazaras, are very different, as Hazara women are much less constrained (although they also face many difficulties) by behavioral norms that limit their activities outside of their households.

I wanted to find out, particularly among the Pashtuns in Jalalabad, how women working for development NGOs "bent the rules" of their community regarding the proper comportment for women by traveling daily to an office and regularly into the surrounding countryside to monitor projects in outlying villages. Pashtuns are generally recognized to be the most conservative group in Afghanistan, particularly regarding the behavior of women. I myself was very restricted in my movements. I could not leave the house without my husband, and I always wore an enveloping, light blue burqa when I went out.

The women working for development NGOs I interviewed in Jalalabad changed many of the assumptions I had when I first arrived. Most importantly, they showed me that rather than subverting Pashtun culture, they embrace it even as they change it. They take what they believed to be the most important aspects of the culture — modesty, hospitality, showing respect for men, and they put it to use for their work. They look to their male colleagues as older brothers who they can depend on to protect them. An office segregated by sex means that women receiving support from an NGO safely and comfortably meets with the female staff. The NGO workers listen carefully to the elders in the villages where they carry out projects and try to provide the most needed services. The women use their culture to justify their work as improving the lives of fellow Pashtuns. They show that cultural norms are not static but can, in holding a variety of meanings for different individuals, be enacted in different, malleable, ways.

What assistance do Afghan women most need?

The Pashtun women NGO workers I interviewed have very strong ideas on what is most necessary for the reconstruction and development of Afghanistan, and they are not always in agreement with international donors. Most of my informants work on income generation projects involving handicraft and carpet production for women living in villages. Almost all of the NGO workers said, however, that if donors really want to help Afghanistan, they would focus on large-scale infrastructure development which would promote business.

Male income generation projects should be given more attention, as a family in which the wife earned while the husband didn't was more vulnerable to discord or abuse. What these women believe is needed to help other women was access to education and health care. I often heard male leaders of development projects state that the important thing is to "get money into the hands of the women," while women working for the same projects told me a different story. Of course, not all women working for such projects share this view, and not all international development organizations focus primarily on women's income generation. One organization reported that they had shifted their main goals to large scale infrastructure projects, such as providing electricity. They realized that these types of projects were what the people felt were most important, and they also recognized that projects related to activities such as carpet weaving, while well meaning, can all too often lead to exploitative relationships between women and children and other family members (my own research confirmed this). The overall sentiment among Pashtun women working for these projects is, however, that there is a disconnect between the types of projects most needed to improve the lives of Afghan women and the types of projects that were being funded. They are willing to accept any help provided, however, despite their frustrations.

What can be done for Afghan women?

I cannot pretend to know the answer to this question, but I can reiterate some of the points that the women I interviewed in Jalalabad made. First, continued military operations in the region will, at least in the short term, make lives more difficult for women living in these areas. They are forced to cope with insecurities arising from both insurgent activity and NATO and US forces. Often, these threats result in a tightening of restrictions on women's lives, either because their family or they themselves fear for their safety if they venture too far from their households. Second, any attempt to provide development projects for Afghan women must take into account that they are embedded in a web of social and familial relations which are deeply important for all involved. For this reason, it is wise to focus on projects that will develop the infrastructure of Afghanistan and put men to work, rather than continuing to over-focus on women's income generation which, while important, should be a secondary consideration. Third, even the most independent Pashtun (insert Hazara, Uzbek, Tajik, etc) woman is most likely going to still consider herself part of the culture she grew up in, and while she might rail against certain aspects of that culture, other aspects will be valued and embraced. The ways that women make use of the dynamic aspects of their culture even as they promote change in some areas of society needs to be better understood.

8

Afghanistan: Education in the Post Taliban Era

When preparing for this trip, Dost made a list of places he wanted to visit in order to evaluate the extent of development in Mazar. The first place we visited with him was the University of Balkh, Afghanistan's second largest university, located in Mazar-i-Sharif. When Dost was last living in Afghanistan, enrollment at University of Balkh stood at 1,000 male students, as women were excluded from public education during the Taliban era. When we visited, men and women passed eachother in the halls on the way to new classes, like journalism. Student enrollment is currently up to 7,000 students. The women we saw wore only loose-fitting head scarves, not the all-encompassing burqa that is still ubiquitous on the streets of Mazar. The male students wore jeans and t-shirts.

Our first stop on the Soviet-built campus was the office of the university chancellor, Habibullah Habib. In the office the chancellor spread out plans for university expansion. "Without education, we cannot move forward," he told us. The land had been purchased for a new campus that would allow the university to increase enrollment and provide its students with an updated study environment outfitted with modern technology. The estimated cost of the project is $200 million, which Habib has been fundraising for to little avail. About $40 million has been raised through World Bank loans and contributions from Pakistan. Habib says he is hopeful, but Western donors have not yet shown interest. It was a frustrating fact to hear, considering the billions of dollars spent each month by the U.S. alone on military operations. I'm inclined to agree with the chancellor that education today will go a long way in pre-emtively stemming conflict in the future.

After leaving the university we headed to the Abraham Lincoln Center, a U.S. State Department-funded center for education about all things American. Reza Hosseini, who runs the center, gave us an enthusiastic tour of the library, which holds both books about the U.S. and classics by American authors. Through the tour Reza, who has never been to the U.S., pulled his favorites from the shelves to show us what he's read. Drawings by local children of George Washington and Rumi, a 13th century poet born in Balkh Province, papered the walls. At the back of the center there was a large, flat-screen television where American movies are screened each week. The movies are a big draw in this area, where TVs were almost non-existent as recently as ten years ago. The center certainly seems to be an extension of the U.S. mission to win "hearts and minds."

As we wrapped up our tour of the library a group of about a dozen girls in black and white school uniforms started to gather at the center table. Before leaving Reza asked me if I could speak to them about Mother's Day traditions in the U.S., since our visit coincided with the holiday. I happily obliged and soon realized that half of the girls I was addressing were the editors of a student newspaper. As a former student newspaper editor myself, we hit it off. Through a translator they fired off a slew of questions about my life in the States, what school was like for girls, and what women did when they left college. They were a fascinating bunch of very smart girls. I asked them some questions back, about what it was like being the first generation of girls to go to school after the Taliban. They told me that they were lucky to be from families that supported education, but that in Balkh Province there are still many families that are against sending girls to school. Many of the girls they know, they told me, are still kept at home, despite schools now being open to female students. They said that they think things will change with their generation, but that change is slow. While a bit of a discouraging fact to hear, it was heartening to speak with such intelligent young women who are concerned about the future of their country, and are doing something about it. I left the talk with a stack of copies of their student newspaper.

IN AFGHANISTAN, UNDERGROUND GIRLS SCHOOL DEFIES TALIBAN AFTER EARLIER EFFORTS FAILED

Every morning in this mountain village in eastern Afghanistan, four dozen girls sneak through a square opening in a mud-baked wall, defying a Taliban edict.

A U.S.-funded girls school about a mile away was shuttered by insurgents in 2007, two years after it opened. They warned residents that despite a new government in Kabul and an international aid effort focused on female education, the daughters of Spina were to stay home. For a while, they all did.

Then two brothers, among the few literate men in the village, began quietly teaching math, reading and writing to their female relatives in a living room on the edge of town. They wanted to keep the classes small, they said, to stay off the Taliban's radar. That turned out to be impossible.

The United States and its allies have spent millions of dollars on female education in the past decade, and Afghan and Western officials have pointed to the issue as one of the most hopeful changes of the post-Taliban era. Female enrollment in public schools has risen from 5,000 under the Taliban to 2.5 million, according to the Afghan Education Ministry.

But Afghanistan is rife with places like Spina, where formal efforts to educate women and girls have crumbled. About 2 million Afghan girls do not attend school.

Those who do sometimes face threats. Last week, suspected militants poisoned more than 100 schoolgirls in northern Afghanistan, according to Amanullah Iman, a spokesman for the Education Ministry, who said an investigation into the incident was ongoing. The girls are recovering.

Because of threats, several schools in eastern Afghanistan have been closed in the past few months, reversing what had been a positive trend, said Vidhya Ganesh, the deputy country representative for UNICEF.

The insurgency had already forced the closure of dozens of girls schools beginning in the middle of past decade, when insurgents started to return to Afghanistan. Many of the schools were built and funded by the United States, and many never reopened. In some villages, the schools have gone underground, hidden in living rooms and guesthouses, as they were during the Taliban's reign.

"It's risky for the teachers and it's risky for the students, but these underground schools show the thirst people have for education under the Taliban," said Shukriya Barakzai, a parliamentarian who ran her own underground school when the Taliban held power in Kabul in the 1990s.

"It doesn't feel much different from those years," said one of the brothers in insurgent-infested Spina. "We live in a community very far from democracy and freedom."

'Something from nothing'

When the insurgency arrived in this patch of Paktika province in 2005, it did so with great force and little resistance. The absence of Afghan or American security forces meant fighters could wield weapons freely and threaten residents without consequence. The warning to girls went unchallenged.

But word soon spread about the underground girls school — part of a shadow education system developed in places such as Spina to elude the Taliban. The full extent of the system is not known, but American and Afghan officials say such underground networks are not uncommon in places with a large insurgent presence.

First, young students — between 5 and 12 years old — would trickle into the home of the two brothers, who for security reasons insisted that their names not be published. Then, teenagers started arriving, the brothers said, a particularly rare and controversial development in eastern Afghanistan, where females are expected to remain home upon reaching adolescence.

The brothers could hardly believe the turnout, which at once worried and excited them. They named the school after their great uncle, Namizad, a religious scholar.

"The girls just kept coming." one brother said. "They were so eager, like they were starving."

When a U.S. army platoon made a rare visit to Spina this month, soldiers saw the school as an example of resilience in the face of a failed development project, a sign of hope in a dismal place. In recent months, according to U.S. officials, the Taliban in Paktika have robbed teachers of their salaries to buy an 82mm mortar and shells.

"I want to thank you for your courage," U.S. Army Lt. Col. Curtis Taylor told the brothers and their students after ducking through the family's living room doorway.

The girls at the Namizad School sit on carpets, beginning each class with a recitation from the Koran. A chalkboard rests on the floor. Less than half the class has textbooks, which have made their way from Kabul. As in the rest of Spina, there is no electricity.

"These students are learning something from nothing," one of the brothers said. The brothers have pleaded for more resources. They have prayed to remain outside the Taliban's reach. But the district's education director claimed he had no money for the education of girls, the brothers said, in an account confirmed by local officials. And the Taliban have crept ever closer.

A few months ago, insurgents posted a letter on the brothers' door. "We will not allow the education of girls," it read, calling the practice "un-Islamic." The letter warned of a violent punishment.

The brothers talked about what to do. Should they end the classes? Should they leave Spina?

The two willowy men in their early 30s have bright eyes and long brown beards and wear flowing white salwar-kameez, the traditional dress here. Their backgrounds are strikingly similar to those of the insurgents who threaten them. Like the Talibs of western Paktika, the brothers were educated in Pakistani madrassas, or religious schools. They, too, were raised to believe in a strict adherence to the Koran, Islam's holiest book.

"I was so close to joining the Taliban," one said. "The men haunting us, they are men we know well."

'I want to learn everything'

The brothers tried to make the case to the Taliban that they would teach only religious material to their students. They warned their students of the risk of attending classes, and they were surprised again when the girls kept coming. There's now a morning class for young children and an afternoon class for teenagers. The brothers beam when talking about recent graduates, eight of whom are now trained midwives.

"I liked the other school better. We had desks and books," said Baranah, 11, who was in first grade when the Taliban closed the U.S.-funded school. "But this place is still good. We still learn here. I want to learn everything."

The insurgency has not followed through with its threat. The brothers wonder if it ever will — if the Taliban's recent silence signifies its tacit approval or is merely a prelude to violence.

In some cases, the Afghan government and international organizations have been able to reach compromises with insurgents to keep schools open.

"We're beginning to find ways to negotiate with anti-government elements," said UNICEF's Ganesh.

Some here worry that women's rights are being sidelined as the United States prepares to leave and the Afghan government attempts to satisfy a hard-line constituency. In March, top religious leaders on the country's Ulema Council ruled that men are "fundamental" and women "secondary," barring women from interacting with their male counterparts in schools or the workplace.

In Spina, only boys are educated in the U.S.-funded, one-story yellow building constructed five years ago to educate girls. Most of the windows are broken, and the paint is chipping.

"That place seemed perfect," one brother said. "But we knew it wouldn't last long."

EDUCATION IN AFGHANISTAN

Education in Afghanistan includes K-12 and Higher education, which is supervised by the Ministry of Education andMinistry of Higher Education in Kabul, Afghanistan. Afghanistan is going through a nationwide rebuilding process, and despite setbacks, institutions are established all across the country. By 2013 there were 10.5 million students attendingschools in Afghanistan, a country which has around 27.5 million people living in it.

History

One of the oldest schools in Afghanistan is the Habibia High School in Kabul, which was built by King Habibullah Khan in 1903 to educate students from the nation's elite class. In the 1920s, the German-funded Amani High School opened in Kabul, and about a decade later two French lycées (secondary schools) began, the AEFE and the Lycée Esteqlal. The Kabul University was established in 1932. Education was improved under the rule of King Zahir Shah between 1933 and 1973, making primary schools available to about half the population who were younger than 12 years of age, and expanding the secondary school system and Kabul University.

During the Democratic Republic of Afghanistan, the government of the People's Democratic Party of Afghanistan (PDPA) reformed the education system; education was stressed for both sexes, and widespread literacy programmes were set up. By 1988, women made up 40 percent of the doctors and 60 percent of the teachers at Kabul University; 440,000 female students were enrolled in different educational institutions and 80,000 more in literacy programs. Despite improvements, large percentage of the population remained illiterate. Beginning with the Soviet invasion of Afghanistan in 1979, successive wars virtually destroyed the nation's education system. Most teachers fled during the wars to neighboring countries. In the middle of the 1990s, about 650 schools were functioning throughout the country.

In 1996 the Taliban regime restricted education for females, and the madrassa (mosque school) became the main source of primary andsecondary education. About 1.2 million students were enrolled in schools during the Taliban, with less than 50,000 of them girls.

After the overthrow of the Taliban in late 2001, the Karzai administration received substantial international aid to restore the education system. Around 7,000 schools were operating in 20 of the 32 provinces by the end of 2003, with 27,000 teachers teaching 4.2 million children (including 1.2 million girls). Of that number, about 3.9 million were in primary schools. An estimated 57 percent of men and 86 percent of women were reported to be illiterate, and the lack of skilled and educated workers was a major economic disadvantage. When Kabul University reopened in 2002, some 24,000 male and female students enrolled for higher education. In the meantime, five other universities were being rehabilitated in different parts of the country. Public school curricula have included religious subjects but detailed instruction is left to religious teachers.

By 2006, over 4 million male and female students were enrolled in schools throughout Afghanistan. At the same time school facilities or institutions were also being refurbished or improved, with more modern-style schools being built each year. The American University of Afghanistan (AUAF) in Kabul was established in 2006. Other universities were also renovated or rebuilt, such as Kandahar University in the south, Nangarhar University and Khost University in the east, Herat University in the west and Balkh University in the north. Despite these achievements, there were still significant obstacles to education in Afghanistan, many of which stem from a lack of funding. Planning curricula and school programs is difficult for the Ministry of Education because a significant amount of the budget for education comes from varying external donors each year, making it difficult to predict what the annual budget would be.

The obstacles to education were even more numerous for Afghan girls. Afghanistan's then Education Minister, Mohammad Hanif Atmar, said in 2007 that 60% of students were studying in tents or other unprotected structures, and some parents refused to let their daughters attend schools in such conditions. A lack of women teachers was another issue that concerned some parents, especially in more conservative areas. Some parents were not allowing their daughters to be taught by men. But this often meant that girls were not allowed to attend school, as the international aid agency Oxfam reported in 2007 that about one quarter of Afghan teachers were women. In 2009, another concern was the destruction of schools by the Taliban, especially schools for females. Following the destruction of over 150 schools in a year, many parents had doubts about the government's ability to protect them.

The following achievements were made the last decade:

- Between 2001 and 2010, primary school enrolment rose from around 1 million to nearly 7 million (a sevenfold increase in eight years) and the proportion of girls from virtually zero to 37%.
- The number of teachers in general education has risen sevenfold, but their qualifications are low. About 31% are women.
- Since 2003, over 5,000 school buildings have been rehabilitated or newly constructed. Just over 50% of schools have usable buildings.

Enrollment is still low, the average is 1,983 students per institution, three institutions have less than 200 students. Furthermore, there is a deficiency of qualified faculty members: only 4.7 % (166 of total 3,522) of the teaching staff held a Ph.D.— In "addition to problems of inadequate resources, and lack of qualiûed teaching staff are issues of corruption, of various kinds."

In 2010, the United States began establishing a number of Lincoln learning centers in Afghanistan. They are set up to serve as programming platforms offering English language classes, library facilities, programming venues, Internet connectivity, educational and other counseling services. A goal of the program is to reach at least 4,000 Afghan citizens per month per location.

According to the Human Development Index, in 2011, Afghanistan was the 15th least developed country in the world.

In June 2011, officials from the United States signed a joint statement with Education Minister Ghulam Farooq Wardak to expand future opportunities for direct financial support from USAID to the Afghan Ministry of Education. In December 2011, the *Baghch-e-Simsim* (Afghan version of *Sesame Street*) children's television series was launched in Afghanistan, which is funded by the U.S. Department of State and is produced in consultation with Afghanistan's Ministry of Education. The project is designed to help educate Afghans from pre-school stage and onward. It was reported in May 2013 that there were 16,000 schools across Afghanistan, with 10.5 million students. Education Minister Wardak stated that three millions children remained deprived of education and requested $3 billion to construct 8,000 additional schools over next two years.

CURRENT CHALLENGES TO EDUCATION DEVELOPMENT

Violence

Afghanistan is one of the worst affected countries by violence against schools, with 670 incidents of attacks on education in 2008. Violence on students have prevented close to 5 million afghan children from attending school in year 2010. In terms of death rates, Afghanistan had 439 teachers, education employees and students killed in 2006-9, one of the highest in the world.

Teacher's credentials

Since the Taliban regime was toppled in 2001, up to 6 million girls and boys started attending school. In 2012, the supply of students far exceeded the pool of qualified teachers. According to statistics provided by the Ministry of Education, 80 percent of the country's 165,000 teachers have achieved the equivalent of a high school education or did not complete their post-secondary studies.

Extremist curriculum

Since the toppling of the Taliban regime, under the combined efforts of Afghan and international experts, the curriculum has been changed from extremist Islamic teachings to one relatively better with new books, and better training. Yet, there still remains no standard curriculum for secondary school textbooks and high school textbooks remain woefully inadequate in number and content.

Infrastructure

In 2012, there were insufficient schools. Around 4,500 schools are being built according to a recent government report. 40 percent of schools were conducted in permanent buildings. The rest held classes in the UNICEF shelters or were "desert schools" with students and teachers gathering in the desert near a village.

Child Labour

In 2007, more that half of the population of Afghanistan was under the age of 18. UNICEF estimates that close to a quarter of Afghan children between the ages of seven and fourteen were working. In rural areas, the problem is worse and there are more girls working than boys. This disrupts children's education and possibly prevents them from schooling completely.

Bibliography

Ahmad, Ilyas : *Sovereignty, Islamic and Modern,* Allies Book Corporation, Karachi, 1965.

Ahmad, Khurshid : *Islam : its Meaning and Message,* Islamic Council of Europe, London, 1976.

Allison, Graham: *Nuclear Terrorism: The Ultimate Preventable Catastrophe,* New York: Times Books, 2004.

Bahedur, Kalim : *The Jamaat-i-Islami of Pakistan,* Progressive Books, Lahore, 1978.

Basrur, Rajesh M., and Hasan-Askari Rizvi, *Nuclear Terrorism and South Asia,* Albuquerque, NM: Sandia National Laboratories, February 2003.

Dhagamwar, Vasudha : *Law, Power and Justice : Protection of Personal Rights under Islam,* Popular Prakashan, Bombay, 2001.

Evelyn Goh, *Meeting the Afghanistan Challenge: The U.S. in Southeast Asian Regional Security Strategies*, DC: East-West Center, 2005.

Fletcher, Arnold: *Afghanistan, Highway of Conquest*, Ithaca, New York, Cornell University, 1965.

Friedman, G.: *The Future of War of Cyber Crimes*, N.Y., Random House, 1996.

Habberton, William: *Anglo-Russian Relations Concerning Afghanistan 1837-1907*, Urbana, University of Illinois, 1937.

Hoffman, Bruce, *Inside Terrorism in Afghanistan,* New York: Columbia University Press, 1998.

Ikram, S.M. : *Muslim Civilization in India,* Oxford, New York, 1981.

James, Piscarton : *Islam in the World of National States,* Macmillan, New York, 1982.

Janowitz, M.: *The Professional Soldier: A Social and Political Portrait,* N.Y., The Free Press, 1960.

Kalim, M. Siddiq : *Studies in Pakistan Culture : an International Perspective,* Manohar Publications, New Delhi, 1993.

Kaplan, David, *The Cult At the End of the World,* New York: Crown Publishers, 1996.

Keane J.: *Democracy and Civil Liberty in Afghanistan,* London, Verso, 1988.

Laquer, Walter: *The New Terrorism: Fanaticism and the Arms of Mass Destruction,* Oxford: Oxford University Press, 1999.

Levitas, D.: *The terrorist next door: The militia movement and the radical right,* New York: Thomas Dunne Books, 2002.

Norris, James A.: *The First Afghan War 1838-1842,* Cambridge, University Press, 1967.

Oudha, Abdul Qadir : *Criminal Law of Islam,* Kitab Bhavan, New Delhi, 1999.

Puryear, V. J.: *International Economics and Diplomacy in the Near East,* London, Oxford University, 1935.

Robert M. Young: *Darwinian Evolution and Human History,* Historical Studies on Science and Belief, 1980.

Rosen, P.: *Societies and Military Power: India and its Armies,* Ithaca, Cornell University Press, 1996.

Saxena, V. K. : *Muslims and the Indian National Congress,* Discovery Publishing House, New Delhi, 1985.

Smith, W. C. : *Modern Islam in India : a Social Analysis,* Manohar Publishers, New Delhi, 1985.

Thomas Arnold: *The Spread of Islam in the World, A History of Peaceful Preaching,* Goodword Books, 2001.

Walker, Benjamin : *Foundation of Islam : the Making of World Faith,* Rupa & Co., New Delhi, 2001.

Zafeeruddin, M.M. : *System of Modesty and Chastity in Islam,* Idara Ishaat-e-Diniyat Pvt. Ltd, New Delhi, 1995.

Index

❑❑❑